**Suffolk**
County Council

Please return/renew this item
by the last date shown.
Books may also be renewed by
phone or the Internet.
Libraries & Heritage
www.suffolkcc.gov.uk/libraries/

FROM TILBURY TO TYNESIDE

EASTERN REGION RAILWAY SHIPPING PUBLICISED

ROBERT N. FORSYTHE

TEMPUS

In respect of those family and friends who brought me up on the Norfolk Broads, to them this volume is dedicated.

Front cover illustration: The *Avalon* crossing the North Sea on the Harwich-Hook of Holland route. An unsigned British Railways-commissioned image intended for brochure and poster use.

First published 2006

Tempus Publishing Limited
The Mill, Brimscombe Port,
Stroud, Gloucestershire, GL5 2QG
www.tempus-publishing.com

British Library Cataloguing in Publication Data.
A catalogue record for this book is available from the British Library.

ISBN 0 7524 3882 4

Typesetting and origination by Tempus Publishing Limited
Printed in Great Britain

Contents

Foreword by Ambrose Greenway, Chairman of
    the World Ship Trust   7

Introduction   9

Acknowledgements   11

Selected Brief Chronology   13

Chapter 1   From the Thames   15

Chapter 2   The Haven Ports – Harwich   37

Chapter 3   Beyond the Hook   89

Chapter 4   Not to the Low Countries   143

Chapter 5   The Haven Ports – Felixstowe   179

Chapter 6   Onwards to Hull   199

Chapter 7   To Tyne Commission Quay   233

Select Bibliography   255

Foreword

by Ambrose Greenway, Chairman of the World Ship Trust

The North Sea has been a corridor of communication to the Continent of Europe and Scandinavia for centuries, none more so than in the period of time covered by this fascinating compilation of travel ephemera. On a daily basis, relatively small steamers by today's standards departed with their passengers and cargo, more often than not following the arrival of the relevant boat train, on what was often a rough and uncomfortable voyage lasting anything between six and twenty-four hours. Despite the vagaries of weather, these services ran more or less to schedule, in those days a matter of considerable pride to officers and crew, but inevitably over time some came to founder and others fell prey to wartime military action.

When doing research for my book *North Sea Passenger Steamers* back in the early 1980s, I became totally absorbed by the types of ship involved in these North Sea services, so different from the sleek English Channel packets and the rather more stately Irish Sea ferries, ranging from the Railway services out of Harwich which needed more substantial steamers than the former and the longer Esbjerg and Bergen services which required virtual mini liners. In between were the secondary services such as those of the Great Central and the Lancashire and Yorkshire Railways and Holland's Batavier Line, whose ships were generally no more than seaworthy cargo ships with limited passenger accommodation. In addition there were the well-known and popular excursion ships of the General Steam Navigation Co. and the Bell Steamers on the Thames as well as the estuary ferry services which also traversed the Stour and Humber.

This whole glorious miscellany of railway connected shipping services and their attendant publicity material is brought back to life in the author's informative text and carefully chosen illustrations. I wish him well in his endeavour which I know will bring joy to many who read it.

Ambrose Greenway
House of Lords

Introduction

This is now the third book in this series I have written examining shipping services through their publicity literature. The phrase 'Eastern Region' indicates a geographical and a business concept. Geographically, the Eastern Region consists of the controlling ports which run up the East Coast from Tilbury to Tyneside. As a business concept the Eastern Region, formed lineally from the London and North Eastern Railway and before that the Great Eastern Railway, was a part of British Railways and thereby connected with railway-owned shipping at Tilbury, Harwich and in the Humber. Much of this book reflects this direct railway involvement, and explores the heyday of the actual Eastern Region. That heyday is well and truly history. When the Eastern Region was formed in 1948, it was the direct inheritor of the London and North Eastern Railway's well established and widespread shipping interests. The Eastern Region would eventually disappear in the run up to privatisation in the 1990s, but long before that its direct operation of ships had ceased, with the creation by British Railways of what came to be called Sealink.

The actual operation of ships by the Eastern Region was therefore restricted to roughly two decades from 1948. So the topic extends beyond the Eastern Region in date and business but retains the railway connection. Earlier material from the Great Eastern and the London and North Eastern railways appears. The famed Manchester Boat Train to Harwich is described. A wealth of railway-issued Harwich material extended far into Europe and this is shown. Likewise, Continental-issued material for travel into Britain is shown. A remarkable artistic quality in this material from the 1950s and 1960s is evident. Until 1978, the railway operated Humber services included steam paddle ships, which also feature.

The railway also connected with other shipping lines. This enabled operators as varied as the General Steam Navigation Thames pleasure sailings, the Swedish Lloyd services from Tilbury, and other Scandinavian operators like DFDS, Fred. Olsen and Tor Line to be involved. These partners extend the narrative to the Tyne.

Freight services are not forgotten. The Harwich train ferry, the adoption of containerisation, and the liner services of Associated Humber Lines are represented through their publicity. Harwich was a railway-owned port. Its opposite companion was built by the Felixstowe Dock & Railway Co. which, avoiding nationalisation, remained an independent port and railway operator. Therefore, services from Felixstowe feature. Between the Haven ports and the Humber the railway had a presence at several other ports, enabling Lowestoft and the Wash to be visited.

In assembling the material, it has been fascinating to see the sheer spread covered from the technical excellence and innovation of vessels like the *Parkeston*, to long-forgotten services like the ALA in the Thames. By coming to the Tyne and encountering the former Tilbury railway ferry *Catherine* still hard at work in 2005, a neat symmetry appeared.

It is stressed that all this material (aside from one item which receives special pleading) comes from our own collection. This has been deliberate policy with these volumes. Partly this is out of practicality: we live physically remote from major collections. Another justification is to show other potential students of the subject what can still be assembled with patience and dedication. Those who approach the subject with their own knowledge will realise that for all that has been assembled, there are still certain sizeable gaps. Should relevant material be in danger of being disposed of, I invite contact via the publisher.

If the reader wishes to explore the subject further, my two previous related volumes were published by Tempus and may still be purchased:

To Western Scottish Waters: By Rail and Steamer to the Isles (2000) 0-7524-2104-2
Irish Sea Shipping Publicised (2002) 0-7524-2355-X

Acknowledgements

To Campbell McCutcheon at Tempus, a big thank you for his interest and support throughout this series. Likewise to my wife Fiona who, strange as it may seem, is easily as enthusiastic about the subject as I am. In recent years we thank baby Clare too who did not really understand why Daddy had to stare at a funny screen so much (and became schoolgirl Clare whilst we wrote this). Specific help with this volume has come from Lindsay Jameson at Associated British Ports, Wendy Hooper-Greenhill at Fred. Olsen, George Robinson and Ron Mapplebeck for the dredger *Goole Bight*, Twan Laan in Holland and Helen Sharkey at Hutchison Ports (UK) Ltd (Felixstowe).

The copyright ambiguities surrounding this material are considerable. I have contacted and acknowledge the courtesy of the following interested organisations: Associated British Ports, British Railways Board (Residuary) Ltd, DFDS, Fred. Olsen Cruise Lines, Hutchison Ports (UK) Ltd, Nederlandse Spoorwegen, the P&O History and Archives at the National Maritime Museum, Stena Line, Tyne Leisure Line Ltd.

Should anyone feel I have infringed their interests, I am sorry and I plead indulgence.

The material has been collected from many sources and it is usually invidious to single out individual contributors. However not only has John Batts provided significant amounts of the older material but he took on the task of undertaking a proofread of the manuscript through a stranger's eye, which is a job well worth a thank you.

Selected Brief Chronology

1661 First official regular packet service from Harwich
1863 First Great Eastern Railway shipping service from Harwich
1866 DFDS founded
1883 Harwich Parkeston Quay opened
1900 Tyne Commission Quay station opened
1924 Train ferry started from Harwich
1925 DFDS introduced *Parkeston* to Harwich service: world's first short sea motor passenger ship
1930 Opening of Tilbury Landing Stage
1931 World's then fastest motor ship the *Venus* took up Newcastle–Bergen sailings
1964 DFDS introduced *England*, the North Sea's first car ferry
1967 Felixstowe started handling Freightliner services
1968 BR Roll on/Roll off and ISO Freightliner services started at Harwich
1969 Sealink brand introduced
1981 DFDS take over Tor Line and Prins Ferries
1984 British Railways-owned Sealink privatised
1989 Stena Line purchase Zeeland/Crown Line
1990 Stena Line purchase Sealink British Ferries
1997 Stena Line introduce High Speed Superferry (HSS) at Harwich.

Chapter 1

From the Thames

Any examination of railway-owned (and connected) shipping from Tilbury to Tyneside
will need to consider the relatively humble cross-Thames operation between Tilbury and
Gravesend whose 'railway' lineage lasted from the 1862 takeover by the London Tilbury &
Southend Railway to its sale by a then privatised Sealink operation in 1991.

Our focus will be on the 1961 trio of motor vessels which replaced steam on the ferry.
This is not just because of the material available but the subsequent history of the trio links
directly to the end of the volume on Tyneside and across to our earlier book *To Western
Scottish Waters*.

This picture from 21 August 1982 comes from the period when the 1961 sisters *Edith*
and *Catherine* held the service. Ominously, the ferry is not well laden. *Edith* is leaving
Gravesend pier. Her sister was tied up there; the spare boat *Rose* had long since departed
for other waters, as will be explained.

For many decades until the end of 1964, the railway operated two separate services between the towns. *Tessa* and *Mimie* were two 1920s steam-powered vehicle ferries built for the LMS that shuttled between Tilbury and Gravesend (Car Ferry Pier). The accompanying Edmondson card ticket for this service shows that motor coaches could be catered for.

Opposite: The passenger-only vessels worked from Gravesend Town Pier although in 1965 this was changed to the West Pier. The Town Pier, dating to 1834, became derelict, and was only restored after 2000.

The services did not generate a lot of free-standing publicity but had a page to themselves in the British Railways Eastern Region timetable. This extract is from the September 1960 issue and clearly shows the twin services.

Another regular haunt for the service was an entry in the London Transport Gravesend and District timetable book.

Table 17

TILBURY - GRAVESEND FERRY STEAMERS

(Weather and other circumstances permitting).

APPROXIMATE CROSSING TIME 5 MINUTES

TILBURY TO GRAVESEND (Town Pier)

WEEK DAYS								SUNDAYS				
dep am	dep am	dep am	dep pm	dep pm	dep pm	dep pm	dep pm	dep am	dep am	dep pm	dep pm	dep pm
5 25	8 15	10 30	12S30	2 45	5 0	7 15	9 45	7 0	11 50	3 20	6 0	8 15
6 0	8 30	10 52	12 45	3 0	5 20	7 30	10 15	7 35		3 50	6 15	8 30
6 30	8 45	11 10	1 0	3 15	5 30	7 45	10 45	8 6	pm	4 0	6 30	8 50
6 45	9 0	11 30	1 15	3 30	5 45	8 0	11 15	8 50	12 20	4 20	6 45	9 20
7 0	9 15	11 45	1 30	3 45	6 0	8 15	11 45	9 20	12 50	4 45	7 0	9 50
7 15	9 30	noon	1 45	4 0	6 15	8 30	night	9 50	1 20	5 0	7 15	10 15
7 30	9 45	12 0	2 0	4 15	6 30	8 45	12S15	10 20	1 50	5 15	7 30	10 45
7 45	10 0	pm	2 15	4 30	6 45	9 0	12 45	10 50	2 20	5 30	7 45	11 15
8 3	10 15	12 15	2 30	4 45	7 0	9 15		11 20	2 50	5 45	8 0	11 45

GRAVESEND (Town Pier) TO TILBURY

WEEK DAYS								SUNDAYS				
dep am	dep am	dep am	dep pm	dep pm	dep pm	dep pm	dep pm	dep am	dep am	dep pm	dep pm	dep pm
5 15	8 0	10 15	12 15	2 30	4 45	7 0	9 30	6 30	11 30	2 30	6 15	8 30
5 44	8 15	10 30	12 30	2 45	5 0	7 15	10 0	7 25		3 0	6 30	8 40
6 15	8 30	10 45	12S45	3 0	5 18	7 30	10 30	7 50	noon	3 30	6 45	9 0
6 30	8 45	11 0	1 0	3 15	5 30	7 45	11 0	8 16	12 0	4 0	7 0	9 30
6 45	9 0	11 20	1 15	3 30	5 45	8 0	11 30	9 0	pm	4 30	7 15	10 0
7 0	9 15	11 45	1 30	3 45	6 0	8 15		9 30	12 30	5 0	7 30	10 30
7 15	9 30		1 45	4 0	6 15	8 30	night	10 0	1 0	5 30	7 45	11 0
7 29	9 45	noon	2 0	4 15	6 30	8 45	12 0	10 30	1 30	5 45	8 0	11 30
7 45	10 0	12 0	2 15	4 30	6 45	9 0	12S25	11 0	2 0	6 0	8 15	

S—Saturdays only

VEHICLE FERRY

Motor cars, road vehicles and goods traffic are conveyed by ferry steamers between Tilbury and Gravesend (Car Ferry Pier) as under:—

TILBURY TO GRAVESEND (CAR FERRY PIER)		GRAVESEND (CAR FERRY PIER) TO TILBURY	
Week Days Sundays	7 5 am, 7 25, 7 45 am then at 5, 25, 45 minutes past each hour until 10 5 am then at 5, and 35 minutes past each hour until 4 5 pm, then 4 25, 4 45, 5 5, 5 25, 5 45, 6 5, 6 35, 7 5, 7 35, 8 5, 8 45, 9 25, 10 5, and 10 30 pm	Week Days Sundays	7 5 am, 7 25, 7 45 am then at 5, 25, 45 minutes past each hour until 10 5 am then at 5, 35 minutes past each hour until 4 5 pm then 4 25 4 45, 5 5, 5 25, 5 45, 6 5, 6 35, 7 5, 7 35, 8 5, 8 25, 9 5, 9 45 and 10 20 pm

Passengers are also conveyed by the vehicle ferry

CONDITIONS

Passengers and other persons are admitted to the British Transport Commission's piers and quays and are carried in the Commission's vessels upon and subject to the Bye-Laws, Regulations and Conditions, where applicable, published from time to time in the Commission's publications and notices applicable to British Railways.

The Commission hereby give notice that they will not be liable for any loss of, or damage (including any leakage or breakage) or delay to any goods, carriages, live stock, Passenger's Luggage or articles of any kind whatsoever carried or about to be carried on the Steam Ferry from Essex to Kent or vice versa, or to or from any vessel in the Thames whether such loss, damage or delay occurs on the Commission's boats or their premises or in embarking or disembarking, or if left till called for, or held for convenience of the owners or depositors of any such goods except upon proof that such loss, damage, or delay was caused by the wilful misconduct of the Commission's servants.

208

17

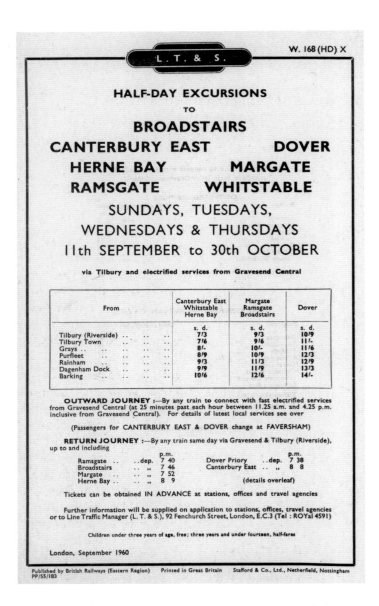

Published by British Railways (Eastern Region)   Printed in Great Britain   Stafford & Co., Ltd., Netherfield, Nottingham
PP/55/183

The ferries made a regular appearance on one genre of handbill issued by both the Southern and Eastern Regions of BR. The ferry offered a route avoiding London for foot excursionists wanting to travel from Essex to South Coast resorts, and for trippers to Southend from south of the Thames. This market was tapped in a series of handbills.

The example shown from the summer of 1960 comes from the tail end of the lives of the first trio of *Rose/Catherine/Edith* sisters. These were steamers built between 1901 and 1911.

Crossing the Thames on them must have come as a contrast to the new Kent Coast electrics on the south bank. On the north bank, the electric trains did not appear until late in 1961, by which time the ferry itself had been modernised to diesel power.

For the collector the handbill has added interest in its LT&S header. This represented a short-lived revival of pre-grouping identities on the Eastern Region.

1966 RIVER TRIPS

by modern diesel ferries

from

Tilbury

Gravesend

Greenwich

and

Tower Bridge

15 June to 8 September

The highlight of the diesel boat's lives at Gravesend is represented by this glossy leaflet. From 1963 a programme of cruises was offered up-river to Tower Bridge and between Tower Bridge and Greenwich. One feature of the 1966 leaflet shown was a map of this section of river.

The Tilbury–Gravesend service remains in operation. Until 2002 a modern fast ferry of White Horse Ferries undertook the crossing, although this was an operator then in financial difficulties. More recently Thames Fast Ferries have been the operator of what is a subsidised service. The train service on the north bank at Tilbury Riverside, which had been an impressive terminal station, was replaced by a bus link to Tilbury Town from 30 November 1992. The station was mouldering away as this book was written.

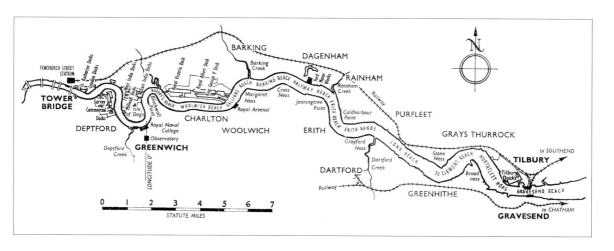

Was the ability to offer cruises affected by the 1967 sale of the *Rose*? On 13 May 1987 *Keppel*, née *Rose*, was approaching Wemyss Bay on the Firth of Clyde after two decades in Scotland. She had gone north in 1967 to handle the Largs–Millport service. Her final use by Caledonian MacBrayne was as an excursion vessel between 1987 and 1992, in which guise she is portrayed.

Opposite: Up-river of Tilbury, railway maritime interests were not restricted to a few cruises. As far inland as Brentford, there was a rail-connected dock. Around 1960 this lavish fourteen-page brochure was printed for British Railways by The Curwen Press, often used by BR for prestigious work.

The Eastern Region was able to serve the West and East India Docks, the Royal Docks complex, which the branch line to North Woolwich bisected by tunnel, and the Tilbury Docks.

At the time Freightliner had not been heard of. Great weight was given to the Export Express Service promising next day delivery between selected stations and the docks for wagonload traffic. The selection of stations in the list owed much to established customers who were present at certain locations and had call on this facility. This explained how such wayside locations as Birtley and Saffron Walden entered the lists. Saffron Walden had Acrow's engineering works with a healthy export trade. By the end of 1964 Saffron Walden had no railway at all.

British Railways

Services

to the Export

& Import Trade

at the

Port of London

Opposite: Railway passengers did not just arrive at the commodious Tilbury Riverside station for the Gravesend ferry. From the moment the railway had arrived at Tilbury in 1854 all sorts of maritime possibilities loomed. The 1882 Act that created Tilbury Docks ensured Tilbury's maritime importance although elements of the railway-connected steamer and liner traffic used riverside berths adjacent to the station. This was particularly the case after 1930 when the Tilbury (Floating) Landing Stage was opened by Ramsay MacDonald. Such an event was bound to produce nice publicity. One I only know of by repute is deep in the third volume of Ottley's *Bibliography of Railway History*. Item 16390 is a Public Record Office copy of a descriptive brochure jointly produced by the LMS railway and the Port of London Authority to celebrate this opening. Ottley's recording of ephemera is variable, so this record is pleasing, as, doubtless, is the actual item.

What is illustrated spins out a yarn. The initials ALA are recognised by relatively modern ship enthusiasts in association with the Dover train ferries *Twickenham Ferry* and *St Eloi* which ultimately led to ALA in 1977 becoming a French company wholly owned by British Railways.

ALA stood for Angleterre Lorraine Alsace. The original plan of this French company was to run a Tilbury–Dunkirk service. This started in 1927 and used ex-LMS Irish Sea steamers. The depression years did not help and by 1932 ALA had moved operations to Folkestone and became closely associated instead with the Southern Railway. The collector's challenge is to find ALA material from Tilbury. That is a challenge I cannot yet rise to, and what is shown is probably even more unusual. For a brief period in 1930, the (desperate) company tried Channel cruises to Dunkirk from Southend and here is a handbill for that operation. The ship was the *Lorrain* which would go to Belgian breakers in 1932. Originally she had been the LNWR's *Rathmore* on the Holyhead–Greenore service. Truly this vessel was a master of the commercial backwater.

A. L. A.

SUMMER PLEASURE STEAMERS
DAY TRIPS TO FRANCE.

SOUTHEND PIER to
DUNKERQUE

For the Seaside Resort—MALO-LES-BAINS

NO PASSPORTS REQUIRED————————4½ HOURS IN FRANCE

The fast luxurious twin-screw

S.S. "LORRAIN"

(2014 tons—Accommodating 940 passengers)

will leave Southend Pier at 9 a.m.

Every Saturday, Sunday and Monday

UNTIL FURTHER NOTICE.

Due at Dunkerque 1.30 p.m.—Leave at 6 p.m.

Fares
(Light hand luggage only)

To Return same Day	. .	**12/6**
Children 6/6		
To Return on following day or day after . .	. .	**20/4**
Children 12/4		

CABINS CAN BE ENGAGED: 2/6 each way.

Fully licensed bars on board ; BREAKFAST 2/- — LUNCH 3/- — TEA 1/- — DINNER 3/-

PASSENGERS PERMITTED ON BOARD AT 8 a.m.

Subject to fourteen or more passengers desiring the same, motor-coach trips, for which tickets may be obtained from Mr. Chas. DALE, can be arranged as follows :—

FOR DAY EXCURSION.—Poperinghe and Ypres: 7/5. Ostend: 6/6.

Buses to Malo-les-Bains: 3 francs.

FOR WEEK-END EXCURSION.—*Saturday and Sunday:* Cassel, Lille (night), Vimy, Arras: 17/3. *Sunday and Monday:* Ghent, Brussels (night) Bruges: 25/-

---

Agent: **Chas. DALE**, 5, Clarence Street, SOUTHEND-ON-SEA.

TELEPHONE 6314.

Passengers can also book at the Pier Head on day of sailing.

B. H. PRIEST. Printer, 22a & 24 Balmoral Road, Westcliff-on-Sea.

As the 24-hour system for Railway Time operates on the Continent, it is used in this time-table thus :—12.00 noon, 18.00 6 p.m., 24.00 arrival midnight, 0.00 departure midnight.

LONDON—SCANDINAVIA

Via TILBURY—GOTHENBURG

SWEDISH LLOYD LINE

(Swedish Lloyd Steamship Co., Gothenburg)

(The British & Northern Shipping Agency Ltd.)

Miles.	OUTWARDS.			Until May 29	June 1 to Sept. 30
				M.S. SAGA. S.S. BRITANNIA. S.S. SUECIA. Mondays, Thursdays and Saturdays, except May 15 & 22 (See Note " a.")	M.S. SAGA. S.S. BRITANNIA. S.S. SUECIA. Mondays, Wednesdays, Thursdays and Saturdays, except Sept. 21 & 28 (See Note " a.")
—	London (St. Pancras Station) (Riverside Station)	… … … … … …	dep. arr.	1 & 3 Cl. 15 55 16 55	SWEDISH LLOYD SPECIAL
29	Tilbury { (Landing Stage)	… … … … … …	arr.	1 & 3 Cl. (b) 18 30	
618	Gothenburg (Stigbergskajen) 🚉	… (C.E.T.) third day, arr. about		7 00	
				Until Aug. 27	
618	Gothenburg (C)	… … … … … …	dep.	2 & 3 Cl. 8R25	2 & 3 Cl. 12R05
901	Stockholm (C)	… … … … … …	arr.	15 00	18 35
				Daily (See Note " c ")	
901	Stockholm (Skeppsbron) 🚉	… … … … … …	dep.	1 & 2 Cl. 11 00	
1137	Helsingfors—Helsinki (South Harbour) 🚉 (E.E.T.) next day, arr. about			10 00	
				Daily (See Note " d ")	
901	Stockholm (Skeppsbron) 🚉	… … … … (C.E.T.)	dep.	1 & 2 Cl. 16 00	
1066	Åbo-Turku (Harbour) 🚉 … … (E.E.T.) { next day, arr. about dep.			8 00 10R50h	
1192	Helsingfors—Helsinki (C)	… … … … … …	arr.	16 37h	
				Until June 9	June 10 to Aug. 27
618	Gothenburg (C)	… … … … … … (C.E.T.)	dep.	1, 2 & 3 Cl. 16R15	2 & 3 Cl. 12s35	1, 2 & 3 Cl. 21 15	16 15	20 26
804	Malmö (C)	… … … … … …	arr.		
618	Gothenburg (C)	… … … … … …	dep.	1, 2 & 3 Cl. 16R15	2 & 3 Cl. 12s35	1, 2 & 3 Cl. 20 06	15 43	20 01
769	Hälsingborg (F) 🚉	… … … … … { arr. dep.		20 27	2 & 3 Cl. 15s48	20 27
772	Helsingör 🚉	… … … … … { arr. dep.		20 56	16 32	20 54
800	Copenhagen (H)	… … … … … …	arr.	21 23	16 32	21 23	22 15	17s20	22 15
618	Gothenburg (C)	… … … … … …	dep.	1, 2 & 3 Cl. 13R26	1, 2 & 3 Cl. 13R26
735	Kornsjö 🚉	… … … … … { arr. dep.		16 30 16 45	16 30 16 45
840	Oslo (Ö)	… … … … … …	arr.	19 45	19 45

R—Restaurant Car. 🚉—Frontier Station.

(a)—Actual sailings :—
M.S. SAGA—May 18, 25, June 1, 7, 12, 17, 22, 28, July 3, 8, 13, 19, 24, 29, Sept. 4, 9, 14, 20, 27.
S.S. BRITANNIA—May 27, June 5, 10, 15, 21, 26, July 1, 6, 12, 17, 22, 27, Aug. 2, 7, 12, 17, 23, 28, Sept. 2, 7, 13, 18, 23.
S.S. SUECIA—May 20, 29, June 3, 8, 14, 19, 24, 29, July 5, 10, 15, 20, 26, 31, Aug. 5, 10, 16, 21, 26, 31, Sept. 6, 11, 16, 25, 30.
(b)—M.S. SAGA has accommodation for 2nd Class passengers at a supplement of £3 0s. 0d. above 3rd Class fares.
(c)—Daily until Sept. 8 (except Mondays and May 16, 18, 20, 23, 25 & 27.)
(d)—Daily until Sept. 2 (except May 21 & 28.)
(e)—Limited to passengers holding seat reservations. (reservation fee 4s. 6d. per seat.)
(g)—Change at, and depart from, Angelholm 15.19
(h)—Alternative service by motor coach. Åbo dep. 8.40. Helsingfors arr. 12.40.

For fares, see Fares section at end of Handbook.

— 144 —

SCANDINAVIA—LONDON

Via GOTHENBURG—TILBURY

SWEDISH LLOYD LINE

(Swedish Lloyd Steamship Co., Gothenburg)

(The British & Northern Shipping Agency Ltd.)

	INWARDS.			Until June 9	June 10 to Aug. 27
Oslo (Ö)	… … … … … … (C.E.T.)	dep.		1, 2 & 3 Cl. 9R35	1, 2 & 3 Cl. 9R35
Kornsjö 🚉	… … … … … { arr. dep.			12 30 12 46	12 35 12 50
Gothenburg (C)	… … … … … …	arr.		15 55	16 02
Copenhagen (H)	… … … … … …	dep.		2 & 3 Cl. 7 05	2 & 3 Cl. 7 30	2 & 3 Cl. 13s00g
Helsingör 🚉	… … … … … { arr. dep.			7 55 8 25	8 20 8 50	13 47 14 00
Hälsingborg (F) 🚉	… … … … … { arr. dep.			8 46 1, 2 & 3 Cl. 9R21	9 17 1, 2 & 3 Cl. 9R50	14 27 2 & 3 Cl. 14 44g
Gothenburg (C)	… … … … … …	arr.		13 11	13 09	17 54
Malmö (C)	… … … … … …	dep.		2 & 3 Cl. 8R20	2 & 3 Cl. 9R35	2 & 3 Cl. 14e12
Gothenburg (C)	… … … … … …	arr.		13 11	14 38	17 54
				Daily (See Note " c ")	
Helsingfors—Helsinki (C)	… … … … (E.E.T.)	dep.		1 & 2 Cl. 12R30h	
Åbo-Turku (Harbour) 🚉	… … … … … { arr. dep.			17 05h 19 00	
Stockholm (Skeppsbron) 🚉 … (C.E.T.) next day, arr. about				9 00	
				Daily (See Note " d ")	
Helsingfors—Helsinki (South Harbour) 🚉	… … … …	dep.		1 & 2 Cl. 11 00	
Stockholm (Skeppsbron) 🚉 … next day, arr. about				8 00	
				Until June 9	June 10 to Aug. 27
Stockholm (C)	… … … … … (E.E.T.)	dep.		2 & 3 Cl. 8R30	1, 2 & 3 Cl. 9R20
Gothenburg (C)	… … … … … (C.E.T.)	arr.		15 10	15 25
				Until May 31	From June 1 to Sept. 30
				M.S. SAGA. S.S. BRITANNIA. S.S. SUECIA. Tuesdays and Saturdays only (See Note " a.")	M.S. SAGA. S.S. BRITANNIA. S.S. SUECIA. Mondays, Tuesdays, Thursdays and Saturdays, except Sept. 19 & 26 (See Note " a.")
Gothenburg (Stigbergskajen) 🚉 … … (C.E.T.)	dep.			1 & 3 Cl. (b) 19 00	SWEDISH LLOYD SPECIAL
Tilbury { (Landing Stage) 🚉 third day, dep. about				7 00	
	(Riverside Station)	… … … …	dep. about	1 & 3 Cl. 9 00	
London (St. Pancras Station)	… … … …	arr. about	10 00		

R—Restaurant Car. 🚉—Frontier Station.

(a)—Actual sailings :—
M.S. SAGA—May 16, 23, 30. June 5, 10, 15, 20, 26, July 1, 6, 11, 17, 22, 27, Aug. 1, 7, 12, 17, 22, 28, Sept. 2, 7, 12, 18, 25.
S.S. BRITANNIA—May 20, June 3, 8, 13, 19, 24, 29, July 4, 10, 15, 20, 25, 31, Aug. 5, 10, 15, 21, 26, 31, Sept. 5, 11, 16, 21, 30.
S.S. SUECIA—May 27, June, 1, 6, 12, 17, 22, 27, July 3, 8, 13, 18, 24, 29, Aug. 3, 8, 14, 19, 24, 29, Sept. 4, 9, 14, 23, 28.
(b)—M.S. SAGA has also accommodation for 2nd Class passengers at a supplement of £3 0s. 0d. above 3rd Class fares.
(c)—Daily until Sept. 2 (except May 21 & 28.)
(d)—Daily until Sept.B (except Mondays and June 24, 26, 27).
(e)—Limited to passengers holding seat reservations (reservations fee equivalent to sterling charge of 4s. 6d. per seat).
(g)—Change at, and depart from, Angelholm 15.14.
(h)—Alternative service by motor coach Helsingfors dep. 14.00, Åbo arr. 18.00.

For fares, see Fares section at end of Handbook.

— 145 —

For several other Tilbury shipping operators, the train connection was worked to London St Pancras, the former Midland Railway station which offered good connections beyond London.

One such was Swedish Lloyd whose Tilbury service made the change to a car ferry. Their history from 1916 means that a range of Swedish Lloyd ephemera can be found. Two passenger-only ships were built for the route after the Second World War. The 1946 *Saga* and the 1951 *Patricia* were virtually mini liners. The latter was Tyne-built.

Their service, along with the named train connection *The Swedish Lloyd Special*, could be traced after 1950 in the British Railways *Continental Handbook*. This had grown out of an expanded Southern Railway production. Its twice yearly issues are a key source until it was abandoned in May 1960 and replaced by the series of national booklets. The St Pancras boat trains were discontinued from 1 April 1963.

24

An actual Swedish Lloyd-published item is this autumn 1952 timetable. A very characterful cover with the funnel emblem prominent. How I wish I knew whether they owned any tugs! If so, they were probably at the Gothenburg end of the route. The sixteen-page timetable contained colour fold-out plans for the 1946 *Saga* and the 1929 Swan Hunter twins the *Britannia* and the *Suecia*. The 1951 *Patricia* was absent because this was the winter timetable. She was experimenting with a winter cruise to Bermuda. Her side profile is the cover!

The train connection in Sweden to the capital was a much longer journey than to St Pancras, but it was a named train too – the *Londonpilen*. The brochure was illustrated with drawings and monochromes, one of which showed cars being craned aboard ship at the London Pier in Gothenburg.

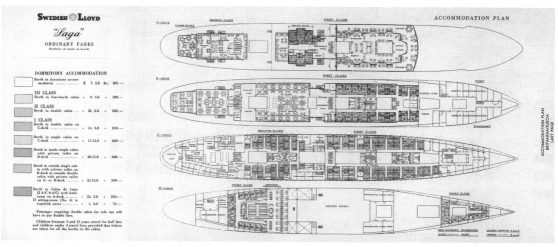

SWEDISH LLOYD
TILBURY
GOTHENBURG
CAR FERRY

SAILINGS AND FARES

1st APRIL 1976
30th SEPTEMBER 1976

When the passenger-only service changed to car ferries, the thirty-seven-year-old *Suecia* and *Britannia* closed the service in 1966. They then went to the Greeks for Mediterranean cruising.

The replacement was more than a car ferry – it was a consortium. For a while Swedish Lloyd joined forces with Wilson Line's Hull–Gothenburg operation. Swedish Lloyd ran the Tilbury car ferry service with the 1966 *Saga* and Wilson's 1966 *Spero* maintained the Hull link. A third member of the consortium was Svea Line, with another new ship – the *Svea*.

Wilson's withdrew their service in 1973, which left Swedish Lloyd to re-assert themselves with their own publicity, as in this 1976 leaflet, before their service disappeared. The 1966 *Saga* is the cover vessel.

Tilbury was pre-eminently a port for the world whether with cargo or with passenger lines. For instance both the Clan Line and the Orient Line were long associated with the port. One momentous arrival was the SS *Empire Windrush* in 1948 with the first shipload of organised Caribbean immigrants. An interesting cross between liner and packet services is represented by this leaflet for 1960.

Its cover smacks of the 1960s, hinting at a Pink Panther film credit. The purpose of the leaflet was to tack on 'ferry' crossings to what were really the Europe–Canada schedules of QSS *Arkadia*. Her 20,260 tons would be eclipsed by many a ferry today.

The leaflet advised that getting to Tilbury was the passenger's responsibility: there were no through rail/sea tickets. Nor was it very clear from exactly where the ship sailed, but my guess is that it was from within the docks. Certain liner companies like P&O had arrangements that took boat trains into the docks complex for alongside transfer. The Greek Line's use of Tilbury appears to have been quite short-lived. Their routes used Southampton and not Tilbury in 1954. By 1967 they had abandoned northern Europe altogether.

Germany and Holland by OCEAN LINER

FROM TILBURY TO AMSTERDAM & BREMERHAVEN

Q.s.s. "ARKADIA"
(20,260 tons)

GREEK LINE
28 PICCADILLY LONDON W.I. TEL. REGENT 4141

From JUNE 9th until SEPT. 16th, 1956

P.S. "MEDWAY QUEEN"

will leave **SOUTHEND PIERHEAD** Daily
(FRIDAYS and JUNE 16th excepted)

at 10.55 a.m.

For 3 Hours SEA TRIP and 4½ Hours ASHORE at

HERNE BAY

ALSO offering 3 Hours in the ANCIENT CITY of

CANTERBURY

—arriving Herne Bay 12.30 p.m.; leaving 5.0 p.m.
back at SOUTHEND 6.30 p.m.

HERNE BAY	FARES		CANTERBURY
Single	Day Return	Period Return	Day Ret. (Boat & 'Bus)
6'6	**8'-**	**12'-**	**10'6**
CHILDREN: 3 to 14 years HALF FARE			CHILD 5/6

Sailings are subject to weather and other circumstances permitting

TICKETS INCLUDE ADMISSION TO PIERS

EAGLE & QUEEN LINE STEAMERS

PIER HILL, SOUTHEND-ON-SEA

MAY   Telephone: **66597** (May/Sept.)   P.T.O.

"Medway Queen," last of the paddle steamers on the River Thames, is very popular on the Herne Bay service, and, with the combined East Kent Road service to Canterbury, offers an excellent day's outing at a moderate cost. Passengers for Canterbury join the 'bus or coach at the entrance to Herne Bay pier, and in about half an hour following a pleasant drive through the Kent countryside, arrive in Canterbury, which abounds in historic treasures, apart from the attraction of the great Cathedral. Herne Bay is one of the quieter resorts of Kent, with good fishing facilities, and easy transport to Whitstable, Tankerton, etc.

"Medway Queen" is fully licensed, and luncheons, teas and light refreshments are obtainable aboard at moderate prices.

1.—Passengers are carried only on the terms and conditions printed on the Company's Sailing Bills, Leaflets and Notices and/or bye-laws, regulations and conditions contained in the publications and notices of or applicable to the British Transport Commission.

CONDITIONS OF CARRIAGE

(1) Passengers are carried subject to it being hereby agreed that the General Steam Navigation Co. Ltd. (hereinafter referred to as "the Company" which term shall include the Shipowners, the Line, Charterers, Managers, Operators and the Ship, as the case may be) shall not be liable for the death of or injury, damage, loss, delay or accident to passengers, their apparel or baggage, whensoever, wheresoever and howsoever caused and whether by negligence of their servants or agents, or by unseaworthiness of the vessel (whether existing at the time of embarkation or sailing, or at any other time) or otherwise nor for any sea or river risks whatsoever.

(2) By accepting or receiving a ticket each passenger agrees both on his or her behalf and on behalf of any person or child travelling with him or her or in his or her care that all rights, exemptions from liability, defences and immunities of whatsoever nature referred to in Clause 1 hereof shall in all respects enure also for the benefit of any servant or agents of the Company acting in the course of or in connection with their employment so that in no circumstances shall any such servant or agent as the result of so acting be under any liability to any such passenger or to any such person or child greater than or different from that of the Company. For the purposes of the agreement contained in this clause, the Company is or shall be deemed to be acting on behalf and for the benefit of all persons who are or may be its servants or agents from time to time, and all such persons shall to this extent be or be deemed to be parties to the contract contained in or evidenced by such ticket.

Opposite and above: Taking a ship from Tilbury was not the way most Londoners experienced the Thames estuary. Until the 1960s by far the most popular way to do this was aboard one of the pleasure 'steamers'. Eagle & Queen Line Steamers was itself part of the General Steam Navigation Co., an organisation that, as it abandoned pleasure steamer operation, was to involve itself in car ferries at Southampton and ultimately to become part of P&O Ferries.

In the heyday eighty or more years ago, the pleasure tripper from the Thames was spoilt for choice with names like Belle Steamers, New Medway Steam Packet and General Steam. General Steam was the daddy of the operators, being founded in 1824 and running services from the Thames for 140 years.

General Steam bought New Medway around 1937, and with it came the 1924 paddler *Medway Queen*. She remains in existence in 2006 although she has not carried passengers for decades. Her fame came through her participation in the Dunkirk evacuation and in practically closing regular Thames excursion paddle steamer services with her demise after the 1963 season.

The handbill here is for her 1956 season calls at Southend Pierhead, whose length required its own railway to transport passengers to and from the shore. At Herne Bay the connection to and from Canterbury was by East Kent bus.

The 1950s publicity shouted out Eagle steamers – note how the 'E' is treated – but behind this facade it was the General Steam Co. This brochure was a glossy affair, unlike the previous handbill, and it was targeted at the organiser of group excursions. Although a paddler like *Medway Queen* excited nostalgia, the company had been investing in modern diesel-powered excursion ships since the *Queen of the Channel*, built by Denny's in 1935.

This leaflet cover highlighted the three principal vessels of the 1950s: *Royal Sovereign*, *Royal Daffodil* and *Queen of the Channel*. Only *Royal Daffodil* of 1939 dated from before the war, the other two being replacements of war losses. The ships were illustrated in monochrome inside. At around 1,500 to 2,000 tons each they were a familiar sight anywhere between London's Tower Pier, Clacton, the Kent Coast and beyond to the French and Belgian coasts.

Opposite: General Steam relied largely for its ticketing on the classic Edmondson card. A good number of these have survived, thanks to the Transport Ticket Society.

Those shown illustrate:

1. A voyage from Clacton to Yarmouth (the northern extremity of operations).
2. A Tilbury to Calais trip (note the mention of British Railways, which will be explained shortly, and the Passport Essential over-stamp).
3. An evening cruise from London's Tower Pier at the end of operations, it is dated 9 June 1966 and the vessel is named.
4. A ticket which could hardly be more basic – for that British staple of 'Fish and Chips'. Others in this vein included 'Hot Lunch' or 'Cold Lunch'.

0265

Ticket issued subject to Conditions
on Sailing Bills, Leaflets & Notices.
General Steam Navigation Co. Ltd.

AVAILABLE DAY OF ISSUE ONLY

CLACTON to YARMOUTH

Does NOT admit to Sun Deck Enclosure
SINGLE FARE 15/-

0265

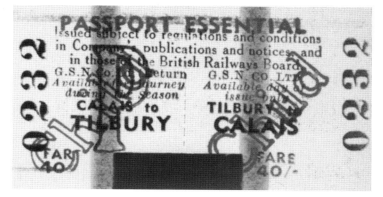

0232

PASSPORT ESSENTIAL

Issued subject to regulations and conditions
in Company's publications and notices, and
in those of the British Railways Board
G.S.N. Co. Ltd. return   G.S.N. Co. Ltd.
Available for journey   Available day of
during the season   issue only

CALAIS to TILBURY   TILBURY to CALAIS

FARE 40/-   FARE 40/-

0232

0462

M.V. ROYAL DAFFODIL
Ticket issued subject to Conditions
on Sailing Bills, Leaflets & Notices.
General Steam Navigation Co. Ltd.

AVAILABLE DAY OF ISSUE ONLY

EVENING RIVER CRUISE
FROM
TOWER PIER
THURSDAY, 9th JUNE, 1966
FARE 10/-

0462

General Steam Navigation Co. Ltd.

FISH & CHIPS
(No. 1)

4623

DAY EXCURSIONS by RAIL and STEAMER

W.303

CALAIS AND BOULOGNE

54/-

DAY RETURN FARE

from
FENCHURCH STREET or LIVERPOOL STREET
(via Southend-on-Sea)
with bookings from intermediate stations

BRITISH RAILWAYS in conjunction with the General Steam Navigation Co. Ltd.

This talk of General Steam might seem to have little to do with the Eastern Region of British Railways. Indeed the vessel name *Queen of the Channel* suggests an activity at first sight far removed from Fenchurch Street station.

One of the highlights of the General Steam programme was the 'no passport' day cruise to Calais or Boulogne. This was revived after the war in 1954 when *Royal Daffodil* took up the Gravesend–Southend–Boulogne run and *Queen of the Channel* took French trips from Clacton and Ramsgate.

Rail connections made a day out to France using the General Steam service possible from Essex and the East End of London. The BR-issued handbill probably existed in a series from 1954. I have several – this is from 1963. If taken from the London terminals the full day started at about 8 a.m., ended shortly after midnight, and offered three hours in the French port. These excursions ran, in 1963, four days a week and a footnote ties in with a ticket just seen. The connection was usually made at Southend Pier and a considerable note was needed to explain to patrons how to get to the pier from either of the two Southend stations – this must have been the longest cross-channel train/ship interchange. On Mondays the handbill advised that the ship started from Tilbury (Landing Stage) at 9 a.m., an hour before the Southend call, and that tickets would be valid via that connection.

The tickets were issued on demand at only a few stations. If travelling from the majority of suburban stations along the two routes to Southend, a day's notice was required. BR also hoped for the favour of party bookings, and special tickets for a BR/GSN party on this route were printed.

The handbill was replaced by a leaflet for the final three seasons prior to the General Steam motor ships being withdrawn after the 1966 season. The cover for 1964 is shown. One of the General Steam's motor ships did the honours along with an electric multiple unit. The latter must have been the most unromantic BR ship-connecting train anywhere. About the only positive thing was that these electric trains, later to be Classes 302 and 307, were new, being built from 1956. Their design was very old fashioned with slam-door compartments. Despite their conservatism they were to last a lot longer than the General Steam motor ships. Many provided forty years' service.

British Railways
in conjunction with
The General Steam Navigation Co. Ltd.

DAY EXCURSIONS

from

LONDON
(Fenchurch Street or Liverpool Street)

to

CALAIS or BOULOGNE
via Southend

Visit two resorts in one day

LONDON
SOUTHEND-MARGATE
LONDON

rail-sea-rail

Above and opposite: To conclude this glance at the Thames estuary, there are two brochures one year apart. Both represent very short-lived operations but they could not have been more different in character. 'New this year… London's latest pleasure steamer' was the headline as newly formed Coastal Steam Packet attempted to revive a steam paddler service on the Thames and compete with the surviving General Steam motor ships. The attempt only lasted for the 1966 and 1967 seasons (this is the 1966 brochure). It was an impressive six-side piece, complete with its colour illustration of PS *Queen of the South*.

She was the 1931 Fairfield built, erstwhile London & North Eastern Railway, paddler *Jeanie Deans*. She was part of the Clyde fleet until she was sold in 1965, effectively, to a group of enthusiasts. Despite an impressive programme, her Thames service was blighted by flotsam damaging the paddle wheels and she failed frequently, hardly offering any sailings from her 1967 programme. There were no through tickets with British Railways who, it must be assumed, did not have much faith in the operation of a vessel that their organisation had owned only months before.

'The Londoner'

Continental cruise-a-car Passenger Ferry

Sails daily London to Calais

with coach services to

PARIS	3 DAY	2 DAY
Only £6.19.0 return	Mini Holiday in Paris for 2 £9.14.0 per person	Mini Holiday in Calais for 2 £6.2.0 per person
Adult 79/- single Child 79/- return Child 49/- single		

STENA BALTICA — THE LONDONER

STENA LINE
THE FRIENDLY LINE

Someone else felt that General Steam could do with some competition but their approach could not have been more different. Stena Line had started operations in 1962 between Gothenburg and Skagen. Only three years passed before the English market tempted and a car ferry was put on between Tilbury and Calais. The aim was to tap both the car owner in cutting out the drive to and through Kent, and reach the residual day cruise market from the Thames. The service was summer season only and was branded 'The Londoner'. There were advertised train connections to Tilbury Riverside.

This was certainly innovative and, in the light of the role Stena would come to play in British ferry operations from the 1990s, very prescient. At the time the initiative did not quite work. Three different ships were used in as many seasons. The 1967 choice was the one-year-old *Stena Baltica*. Her speed of fourteen knots was not really good enough making for a six-and-a-quarter hour crossing. The service did not run in 1968 and for the 1970 season the ship took on a new and much more familiar guise in British waters as she started two decades of work for soon-to-be Caledonian MacBrayne as the *Caledonia*.

Chapter 2

The Haven Ports – Harwich

Next page: The Haven, created by the confluence of the Stour and Orwell, offered East Anglia's greatest natural harbour, and for centuries has attracted trade. Harwich had a borough charter in 1319, after Ipswich's. A landmark date was 1661 when an agreement between the English Postmaster General and the City of Amsterdam opened a packet service to Hellevoetsluis. Defoe later wrote: 'Harwich is known for being the port where Packet Boats between England and Holland go out and come in.'

Harwich had a naval dockyard. In 1826 the town built its first steamships (ironically, for a service from Dover). Harwich had one drawback as the nineteenth century progressed: it was 70 miles from London and needed a railway. In 1832 the packet service had been transferred to steamboats of the General Steam Navigation Co. working from the Thames. It would not return until 1898.

Stagnation took place until the railway reached the town in 1854 (only the town, since Parkeston Quay was then a marsh). It was not until the Great Eastern Railway came on the scene in 1862 that the pace quickened. A year later a steamer service started from near the town station to Rotterdam and in the next year one commenced to Antwerp.

After various tensions with the town authorities, the railway elected to create *ex nihilo* Parkeston Quay named after the company chairman C.H. Parkes. This opened in 1883. Services to Esbjerg had started in 1880 and Hamburg became a destination in 1884 (bringing General Steam to the port). The modern era had arrived thanks to the railway.

Accordingly, the heyday of the Great Eastern is marked by these two postcards produced in the decade or so before the First World War and showing the boat trains. The engines are examples of the Great Eastern's *Claud Hamilton* Class and the train passing under a bridge is decidely the most antique. The stock appears to be six wheeled and perhaps could have occasioned the comments of Gilbert and Sullivan. In the 1880s neither train nor steamer were the acme of comfort, leading to this quip in *Iolanthe* in 1882: 'tossing about in a steamer from Harwich which is something between a bathing machine and a second class carriage'.

According to the postcard the newer train was corridor stock with electric light and steam heating. It is also possible that the six-wheeled stock indicates an Antwerp boat train since these continued with the older coaches much longer than the Dutch connections.

Great Eastern Railway.   Harwich Boat Train

"Continental Express" G.E.R.
NEAR BRENTWOOD.

Matters improved. By 1908 C.B. Black's guide to Holland was in its third edition and summarised the three main routes by ship to Holland from England as Queenborough–Flushing (which we would recognise as Sheerness–Vlissingen), Harwich–Hook, and a new improved service from Hull, which had started in 1907. The Queenborough service was run by the Zeeland Stoomvaart Maatchappij who would not appear at Harwich until 1927.

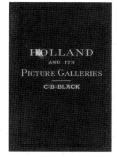

The Hook of Holland had entered the plot on the 3 June 1893 when the Dutch opened a combined quay and railway terminal there, saving the 10-mile steam into Rotterdam.

Black's guide concentrates on Dutch artistic treasures but not before twenty to thirty pages have described, in some detail, the crossings. The book had a subtitle inside: 'Holland: Its rail, tram and waterways'. Holland's intensive public transport network was a wonder to read about even a century ago.

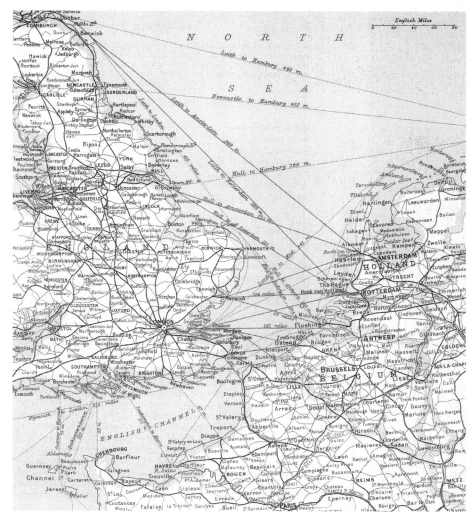

HOLLAND

Anyone with ephemera from the Harwich–Hook route much before the 1920s is very lucky, and the earliest railway-issued publicity we can submit comes from that time.

Numerous developments took place at Harwich in the 1920s. A train ferry started in 1924 (more will follow about that later). The Zeeland ships arrived in 1927 although a joint service to the Hook with the LNER on what became the classic day/night split was a post-Second World War development. Until that point although the two services were co-ordinated and publicised together, the Zeeland day service went to Flushing, and the LNER night service to the Hook.

This undated leaflet had as its main element a descriptive text by G.B. Thomas to entrance the traveller and some final pages of travel information.

Holland
via

HARWICH—FLUSHING	HARWICH—HOOK OF HOLLAND
Every Morning	Every Night
London (Liverpool Street Station) dep. 10 0 a.m.	London (Liverpool Street Station) dep. 8 30 p.m.
Harwich (Parkeston Quay) .. ,, 11 30 a.m.	Harwich (Parkeston Quay) .. ,, 10 15 p.m.
Flushing .. .. arr. 5 30 p.m.	Hook of Holland .. .. arr. 6 0 a.m.

Restaurant and Pullman Car Boat Trains between London and Harwich (Parkeston Quay).

Restaurant and Pullman Car Boat Trains between London and Harwich (Parkeston Quay).

Through Services between Glasgow, Edinburgh, York, Liverpool, Manchester, Sheffield, Birmingham, and Harwich (Parkeston Quay).

CHEAP TICKETS

Available from 3 to 15 days are issued daily to Flushing from London and East Anglian towns during the months April to September inclusive. Week-end tickets, with which no passports are required, are issued to Flushing, Amsterdam, The Hague, and Rotterdam from London all the year round, and from East Anglian towns from April to September.

Special 8-day tickets are issued for the Easter, Whitsun, and August Bank Holidays.

In connection with these excursions, exceedingly interesting tours are arranged in the vicinity of Flushing, and reduced fares are in operation to many places throughout Holland.

ORDINARY RETURN FARES
(By either Route)

	FROM LONDON				FROM HARWICH			
	SINGLE		RETURN		SINGLE		RETURN	
TO	1st Class	2nd Class	1st Class	2nd Class	1st Class	2nd Class	1st Class	2nd Class
Flushing	1 18 6	1 9 6	3 17 0	2 19 0	2 4 0	1 14 0	4 8 0	3 8 0
Hook of Holland	2 18 6	2 0 6	5 17 0	4 1 0	2 4 0	1 14 0	4 8 0	3 8 0
The Hague	3 1 5	2 2 9	6 2 4	4 5 0	2 6 11	1 16 3	4 13 4	3 12 0
Rotterdam	3 0 10	2 2 4	6 1 2	4 4 2	2 6 4	1 15 10	4 12 2	3 11 2
Utrecht	3 6 2	2 6 7	6 11 10	4 12 8	2 11 8	2 0 1	5 2 10	3 19 8
Haarlem	3 5 1	2 5 8	6 9 8	4 10 10	2 10 7	1 19 2	5 0 8	3 17 10
Amsterdam	3 6 7	2 6 10	6 12 8	4 13 2	2 12 1	2 0 4	5 3 8	4 0 2

Subject to Alteration

For full information apply to addresses given on last page

Three
New Ships

HARWICH
HOOK OF HOLLAND
Service

L·N·E·R

No. 38

Left: The LNER's major inter-war investment in the Hook passenger service produced an order for three products of John Brown in 1929–30. The GER had bought three vessels for the Antwerp service in its dying days which dominated that run until the Second World War. The Hook ships were by 1930 all at least twenty years old and so three ships (to operate one overnight sailing each way each day) were replaced by another three, the *Vienna, Prague* and *Amsterdam.* To celebrate their arrival, this twenty-page illustrated booklet was published in 1930.

Above: The Harwich ships had been the subject of railway-published postcards from as early as 1899. Detailing the GER issues is beyond the present space but there were upwards of thirty. The LNER released further shipping cards. Some of these covered ex-GER ships but the three new ships of 1929–30 were a golden opportunity for further cards.

This card, with its reference number S17625, appears to date from soon after *Vienna's* introduction. It is known in a number of imprints. The origin of these cards was in the W.H. Smith Kingsway series, and the same image would be produced both as LNER officials and straightforward commercial cards. The hilly background would suggest that the image was taken during trials in the Firth of Clyde.

The images used within the *Three New Ships* booklet appear to have constituted individual cards too.

WEEK-END PLEASURE CRUISES FROM HARWICH

The following attractive programme of Week-end Cruises from Harwich has been arranged for 1938.

24th June	...	Cruise A	...	Amsterdam and The Hague (via Hook of Holland).
1st July	...	„ B	...	Antwerp and Zeebrugge.
8th „	...	„ C	...	Rotterdam and Zeebrugge.
15th „	...	„ D	...	"Up the Seine to Rouen."
22nd „	...	„ E	...	Antwerp and Zeebrugge.
29th „ (including Bank Holiday)		„ F	...	Amsterdam, Antwerp and Zeebrugge.
5th Aug.	...	„ G	...	Amsterdam and The Hague (via Hook of Holland).
12th „	...	„ H	...	Antwerp and Flushing (For the Isle of Walcheren).
19th „	...	„ J	...	Le Havre (for French Coast Resorts)
26th „	...	„ K	...	Antwerp and Zeebrugge.
2nd Sept.	...	„ L	...	Amsterdam and The Hague (via Hook of Holland).
9th „	...	„ M	...	Antwerp and Zeebrugge.

The above itineraries are subject to alteration without previous notice.

The steamer leaves Harwich (Parkeston Quay) at 23.00 on the Friday and arrives back at 6.00 on the Monday morning.

For the August Bank Holiday Cruise " F " an extra day is provided, and the steamer arrives back at 6.00 on the Tuesday.

Passengers from London leave Liverpool Street at 20†15 and arrive back at 7†53.

Passengers from the Midlands and the North travel by the North Country train arriving at Harwich (Parkeston Quay) at 21.16 and, on the return journey, leaving Harwich (Parkeston Quay) at 7.25. The tickets are not available via London.

† Should be confirmed. Any modifications made subsequent to the publication of this booklet will be specially announced.

The fares provide for all meals on board ship, i.e. :—

For all Cruises except August Bank Holiday Cruise " F."
Saturday and Sunday.—Early Morning Tea, English Breakfast, Luncheon, Tea and Dinner.
Monday.—Early Morning Tea.
For August Bank Holiday Cruise " F "—
Saturday, Sunday and Monday.—Early Morning Tea, English Breakfast, Luncheon, Tea and Dinner.
Tuesday.—Early Morning Tea.

An attractive folder, giving detailed itineraries and full particulars of the arrangements in connection with the Cruises, may be obtained on application to any of the addresses given on page 51.

INCLUSIVE FARES
Third Class Rail, First Class Steamer
From LONDON (Liverpool Street)

For all Cruises except August Bank Holiday Cruise " F " ...	£3 16 6
For August Bank Holiday Cruise " F "	£5 5 0

Passengers may travel first class between London and Harwich (Parkeston Quay) upon payment of a supplement of 3/6 in each direction for adults and 1/9 in each direction for children under 14 years of age.

From HARWICH (Parkeston Quay)

For all Cruises except August Bank Holiday Cruise " F " ...	£3 5 6
For August Bank Holiday Cruise " F "	£4 14 0

[Fares from Provincial Stations on next page

NO PASSPORTS REQUIRED FOR WEEK-END CRUISES

11

Vienna started the tradition of railway boat cruises from Harwich. This was in 1932. The LNER's own literature for their cruises was most impressive with Frank Mason ship portraits for brochure covers. Our collection has none of these but it is possible to show the 1938 programme. The journey to Rouen was the most far flung. The programme is extracted from a most interesting publication, one of two which seem likely to form the basis of the LNER Harwich shipping publicity machine. Evidently an *LNER Continental Services Handbook* was a regular publication, as was this item – *Cheap Holiday Tickets*. This was issue 42 and its fifty-six pages are a mine of information – if predominently faretables.

Something of the cruising theme in BR days will be seen later when the cruises became considerably more adventurous.

EASTERN REGION MAGAZINE

MARCH 1962   Price threepence

When war came the LNER trio became troopships. *Amsterdam* became a victim of mines off France in 1944. *Vienna* and *Prague* survived the war. *Vienna* returned to Harwich but only to spend a further fifteen years serving the British Army of the Rhine.

So only *Prague* took up the passenger service, from 14 November 1945. The LNER needed new ships. An order for another John Brown vessel was placed and this became the 1947 *Arnhem*.

Within a year the *Prague* was lost in a dockside fire. The nationalisation of 1948 allowed further flexibility and a 1935 LMS Irish Sea ship called the *Duke of York* was transferred to Harwich. With the addition in 1950 of a new *Amsterdam*, the BR element of the Harwich–Hook service took on a stability that would last until the *Avalon*'s arrival in 1963.

Over an eighteen-month period in 1961–63, the three ships all enjoyed cover portraits on the British Railways *Eastern Region Magazine*. In August 1961 the *Amsterdam* had the honour and in January 1963 it was the *Arnhem*. Between them, and shown here, the March 1962 issue portrayed the *Duke of York* at the Hook in a picture by G.H. Mapleston.

The *Duke of York*'s BR career was soon to end but, as the final item of Chapter 4 reveals, her life was far from over.

These three BR ships and those of their Zeeland partners saw considerable growth through the 1950s. Comparing the 1950 and 1954 figures shows this. In the first year passengers carried and cargo tons were 394,034 and 217,763 respectively. The 1954 figures were 529,493 passengers and 304,148 tons. This was before car carrying became dominant.

Naturally publicity played its role, as in all probability did another development shown in this poster. Attractive posters had long been a feature of the route. The cover of *Three New Ships* seen previously used as the colour illustration artwork by Frank Mason that was also the core of an LNER poster entitled *Three New Luxury Ships*. Mason (1876–1965) is recognised as amongst the best of British poster artists and maritime themes figured highly in his work. Around 1932 he undertook a quartet for the LNER called *Rivers of Commerce* which are particularly noteworthy and would inevitably be the cream of any 'Tilbury to Tyneside' railway publicity collection. The image entitled *The Stour and Orwell* showed one of the 1932 trio of steamers, a train ferry and a Thames barge.

Posters are now so collectable that to obtain an original of these at auction would be beyond the ordinary collector. The associated postcards and booklet are, however, more accessible, and this explains why I believe the smaller items justify as much interest as the headline-grabbing posters.

It is churlish though to deny the appeal of the poster, and the one illustrated by Paul Mann (opposite, top) comes from 1954. It has three main elements. The steam engine was a new British Railways standard *Britannia* Class. These were introduced to Liverpool Street services to much acclaim from 1951. Two years before and the first electric services had started out of Liverpool Street. It would not be until 1986 that the wires would reach Harwich. The ship offers nothing unexpected but the third element does go some way to explaining how Continental connections were improving. While it took more than thirty-five years for the British wires to go 70 miles, the Dutch were rather quicker.

They had started before the Second World War, and a major push followed that war. Electric services to the Hook had started on 15 May 1935. The electric engines shown are French Alsthom designs which the Dutch bought in quantity from 1950. The beige colouring was not used for long, being replaced by Berlin blue in 1954. As this volume proceeds, the Dutch electric effect in marketing the Harwich–Hook route will become more apparent.

This has proved a moralising caption at more than one level.

Another poster (opposite, bottom) from the route shows off the Avalon several years into her career (see on p49 and following).

Welcome to
Welkom aan boord
Willkommen an Bord   **s.s. ARNHEM**

HARWICH-HOOK OF HOLLAND

⇌ | British Rail

Nightly Service
Nachtdienst
Nachtdienst

Return then to the smaller items of memorabilia and something that marks the last years of the 1947 *Arnhem*. A stock favourite was a postcard-sized 'Welcome' folder that was issued to each passenger joining the ships for the night. These were individually produced for each ship. Whether they were annual, I cannot say, but they were regularly updated since master and purser names were provided, although a timetable was not. A nice touch was a few paragraphs of history.

Amongst a selection of these known to your author is this item issued in December 1966 – quite possibly the last for the *Arnhem*. Immense change consequent on the need to handle vehicles efficiently would come to the Harwich–Hook route in 1968 and *Arnhem* made her last voyage for BR on 26 April 1968. In her twenty-one years she had carried three colour schemes and, as this item shows, the final one was the BR corporate image rail blue and double arrow scheme – not yet known as Sealink. BR ships were allowed to display the double arrow 'the wrong way around' on their port side, as shown in this image.

In 1966 her master was Captain C.G. Witchell MBE. In 1961 it had been Captain A.P. Sutton who was the subject of an illustrated profile (of ship and man) in what has proved a continual work of reference in these volumes about railway publicity – the *British Railways Magazine* (in this case the Eastern Region April 1961 edition).

For a flavour of the period when it seemed both master and ship should echo the sense of stalwart fight that the name *Arnhem* was intended to conjure, nothing better is needed than Frank Moxley's opening sentence to that feature: 'Captain A.P. Sutton, master of the British Railways ship, SS *Arnhem*, has a back as straight as a cliff and a pair of clear, unflinching eyes, well-trained and accustomed to penetrating whether it be the dark shadows of the sea or, perhaps, the character of men.' The written word would have played just as well had it been a British Transport Films commentary.

This page and next page: Against the character of Captain Sutton the needs of the car owner might have seemed trivial although they proved the commercial force that would dominate services from Harwich from 1968 onwards.

Cars had been shipped, I assume, from early in the twentieth century. The 1938 LNER guide cited previously shows that the LNER and Zeeland companies were making provision for the motorist on the Harwich services. Through the 1950s the pressure to carry vehicles grew. I cannot yet say when BR first published a leaflet dedicated to the needs of the motorist at Harwich but it was certainly by 1960, which is the date of this leaflet. The same design was used in 1961 and 1962.

Loose-leaf booking forms were a feature of this period and are required for the leaflet to be 'mint'. Inside the *Amsterdam* and the *Koningin Wilhelmina* were illustrated since cars could go on either the day or night service, although Zeeland would not carry trailers. As for commercial vehicles…

TAKE YOUR CAR

HARWICH
HOOK OF
HOLLAND

CARS · MOTOR CYCLES · CARAVANS · TRAILERS
accompanied by passengers

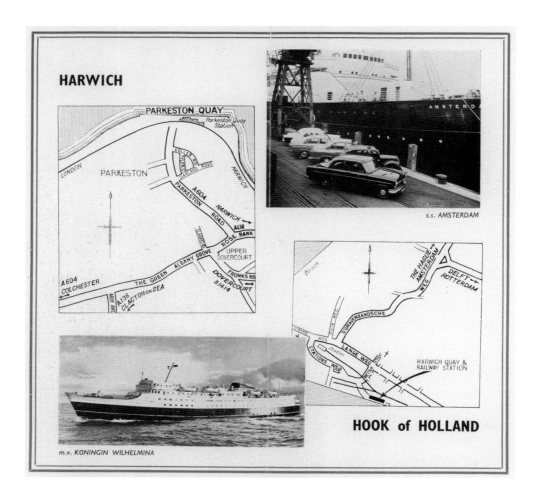

HARWICH

PARKESTON QUAY

s.s. AMSTERDAM

m.v. KONINGIN WILHELMINA

HOOK of HOLLAND

HARWICH QUAY & RAILWAY STATION

The appearance of *Koningin Wilhelmina* within the leaflet does suggests that, at least as far as the design goes, the leaflet was likely to have originated in 1960. The vessel was new that year, the only conventional passenger ferry that Zeeland bought after 1939. The next build, the *Koningin Juliana*, would be one of the 1968 car ferries. The Wilhemina had been built with car space for up to forty cars and side doors for loading them. Nonetheless her design dated rapidly in usefulness if not in outline, which was quite futuristic. She spent her last eleven years prior to sale in 1979 as Zeeland's relief vessel.

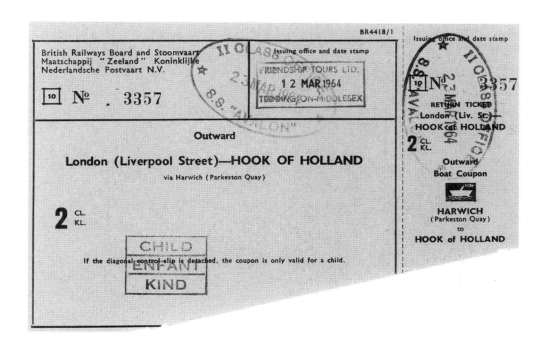

Both Zeeland and British Railways were willing to invest in the Harwich route in the early 1960s and both results went up blind alleys. In BR's case the outcome was the 1963 *Avalon*, an attractive ship, if not quite as visually radical as the Dutch partner. *Avalon* was another Clyde built vessel, in this case by Stephen's of Linthouse. Whereas the Wilhelmina was a motor ship, *Avalon* remained faithful to steam turbines – one argument was that they gave passengers a better night's sleep. The Wilhelmina at twenty-three knots was the faster ship – by a knot and a half.

Two naval architects were closely associated with the BR vessels, namely Messrs Ripley and Rogan. They said of *Avalon*: 'The last classic passenger ship we designed and possibly the finest looking ship we ever built.' At the time she was the largest vessel in the BR fleet and re-used a name of a Harwich–Rotterdam vessel from 1865.

Publicity illustrations of her will follow, but our sympathy for the mundane explains the selection of a ticket for the crossing which bear the ship's stamp. Other collectables from the *Avalon* include posters and an eight-page inaugural guide – 'And all who sail in her' – with a night-time crossing painting cover (as in this book's cover), a Maiden Voyage souvenir envelope and BR's own postcards.

Bright colours, easily-cleaned surfaces in this first-class smoke room are typical of attractive decoration throughout the *Avalon*

Another highbrow contemporary view of *Avalon* was afforded by the British Railways glossy magazine *Transport Age*, whose October 1963 issue carried an article on the new ship including this image (originally in colour) of her 1960s décor, when a first-class smoke room was an essential provision.

Opposite: Choosing to invest in cruising before car carrying is the tale of *Avalon*. After the Second World War, railway ship cruising had restarted in 1948. Incredibly, one such cruise was used by Burgess and Maclean to defect to Russia in 1951. But these were not Harwich initiatives. In 1956 one of the three new Heysham 'Dukes' had a special specification to allow her to cruise, and our previous book – *Irish Sea Shipping Publicised* – covered this. The cruise business seemed to boom and on occasion in 1960 three BR ships were cruising simultaneously. In 1961 the *Duke of Lancaster* even added Harwich to her itinerary. It seemed good sense therefore for the *Avalon* to be a combined packet/cruise ship and to replace older Southern Region ships for that latter task. To that end she was designed to dual specification. As a passenger ferry she could carry 700 passengers on the Harwich–Hook night crossing. When cruising she became a one-class ship for 350.

She was to cruise from 1964 to 1973, and the accompanying illustration shows the covers of leaflets from each of those years. Artwork and not monochrome illustration was used for the latter.

CONTINENTAL CRUISES

by

s.s. AVALON

Spring 1964
HARWICH to
Amsterdam, Hamburg, Kiel and
Copenhagen

Avalon '73
follows the sun

CRUISING TO PORTUGAL, SPAIN, MOROCCO AND FRANCE

Sealink
cruises by ss avalon
for Spring & Autumn 1970
to Russia and Morocco

If I had to set an obscure question for some transport Mastermind it might be 'what was the longest possible bookable journey that could be made entirely by British Railways?' The answer must surely depend on one of *Avalon*'s cruises. She circumnavigated Britain and reached the North Cape, Helsinki, Leningrad and the Moroccan port of Agadir.

A leaflet cover for Sealink cruises to Russia and Morocco has to be irresistible. This was the result for 1970. In this case the Moroccan port was Casablanca. That fortnight cruise included Gibraltar, while the spring voyage at the end of May and beginning of June had made the most of the light nights and reached Leningrad, having included a transit of the Kiel Canal. Rail blue and the double arrow would have made for some noteworthy pictures. Of lesser interest but not insignificant would have been travel on the special cruise boat trains which were put on from Liverpool Street.

When they ended in 1973, after thirty-four (intermittent) seasons of railway cruises, there were two immediate reasons. A new car ferry called *St Edmund* arrived at Harwich in the summer of 1974. *Avalon* was sent to North Shields and was turned into a car ferry for the Fishguard–Rosslare route, in which guise our *Irish Sea Shipping Publicised* volume has previously met her. She went for scrap to Pakistan in 1981.

There is a parallel between the railway cruises and camping coaches. Both were minor but popular attempts to broaden railway business. The camping coaches did not last quite so long. Both relied on a more leisurely use of assets than would be possible subsequently.

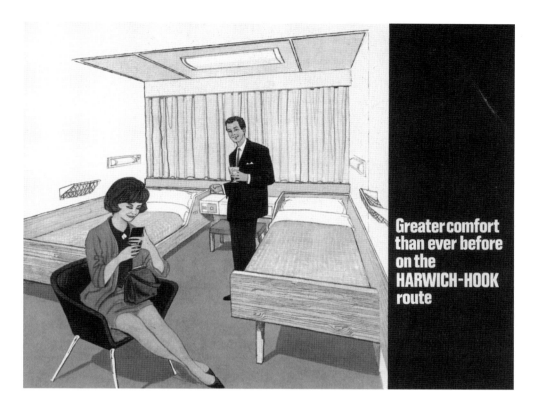

Greater comfort than ever before on the HARWICH-HOOK route

The scene change at Harwich had taken place six years before *Avalon* left. BR and Zeeland, the two partners on the Harwich route ordered one ship each and replaced in total four ships. The two orders were for similar diesel vessels. BR received the *St George* from the Swan Hunter yard on Tyneside. Zeeland took delivery of *Koningin Juliana* from Cammell Laird's at Birkenhead. At the time *St George* was the largest ship to have entered BR's fleet although her 7,356 GRT and 220-car capacity would soon date. Both bow and stern doors were fitted – the modern car ferry had arrived for Harwich-Hook use.

No surprise that the advent of the 1968 pair attracted considerable publicity. This is the rather anonymous cover – featuring improved cabin accommodation – that BR chose for a leaflet about the new *St George*.

The use of artwork reflects the fact that the leaflet was prepared in May 1968, two months before the ship went into service. The ships remained two class but in an operational innovation they now each worked a return sailing every day. This enabled the withdrawal of the four ships and it required both ships to combine the dual role of the night and day ships. Carrying capability for the latter was getting on for double the number of passengers carried at night.

Drive on...
drive off
The new
motorway
to Europe

**HARWICH
-HOOK**

Harwich/Hook of Holland

Some of the same artwork and rather more in the same genre appeared in this fourteen-page 1968 brochure. Whereas the previous brochure concentrated on one ship, this one looked at the route and its connections by both road and rail. Mint copies of this brochure contain two loose blue paper inserts: a timetable and a booking form. The leaflet is a joint affair and covers both ships. The front and back covers which form a unit are shown here. For a while before Sealink had yet to make its appearance, this style of BR/Zeeland route branding was used (as on the reverse).

The new ships had a tremendous effect. Press releases constitute another form of publicity with a poor survival rate. Rarely physically attractive, they can be of enormous note, one such will be shown later. One issued on British Rail Shipping and International Services headed paper in 1970 detailed this growth. The carriage of cars jumped by more than 100 per cent in a year. There were 28,000 in 1968, and virtually 65,000 the next.

SEALINK'S ST. EDMUND IS HERE!

≷ Sealink INTERNATIONAL NEWS "ST. EDMUND" EDITION

April 1975

A luxurious new two-class ship – the 9,000-ton "St. Edmund" – has joined Sealink's busy Harwich-Hook of Holland route.

The largest ship in the Sealink fleet, built for British Rail by Cammell Laird at a cost of £7,500,000. She was launched last November at Birkenhead.

Named after a legendary 9th century King of East Anglia, the "St. Edmund" combines the best of seafaring traditions with the latest in modern design and technology, to make her the showpiece of the Sealink fleet.

A speed of 21 service knots means the ship is capable of making three North Sea crossings daily, carrying a maximum of 1,400 passengers during the day and 1,000 on overnight trips. Comfort is the keynote. All the cabins and public rooms are air-conditioned.

There is cabin accommodation for 670 passengers and sleeping lounges, with comfortable reclining seats for another 177. The spacious lounges are colourful and well-appointed; there are two bars, a cafeteria and a restaurant with waiter service; two television lounges with seating capacity for 71 people; a discotheque and duty-free shopping areas for both classes.

The capacious car deck holds 296 cars or 40 30-foot road haulage vehicles and movement is speeded up by special bow and stern loading and unloading equipment for driving on and driving off.

The "St. Edmund" is the first of the second generation of multi-purpose ships, capable of handling passengers, accompanied motor cars and roll-on roll-off freight, which replaced orthodox passenger vessels in 1968, when car ramps were established at both the British and Dutch terminals. She joins the "St. George", belonging to British Rail and "Koningin Juliana" of the Zeeland Steamship Co.

'The "St. Edmund" will help to realise the full potential of the Harwich-Hook of Holland route,' says Mr David Kirby, General Manager of British Rail Shipping & International Services Division.

Since 1968 motor traffic on the route has risen by 214%, passengers by 33⅓% and road haulage from a trickle to 15,000 vehicles.

STOP PRESS

Third sailing from Harwich

A third service from Harwich to the Hook of Holland for train/ship passengers will be introduced in Summer 1975 (June 27-August 31). This service provides greatly improved train connections to destinations such as Hamburg, Hannover and Cologne.

BR and Zeeland decided that, for the summer of 1975, the service would be pushed up to three return services daily. Sealink replaced *Avalon* with another new and yet larger car ferry. This was the 9,000-ton Cammell Laird-built *St Edmund*. *St Edmund*, launched in November 1973, was still with the builders a year later. Her name commemorated the ninth century St Edmund King and Martyr, whose associations focus on the Suffolk town of Bury St Edmunds.

Her eventual advent at Harwich prompted this four-side A3 folder, fully illustrated in colour, mono and with artwork. A drop-down foldout revealed three monochromes of launch day. This told readers that the naming ceremony was undertaken by Caroline Marsh, wife of the then British Railways Board chairman. *Avalon* had been named by Ella Beeching.

St Edmund's fittings included connections to allow refrigerated containers to continue functioning during the voyage. This reflected the fact that car carrying was being supplemented by road haulage and its requirements. Road haulage was relatively small-scale before 1968, but in this year 3,000 lorries were carried. There were more than 14,000 lorries carried in 1974 and *St Edmund* was intended to double the route's freight capacity.

The Sealink brand began to appear on Harwich's literature in the autumn of 1969. The Dutch partner Zeeland used the brand but retained its joint Hoek van Holland Harwich logo in addition. This went on for many years with examples illustrated in the next chapter. There were rare occasions when this brand was used on English language publicity produced by Zeeland for distribution in the UK.

One such example is this undated (perhaps 1978?) Zeeland brochure for *Prinses Beatrix*'s introduction. This was the Zeeland partner to *St Edmund*. In 1986 this ship became the *Duc de Normandie* with Brittany Ferries.

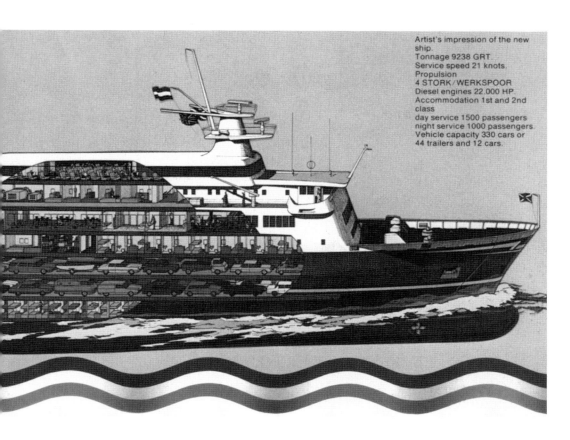

Artist's impression of the new ship.
Tonnage 9238 GRT.
Service speed 21 knots.
Propulsion
4 STORK/WERKSPOOR Diesel engines 22.000 HP.
Accommodation 1st and 2nd class
day service 1500 passengers
night service 1000 passengers.
Vehicle capacity 330 cars or 44 trailers and 12 cars.

Harwich — Hook of Holland a bridge without pillars - Sealink Europe

The Zeeland Steamship Company proudly introduce their new flagship, the "Prinses Beatrix". Reliability, care and comfort are the basis on which the British and Dutch partners established and maintained their unique reputation for well over a century; to sail forth with a completely modern fleet on the premier route linking Britain and the Continent.

hoek van holland
SMZ harwich

HARWICH-HOOK OF HOLLAND

It's the direct route to the "HEART OF EUROPE"

Sealink's Harwich Parkeston Quay to Hook of Holland service is operated jointly by British Rail Shipping and the Zeeland Steamship Company of Holland. This long established DAY and NIGHT service operates throughout the year, with an additional DAY service during the mid-summer peak period, plus many relief sailings. This route is the shortest direct sea crossing to Holland taking about 6½ hours by day and around 8 hours by night.

The overnight crossing is especially popular with motorists who save time by having a comfortable night's sleep en route and enjoy an early morning start on the other side.

The day service operates as a short cruise with ample time to enjoy the delights of the on-ship facilities.

The route is served by a most modern fleet of drive on/drive off Passenger and Car Ferries.

This year a brand new ship, Prinses Beatrix (9000 tons), joined Koningin Juliana (6682 tons), St. Edmund (8987 tons) and St. George (7356 tons) on this service. These ships are custom-built for this route to provide the highest standard of passenger comfort and service. The total capacity of the Sealink Harwich-Hook of Holland Fleet is 5,300 passengers and 1,056 cars daily.

The Harwich-Hook (a two-class) service has established a reputation for quality and reliability, with well appointed cabins, spacious lounges, elegant bars, popular priced cafeterias and full waiter-service restaurants. Each ship has a shopping complex where passengers may purchase a wide range of goods at duty-free prices.

The Sealink Pursers are always available to satisfy your requirements. (ALL passengers on Sealink services are VIP's.)

There are gaming tables on the St. Edmund and the St. George. The St. Edmund also has a disco. All 1st Class cabins on the Prinses Beatrix are equipped with private shower/toilet.

Purpose-built terminals at Harwich Parkeston Quay and The Hook of Holland make the transfer and customs formalities easy, and for motorists the strategic location of the ports gives excellent access to the major motorways of Europe.

For Rail passengers this route is the only truly integrated train/ship service to Holland and beyond. Connecting boat train services operate from Liverpool Street to Harwich Parkeston Quay (journey time under 1¾ hours) and a direct service operates from Manchester via Sheffield, Nottingham and Peterborough to Harwich which offers connecting Inter-City services from Scotland and the North of England, also good connecting services from the Hook of Holland to Northern, Southern, Eastern Europe.

The Hook of Holland terminal is only 10 miles from the whole European Motorway System – an ideal starting point for motor touring or caravan touring journeys, and since the port is also an international rail terminal, Motorail services operate from the terminal to Lorrach (near Basle) also in the summer, from 's-Hertogenbosch (approx. 2 hours drive from the Hook of Holland) to the South of France, Italy, Austria and Yugoslavia.

Timetable and Fares for Rail Passengers and Motorists: 1 November 1978 to 26 May 1979

This page and opposite: Through the 1970s and early 1980s, British Railways via Sealink were issuing a line of route brochure series intended to appeal, as these covers make clear, to both rail passengers and car owners.

The next sentences took hours to write and elaborate. The issue: was *Prinses Beatrix* a partner to *St Edmund* or not? Duncan Haw's *magnum opi* (see bibliography) seemed utterly clear on this point. A whole string of dates asserted that *Prinses Beatrix* went into service in 1974. A worthwhile and extensive article celebrating the route's centenary appeared in *Ships Monthly* in December 1993 by P.J. Cone and gave the same date. So does the same author's book about Harwich.

As remarked in the last caption, the critical piece of ephemera was undated. To see the *Prinses Beatrix* as a partner to *St Edmund* seemed logical but then the research questioned this view. Brian Haresnape's *This Is Sealink* gave a 1978 date.

Here is the punchline: the contents of both these humble brochures disagree with secondary sources that might be relied upon. The November 1978 cover is unfolded and reproduced to show this. The primary evidence dates *Prinses Beatrix* four years later. Since these events are less than thirty years old and the discrepancy is hardly trivial, it is instantly clear just how difficult it is to write accurately and how this under-appreciated genre of transport publicity can play a vital role. Even so, it can contain its own pitfalls.

To make headway it was necessary to find other sources that would support the 1978 date. These came in various Ferry Publications volumes: 1978 it is.

Which discussion has meant that the potential within this leaflet for other subjects is neglected here, but the next chapter will cover in similar leaflets the subject of onward rail connections, which four sides of this leaflet detail. There are timings, briefs on the named trains and this rather nice artwork of the *St Edmund.*

It is worth mentioning that the artwork style of the 1979 leaflet (*right*) with its man clutching ship was a smaller (and altered) version of the style that was used on the overall Sealink brochure in 1979 and again in 1980. Other variants for other routes can also be traced.

Passenger and Car Ferry Services

Harwich- Hook of Holland

It's the direct route to the "Heart of Europe"

27 May - 29 September 1979

Sealink

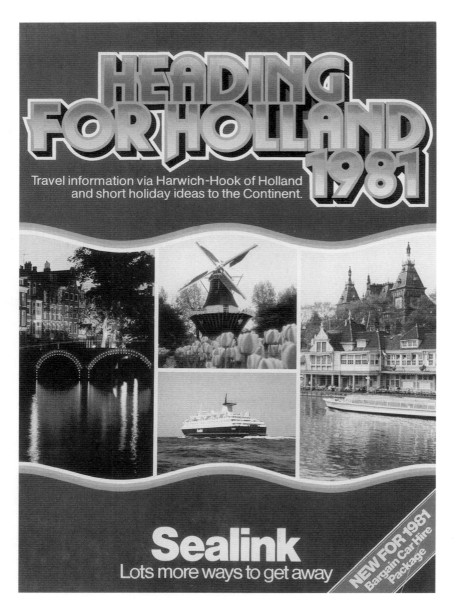

HEADING FOR HOLLAND 1981

Travel information via Harwich-Hook of Holland and short holiday ideas to the Continent.

Sealink
Lots more ways to get away

NEW FOR 1981
Bargain Car Hire Package

Sealink had adopted a fair-sized A4 booklet to publicise its overall services from 1970. Route specific A4 brochures would sometimes follow but never on a totally consistent basis. Even in 2000, Stena's Harwich material tended to be smaller than A4.

It is quite possible (after searching through the generic A4 Sealink brochure which tended to detail and illustrate its offshoots) that this 1981 item was the first A4 timetable brochure for Harwich. Its twenty-four pages clearly used material drawn from the smaller leaflets seen previously. It was also an opportunity to give space to the inclusive holidays available via the route. There was something similar in 1982, although that had a cover that fitted the other routes and destinations that Sealink offered. The main 1983 brochure would suggest that the Harwich version was not done that year.

Sealink

SPECIAL INFORMATION

Sealink U.K. Ltd., Registered Office: Eversholt House, 163-203 Eversholt Street NW1 1BG. Tel: 01-387 1234
Registered in England No.1402237   A Subsidiary of the British Railways Board

IMPORTANT NOTICE FOR PASSENGERS TRAVELLING ON THE HARWICH – HOOK OF HOLLAND
SERVICE TONIGHT

Sealink regret to announce that due to the fact that their ship ST. EDMUND
has been requisitioned by the Government for service in the South Atlantic
in conjunction with the Falkland Islands crisis, the ST. GEORGE or
KONINGIN JULIANA will not be sailing from Harwich tonight.

This means that passengers who were originally reserved to travel on the
ST. GEORGE or KONINGIN JULIANA will be diverted to the Dutch ship
PRINSES BEATRIX but unfortunately it will not be possible to honour your
cabin and seat reservation on board PRINSES BEATRIX.

Will you please write, enclosing the remains of your travel tickets, to
the office of purchase for a refund in respect of the reserved accommodation
we could not provide.

Sealink very much regret the inconvenience caused to their passengers due
to circumstances beyond their control.

The accompanying item is not unique I guess, although it is the only Harwich example in my selection and it is the most recent.

The despatch of ships for war service was something that the route's operators had probably thought was ancient history as the 1980s opened. When such events do take place, they are often sudden and not celebratory. That is the excuse for this visually bland (and undated) sheet of typescript.

The Falklands War proved quite a catalyst for change at Harwich. On 12 May 1982 *St Edmund* was requisitioned for Government service. She was never to return to the Harwich service. Instead, sale to the Army followed after some months as a Falklands troopship and she became the *Keren* in March 1983, doing much the same thing. Eventually she became the *Rozel* in British Channel Islands Ferries' fleet.

Opposite: The BR and Zeeland Sealink partners had entered the 1980s with two car ferries apiece to run a service that was largely two return sailings a day.

With *St Edmund* gone, Sealink was relying on the now elderly and quite small *St George*. A drastic solution was the answer, and one in tune with the cost-cutting ethos of the imminent privatisation that was to take place in July 1984. In June 1983 the *St Nicholas* arrived to replace the *St George* and the service became a two-ship operation, with *Prinses Beatrix* as partner. This was spelt out in the accompanying leaflets.

'The Big One' leaflet was an advance monochrome A5 flyer. It rather gave the game away. The ship that had Sealink on its side bore the name *Princessan Birgitta*. This 1982 14,300 GRT vessel had been intended for Sessan's Gothenburg–Fredikshavn service, which it briefly worked (and about which there is some complex history). Stena owned Sessan and chartered the new ship to Sealink UK in 1983.

A glossy colour brochure followed the monochrome flyer. *St Nicholas* never received the Sealink rail blue hull colours. Instead she epitomised the continual change that seemed to be the story of the 1980s and privatisation.

Sealink News, the in-house A4 magazine, was dominated by the problems or challenges at Harwich in the first half of 1983. The June issue had a back cover colour illustration of *St Nicholas*. It was evidently the same image as that shown on the glossy brochure. One difference: the brochure went for a red (Stena?) funnel, and the magazine replaced the red with blue (for Sealink?).

Sealink had to gain union approval for the one-ship situation at Harwich before *St Nicholas* could be introduced and this only took place after Sealink threatened to completely withdraw from the route, claiming that savings of £1.3 million per annum were needed. The same issues were also reporting how the sale and re-crewing of *St Edmund/Keren* had virtually precipitated a worldwide National Union of Seamen strike and had led to the occupation of a cargo vessel called the *Browning* by Harwich seamen.

In the midst of all this, Sealink managed to celebrate Harwich's centenary on 15 March 1983 with a visit by BRB chairman Sir Peter Parker for quite a party, aboard the DFDS vessel *Prinz Oberon*, on charter until *St Nicholas* could appear.

Sealink announces the coming of 'The Big One'

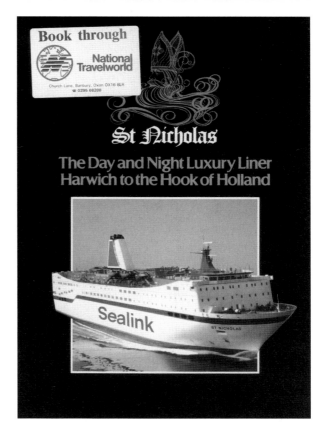

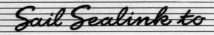

In time *St Nicholas* would leave Harwich (in 1991) but by then she was renamed the *Stena Normandy*. In her years on the route (one which must have appeared a money spinner back in the early 1970s), it was involved in a struggle for survival, with the route recording a loss of £1.5 million in 1987.

For the publicity collector, the *St Nicholas* offered quite a lot. Her Sealink railway era appearances were few. She appeared quite often though on BR rail/ship publicity issued after the privatisation. She was a regular on Sealink British Ferries material. She graced the cover of their overall A4 ferry guide in 1989 and the first issues for 1990 (before *Fantasia* replaced her). Harwich tended to use a smaller brochure, and in 1987 this produced the artwork cover illustrated.

Inside, much was made of the two big ships by then on the service. *St Nicholas* had been outstripped by *Koningin Beatrix*.

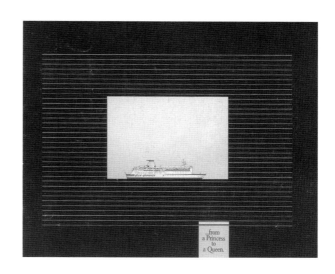

from
a Princess
to
a Queen.

The hospitable coffee shop

This modernly furnished meeting place with its friendly atmosphere will be open round the clock for that bite to eat between times.
It will serve sandwiches, hot and cold snacks, cakes and - of course - delicious coffee.
For the non-coffee drinkers there's a wide selection of drinks available such as tea, beer, soft drinks, ice-cream and milk shakes.

from
a Princess
to
a Queen.

Welcome aboard

In the spacious boarding area with its welcoming atmosphere is the reception desk with a purser who is always standing by, ready to help. Here passengers with cabin accommodation can also collect their keys. Immediately behind the reception desk is the generously dimensioned North Sea Shopping Centre where you can choose from a tremendous selection of tax-free goods. That also goes for the separate boutique where countless attractive souvenirs and useful gifts will be on sale.

Zeeland's follow-up *to St Nicholas* had had to wait until 1986 and the introduction of the brand new *Koningin Beatrix*. Zeeland produced three marvellous large format brochures for her introduction in German, Dutch and English. Their title: 'from a Princess to a Queen' reflected the replacement of the *Prinses Beatrix* with the *Koningin Beatrix*. It was hailed as 'the largest and finest passenger and car ferry vessel... to maintain... service between Holland and Great Britain'.

She came from the Van Der Giessen-De Noord yard and in the brochure was the subject of large double-page artwork spreads and cut-outs. Her size reflected her task, which was to replace the two remaining conventional ferries in Zeeland's fleet.

With the arrival of *Koningin Beatrix*, the narrative is in technology only one step away from the millennial scene. That next step was the immensely radical advent of the High Speed Superferry or HSS craft, which came to dominate the seaways and the publicity in the years either side of 2000.

This change is illustrated with one brochure. The little box referring to Anglia Railways prompts a follow-up. What had once been British Railways Sealink had by 1998 become pure Stena Line. On the rail tracks the parallel process had changed British Railways Eastern Region into Anglia Railways. Anglia Railways themselves produced an attractive series of brochures for through rail/sea journeys, often under the heading of 'Amsterdam Express'.

One other leap has to be explained for here is an image of *Koningin Beatrix* in Stena Line colours and, while the British 'Sealink' operations have obviously made their way to Stena, it may need explaining how the Zeeland (Dutch partner) ship made the transition. In 1989 Stena Line purchased a majority stake in Zeeland and effectively the twin-partnered route became completely owned by Stena when in 1990 they purchased Sealink British Ferries. Stena had warmed up their route knowledge previously, for the *St Nicholas* was a vessel chartered from them.

Once the HSS had displaced the *Koningin Beatrix* at Harwich in 1997, she became associated with the Fishguard–Rosslare route, retaining her Dutch name.

Opposite: The chapter thus far has concentrated on the classic Harwich-Hook route. However, between the various means by which one reached Harwich, port activities at Harwich, specialist freight initiatives, and the other main users of Parkeston Quay, there remains quite a gazetteer of other headings.

From the British angle, one of these operations made Harwich a familiar name to rail users across a wide spread of Northern England. The boat train connection to Harwich from London Liverpool Street was the more straightforward.

No longer formally named, boat trains ran from London to Parkeston Quay in the shape of two non-stop Anglia Railways locomotive-hauled expresses in the winter 2002 timetable. These were the 08.50 and the 17.27 from London and seemed quite anachronistic. Diesel traction may be history but the electric engines dated from the 1960s. The 2002 timetable had an optional third boat train at lunchtime for connections with Scandinavian Seaways (surely this was three years out of date, and the timetable meant to say DFDS once again!). This structure is not dissimilar to what the Eastern Region timetable showed forty years ago. The issue for the winter of 1961 gave over four pages (after the 'Blue Page' named trains section) to the heading 'Continent via Harwich' and in there the magical terms *The Hook Continental*, *The Day Continental* and *The Scandinavian* appeared, by which Harwich contributed three named trains for many years to the roster of BR namers. Parkeston Quay in those forty years had become Harwich International in 1995.

The namers need a fourth addition and to that we shall give more space. This was the cross country connection to the North, widely known (at times officially) as *The North Country Continental*.

Unfortunately I can show no pure and simple Named Train leaflets produced specifically for any of these four named trains under those names. They may exist but I have yet to source one.

Part of the appeal of the boat train running north-west from Harwich was that it was available for ordinary passengers, and for many years was one of the few and, therefore, important, cross country trains out of East Anglia. One type of item in which it featured was this tri-lingual guide to services from the North into Harwich and beyond into Europe. This item comes from the summer of 1973, various editions like it being published thereabouts. The Harwich boat train was shown with no fanfare as the 15.17 from Manchester Piccadilly.

NEWCASTLE, LEEDS, MANCHESTER, HULL, GRIMSBY, DERBY, NORWICH, YARMOUTH, CLACTON, SOUTHEND

To/Naar/Nach

Rotterdam-Amsterdam Köln (Cologne)

Via/Over/Über Harwich

From/Van/Vom 7.V.73
Until/tot en met/bis 5.V.74

(except/niet/ausser 25.XII.73)

The services shown in this publication are subject to alteration (especially during Public Holiday periods).

De dienstregeling van de aansluitende treinen in Groot Brittannië kan eventueel gewijzigd worden, in het bijzonder op zon-en feest-dagen.

Die in dieser Broschüre erwähnten Fahrpläne der anschliessenden Züge in Grossbritannien können verändert werden, besonders an Sonn-und Feiertagen.

Sealink Zeeland

Passenger Timetable
22 May 1977 to 27 May 1978

International
Inter-City, Sealink, Seaspeed services
Great Britain – Continent of Europe

This page and opposite: That May 1973 timetable change had been quite significant. Owing to its pre-grouping origins and its consequent use of the Great Central route to Lincoln and thence the Great Eastern route south to March, the train avoided most population centres beyond Sheffield. It was, therefore, re-routed via Nottingham in May 1973. A leaflet all about the change was produced, simply headed: 'Harwich Boat Train Direct from Nottingham.'

The train had originated as far back as 1885 and, in its steam-hauled golden era, had through coaches for Glasgow, Liverpool and Birmingham in the consist that left Harwich.

Table Z   THROUGH SERVICES   Mondays to Saturdays

Manchester, Sheffield, Peterborough and Harwich Parkeston Quay

To Harwich

		⚐
Manchester Piccadilly	d	15 15
Sheffield	d	16 25
Chesterfield	d	16 41
Alfreton & Mansfield Parkway	d	16 56
Derby	d	16 20
Nottingham	d	17 24
Newcastle	d	15 10
York	d	16 29
Doncaster	d	17b04
Grantham	d	18 03
Leeds	d	16c35
Wakefield Westgate	d	16c52
Leicester	d	16 40
Peterborough	d	18 41
Lincoln Central	d	17 20
March	d	19 03
Ely	d	19 28
Cambridge	d	18e56
Bury St. Edmunds	d	20 04
Stowmarket	d	20 25
Ipswich	d	20 41
Harwich Parkeston Quay	a	21 10

From Harwich

		⚐
Harwich Parkeston Quay	d	07 28
Ipswich	a	07 53
Stowmarket	a	08 09
Bury St. Edmunds	a	08 30
Cambridge	a	09e35
Ely	a	09 06
March	a	09 28
Lincoln Central	a	11 20
Peterborough	a	09 50
Leicester	a	11 16
Doncaster	a	11 10
Wakefield Westgate	a	11 51
Leeds	a	12 11
York	a	11 48
Newcastle	a	13 06
Grantham	a	10 21
Nottingham	a	11 02
Derby	a	12 18
Alfreton & Mansfield Parkway	a	11 31
Chesterfield	a	11 45
Sheffield	a	12 05
Manchester Piccadilly	a	13 18

b—Saturdays dep. 17 10.
c—Saturdays Leeds dep. 15 25, Wakefield Westgate dep. 15 43.

e—Second class only.

Passengers travelling from Manchester, Sheffield and Harwich may reserve seats in advance on payment of a fee of 40p per seat.

To Harwich

		24 June to 27 August
Newcastle	d	01Z12
York	d	02Z50
Leeds	d	00Z40
Doncaster	d	03Z36
Grantham	d	04Z25
Peterborough	d	05Z43
March	d	06Z05
Ely	d	06Z27
Cambridge	d	06Z56
Bury St. Edmunds	d	07Z44
Stowmarket	d	08Z07
Ipswich	d	08Z27
Harwich Parkeston Quay	a	08Z57

From Harwich

		24 June to 27 August	Tuesdays to Saturdays	Sundays
Harwich Parkeston Quay	d	21Z10		
Ipswich	a	21Z38		
Stowmarket	a	22Z27b		
Bury St. Edmunds	a	22Z28		
Cambridge	a	23Z33b		
Ely	a	23Z03		
March	a	23Z23		
Peterborough	a	23Z46		
Grantham	a		00Z22	00Z46
Doncaster	a		01Z17	02Z07
Wakefield Kirkgate	a		02Z37	03Z18
Leeds	a		02Z45	04Z08
York	a		02Z06	02Z57
Newcastle	a		03Z49	05Z03

b—Saturdays.

For general notes see page 4

Heavy figures denote through coaches.   Light figures denote connecting services.

> Details of alterations to services during Holiday periods will be contained in separate Bank Holiday supplements. Please consult stations or agencies.

Through much of the 1970s, there was a fail-safe means of finding the train publicised: look in Table Z. Table Z was the last table (after Table W for London to Malta) in the BR International timetable book of the period. This was the only internal British service in that volume. As 'The Train in Table Z' the service had a nice feature in the January 1979 *Railway Magazine*. With its nigh on six-hour trek around Britain, the train was a leisurely concept and something of an institution. I particularly remember how in the 1970s it became one of the last resorts of Gresley-designed LNER buffet cars.

The 15.15 from Manchester will serve Sheffield, Chesterfield, Nottingham, Grantham, Peterborough, East Anglia, Parkeston Quay and Holland and Germany!

The train did receive some publicity attention all to itself. This item was issued in July 1979 and had a BR Class 45 loco on the cover. Other leaflets in this vein (with different covers) appeared.

The varying pattern of the British boat trains was also detailed over the years in a series of individual European timetables to be examined in the next chapter. One offshoot of that series was something that looked similar but focussed on all the connections north-west from Harwich. See this as an updated version of the simple red-on-white folder with which this section about the Boat Trains started. That item had been issued in 1973 but seemed older in feel. By 1980 its successor looked like this, and in between a number of styles had been used.

Hoek van Holland
for the Heart of Europe

May 12, 1980 to May 10, 1981

Aberdeen
Dundee
EDINBURGH
NEWCASTLE
Sunderland
Durham
Hartlepool
Darlington
Middlesbrough

Harrogate
LEEDS
York
Bradford
Halifax
Wakefield
Hull
Huddersfield
Liverpool
Doncaster
Grimsby
MANCHESTER
SHEFFIELD
Lincoln
Chesterfield
Retford
Newark
Alfreton & Mansfield
NOTTINGHAM
Derby
Grantham
Leicester
King's Lynn
Stamford
Norwich
PETERBOROUGH
March
Ely
Bury St Edmunds
Cambridge
IPSWICH
Harwich Parkeston Quay

Sealink

Inter-City ⇌ Sealink
direct links via Harwich Parkeston Quay

The European
your direct rail & sea service
Straight to the heart of
HOLLAND

16 May to 24 September 1983

InterCity ⇄ Europe

Left and opposite: Ultimately in the 1980s, new Sprinter DMUs would bring much more frequent services from North West England into East Anglia and make a special train to Harwich redundant (along with the complexities of privatisation).

Before that there was one last glorious attempt to emulate history. The Glasgow connection re-appeared when, from 16 May 1983 the service was formally christened *The European* and operated from both Glasgow and Edinburgh (the portions being married at Carstairs), up to

Manchester and then forwards at 15.02 to Harwich. This is the introductory leaflet. In a short life this train produced a variety of attractive material.

Later in the 1980s (11 May 1987 I think), this train – now part of the Intercity Sector – was altered to run via Watford and Shenfield and the north of London. This allowed electric haulage throughout, but it was not long lived. Nor were some named services like *The Loreley*, which were publicised around 1988 by the Express brand of BR's Provincial operation and used the new Sprinter DMUs from the North West.

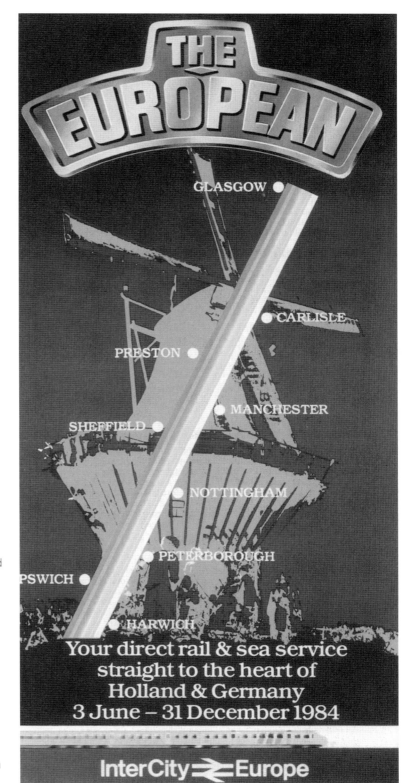

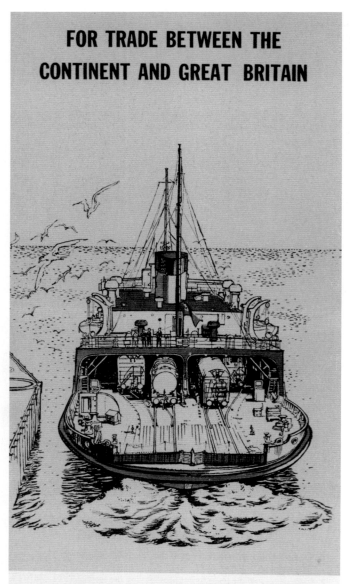

FOR TRADE BETWEEN THE CONTINENT AND GREAT BRITAIN

TRAIN FERRIES

daily services via

DOVER-DUNKERQUE   HARWICH-ZEEBRUGGE

The boat trains were particularly expressive of the railway connection to Harwich. So was another very special operation at the port: the train ferry. The cover of what was a hardy annual is shown – this is from 1962. In 1965 this was replaced by a substantial booklet and foldout map and received the BR corporate image.

Train ferry services from Harwich had started with a Royal opening on 24 April 1924. A new terminal was built beyond Harwich Town station, the train ferries were quite separate in their handling from Parkeston Quay.

The last of the original trio of vessels had been replaced in 1957. A sequence of post-war ferries appeared: *Suffolk Ferry* in 1947, *Norfolk Ferry* in 1951, *Essex Ferry* in 1956 and *Cambridge Ferry* in 1963. The latter had a particularly long life with Sealink. These ferries operated the link for many years. A further vessel called the *Speedlink Vanguard* appeared in 1980 and with her the service ceased in 1987.

The BR issued leaflets in the 1960s covered both the Eastern and Southern Region routes. The ship profile, whether on these drawing covers or on the mid-1960s monochromes, showcased the same vessel, one of the Harwich fleet like the *Essex* or *Norfolk*.

Scene at the inauguration ceremony which was attended by many distinguished personalities of Great Britain and Belgium. Our C.R.O., Mr. C. K. Bird, is on the extreme right and Mr. L. H. K. Neil, Continental Traffic Manager, on the extreme left. Sir Michael Barrington-Ward, Member of the Railway Executive, is third from the right, front row

A NEW
CAR FERRY TERMINAL

An important development at Zeebrugge which should do much to foster "Eastern" trade links with the Continent.

BRIEF reference was made in August issue of the *Magazine* to a marine development at Zeebrugge, the Continental terminal of the Eastern Region route via Harwich, and it is now our pleasure to provide space for a little more information about this important event.

The new facility, which consists of a new berth to accommodate our train-ferry vessels in the outer harbour at Zeebrugge, has a link bridge about 160 ft. long hinged in the middle and electrically operated.

On the seaward end of the movable portion the single track from the land bifurcates so as to couple with the tracks at the stern of the ferry vessels. From the link bridge, which enables loading over a wide variation in water level according to the height of the tide, the railway tracks continue towards a marshalling yard for ferry wagons. At a point where the railway track emerges from its cutting to rise to the general level of the shore terrain, the roadway is taken off on a concrete raft to the east to climb more steeply by a hairpin bend to the immediate vicinity of the ferry company's new offices from which point there is a connection to the public road. This arrangement will enable the Harwich-Zeebrugge train ferry vessels to be used to an increasing degree for the movement of road vehicles to and from the Continent. Civil engineering was carried out by the Société d'Etudes et de Travaux S.E.T.R.A. The engineer for the scheme was Monsieur Joseph Lagrou.

It is anticipated that the new berth will save approximately 1½ hours in each

The link bridge, suspended from two towers, provides a connection 55 yards long between the train deck of the ship and the railway. This facility provides for loading over a wide variety of water levels

direction in getting to the lock and canal berth.

Among many distinguished guests who attended the inaugural function on June 27 were Sir Michael Barrington-Ward, Member of the Railway Executive; Messrs. C. K. Bird, Chief Regional Officer, Eastern Region; L. H. K. Neil, Continental Traffic Manager, Eastern and North Eastern Regions, who is also Vice Chairman of the Société Belgo-Anglaise des Ferry-Boats, and Captain R. Davis, Manager (Shipping Services), Eastern Region.

175

Zeebrugge's linkspan had originated with the British Government's Richborough project in the First World War. It was badly damaged in the Second World War. Some time after the war, it was decided to berth the train ferry in Zeebrugge's Outer Harbour and save the passage through the lock. This was a major project and its inauguration on 27 June 1953 saw a sizeable party of BR's great and the good make passage to Zeebrugge. A report (reproduced) followed in the *British Railways Magazine Eastern Region* of September 1953. That class of document is often useful in respect of British Railway's commercial history.

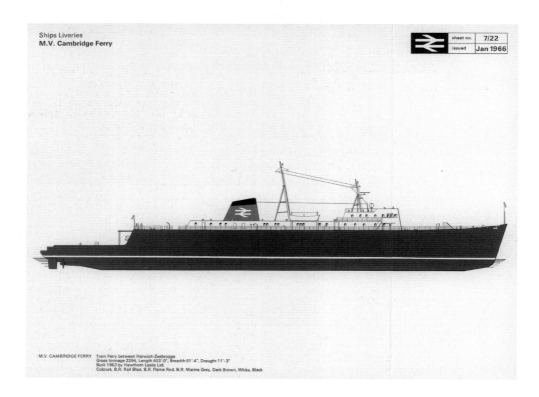

Ships Liveries
M.V. Cambridge Ferry

sheet no. 7/22
issued Jan 1966

M.V. CAMBRIDGE FERRY Train Ferry between Harwich-Zeebrugge
Gross tonnage 3294, Length 403'-0", Breadth 61'-4", Draught 11'-3"
Built 1963 by Hawthorn Leslie Ltd.
Colours, B.R. Rail Blue, B.R. Flame Red, B.R. Marine Grey, Dark Brown, White, Black

The 1963 *Cambridge Ferry* was a product of Tyneside's Hawthorn Leslie yard. An unusual claim to fame was her appearance in the *BR Corporate Identity Manual*. She was shown in her new rail blue livery with double arrow in a drawing issued in January 1966, just a year after the new image was inaugurated. The side profile of the rear deck was similar to her sisters. In 1977, the boat deck was extended to increase carrying capacity and in this guise she served Sealink and privatised successors until 1992.

Opposite: As the years passed a considerable array of 'ferry train' publicity must have been distributed to a relatively small audience. The item reproduced dates from October 1978 and is one of a number of inserts from an information wallet. That was a favourite means of dealing with low print-run materials that might need updating or differing elements distributed. The obvious interest is seeing in colour-coded diagrammatic form both the physical extent and the timetable for the services to Harwich serving up to three train ferry sailings a day. The focal role of the famous marshalling yards at March is evident.

FERRY TRAIN

Sealink   through to Europe

SPEEDLINK EXPORT CONNECTIONS
via Harwich-Zeebrugge

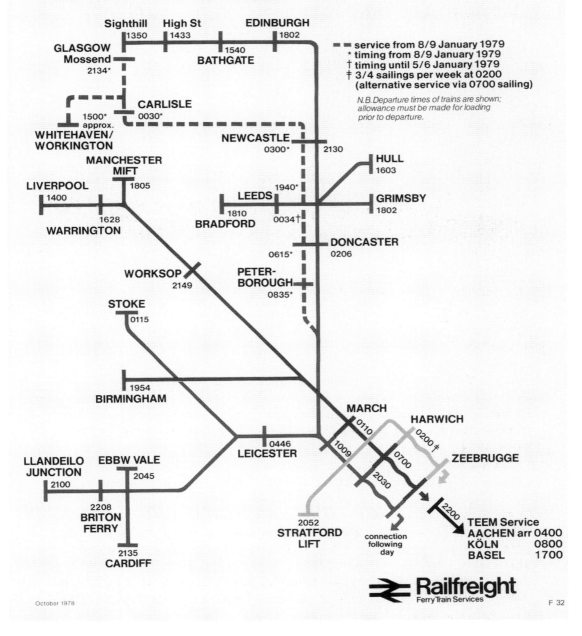

Sighthill 1350   High St 1433   EDINBURGH 1802

GLASGOW
Mossend 2134*   BATHGATE 1540

CARLISLE 0030*
1500* approx.
WHITEHAVEN/
WORKINGTON

NEWCASTLE 0300*   2130

MANCHESTER MIFT 1805
LIVERPOOL 1400
WARRINGTON 1628

HULL 1603

LEEDS 1940*
BRADFORD 1810   0034†

GRIMSBY 1802

DONCASTER
0615*   0206

WORKSOP 2149

PETER-BOROUGH 0835*

STOKE 0115

BIRMINGHAM 1954

MARCH 0110
1009

HARWICH 0200‡
0700

ZEEBRUGGE
2030
2200

LLANDEILO JUNCTION 2100
EBBW VALE 2045
LEICESTER 0446

BRITON FERRY 2208
CARDIFF 2135

STRATFORD LIFT 2052

connection following day

TEEM Service
AACHEN arr 0400
KÖLN 0800
BASEL 1700

-- service from 8/9 January 1979
* timing from 8/9 January 1979
† timing until 5/6 January 1979
‡ 3/4 sailings per week at 0200
(alternative service via 0700 sailing)

N.B. Departure times of trains are shown;
allowance must be made for loading
prior to departure.

Railfreight
Ferry Train Services

October 1978

F 32

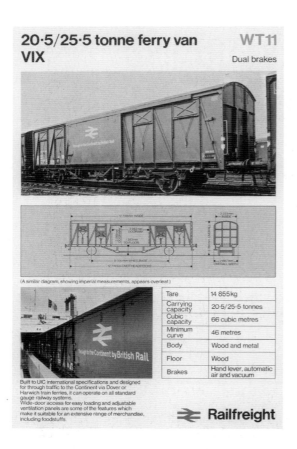

20·5/25·5 tonne ferry van   **WT 11**

VIX   Dual brakes

(A similar diagram, showing imperial measurements, appears overleaf.)

Tare	14 855kg
Carrying capacity	20·5/25·5 tonnes
Cubic capacity	66 cubic metres
Minimum curve	46 metres
Body	Wood and metal
Floor	Wood
Brakes	Hand lever, automatic air and vacuum

Built to UIC international specifications and designed for through traffic to the Continent via Dover or Harwich train ferries, it can operate on all standard gauge railway systems.
Wide-door access for easy loading and adjustable ventilation panels are some of the features which make it suitable for an extensive range of merchandise, including foodstuffs.

≋ Railfreight

Amongst these inserts, the information sheets about the special rolling stock used are a favoured subject. Although the gauge between the tracks on either side of the North Sea was the same, the clearances known as the 'loading gauge' were not. Nor were the brake systems identical. A whole breed of special wagons was developed to make the sea crossing. It can be interesting, for a range exists, to trace European railway administration publicity featuring their stock headed for Britain.

Shown here is one of the dedicated BR designs of vehicle: the VIX coded 25.5 tonnes ferry van, first built in 1961. The original January 1978 leaflet is colour, when only months before a different monochrome version had been issued. There is likely to be a surprising amount of publicity purely for the one-wagon design! Whisky was one kind of traffic to use these vans.

The modeller is familiar with the design because Tri-ang Hornby in 1970 manufactured a 4mm scale example R738. The prototype's 26ft 3in wheelbase was correctly followed which generated some problems for the radius of curves Tri-ang used. They managed to design some play in the wheel sets and produced a model that was not at all run-of-the-mill. Various versions have been made over the years, not always completely accurate, but the original, specifically based on the first 150-strong batch, was very appropriate for the . Harwich route.

On the real railway, there were some 400 of these vans which, at 41ft 11in overall length seemed far more in tune with European railway design than the usual British van. Both prototype and model turned heads when new.

PORTRAIT
OF AN
Old Lady

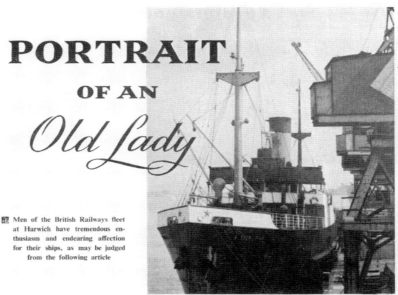

The s.s. "Sheringham" at Parkeston Quay

Men of the British Railways fleet at Harwich have tremendous enthusiasm and endearing affection for their ships, as may be judged from the following article

— By —

F. S. Leonard

AS seafarers know, every ship has a personality. They are like human beings, more than the sum of their parts, and s.s. *Sheringham*, which carries on the Eastern Region cargo service between Harwich (Parkeston Quay) and Rotterdam, is not just another ship; she is *herself*.

Built in 1926 by Earles Shipbuilding Company of Hull, the *Sheringham* is fitted with reciprocating engines, capable of a speed of 14 knots, and is a coal burning vessel. She is 266 feet long, 36 feet broad with a gross registered tonnage of 1,088 tons.

A Hectic Life

Her life has not been uneventful. When the cargo service between Harwich (Parkeston Quay) and Rotterdam, which was suspended on 31 August 1939, re-opened in December 1939 the *Sheringham* sailed from Ipswich, this because Parkeston Quay closed temporarily for commercial purposes on 3 September 1939. Until May 1940, when the Low Countries were invaded, she took out horses, machinery, motor cars and general cargo, bringing in foodstuffs, wireless parts and general cargo.

In June 1940 she was loaned to the Great Western Railway for the Channel Islands/Weymouth vegetable traffic service, but at the end of that month she was engaged in sterner responsibilities—the evacuation of civilians from the Islands. Two voyages were made and on each homeward passage she carried 700 women and children.

Captain D. A. Williams and Bosun F. W. H. Moore on the bridge of s.s. "Sheringham"

Later she was chartered as a military transport between Preston and Northern Ireland ports. Then followed a period when she was placed at the disposal of the Coasting and Short Sea Service, when she sailed from the Clyde to London via the North of Scotland route.

One particularly thrilling incident in her wartime history was the rescue, in very bad weather, of an airman in the Irish Sea near the Chicken Rock Lighthouse in 1941. She was then under the command of Captain R. V. Adams.

Home — to Harwich

In March 1946 she came home—home to Harwich, where, of course, she belongs. From Harwich (Parkeston Quay) she now sails twice a week to Hudig & Pieters' Wharf, Merwehaven, Schiedam, close to Rotterdam. She is about eleven hours on passage and carries general cargoes, bulbs, machinery, horses (there are special "stables" on board and not long ago the famous Olympic jumper "Foxhunter" occupied one of the stalls).

Twenty-five men attend the s.s. *Sheringham*. The last in a succession of fine seamen, Captain D. A. Williams, is her present Master. Her *Bosun*, Boatswain F. W. H. Moore, has been with her since 1938. Others of the crew have been with her for years, notably Able Seaman P. Gooch, Donkeymen 'Ted' Cogger and S. H. Thorne, Greaser 'Chicken' Fenner and the 2nd Engineer, Mr. A. C. Banks. They and their fellows attend her with that peculiar attachment which seamen have for their ships.

9

Another look into the Eastern Region magazine and the chance to eyeball more conventional sea-borne freight. A number of Eastern Region railway ships were profiled in this source through the years. Here the January 1953 subject was the SS *Sheringham* in a short feature by F.S. Leonard. The LNER had had her built for the Harwich–Rotterdam route in 1926 by Earles of Hull. She lasted at Harwich until 1958 and her demise. During that time her only substantial break was her war service. This was quite notable, and included evacuation duty from the Channel Islands in June 1940. Her profile was that of the conventional bridge amidships cargo steamer.

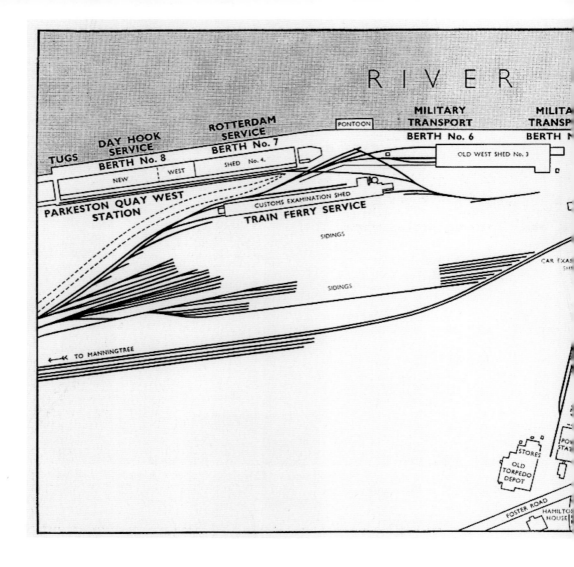

The train ferries may have gradually eaten into the work of the classic freighters like the *Sheringham*. From the late 1950s something far more radical happened, something which would change the estuary at Harwich and Felixstowe utterly. In ten years and involving two generations of ship, freight through the port was largely containerised (or went onto the Ro-Ro ferries).

Firstly, two motor ships called the *Colchester* and *Isle of Ely* arrived in 1958/59 to handle the classic railway container (already more than thirty years old in design). Their arrival and effect was well covered in the Eastern Region magazine in 1959. Within ten years everything was then upgraded to full ISO standards, with yet another pair of ships. Along the way various claims were notched up at Harwich. MV *Colchester* became the first rail blue BR ship in October 1964, some months before the official launch of corporate image in January 1965. This pair had been the first unit load vessels built for Eastern Region and they were supplanted by the first purpose built ISO container ship to come from a UK yard – MV *Sea Freightliner 1* – late in 1967.

Various Eastern Region freight centres like Temple Mills gained their own monochrome brochures to be given away. In 1960 Parkeston Quay received the same treatment, building

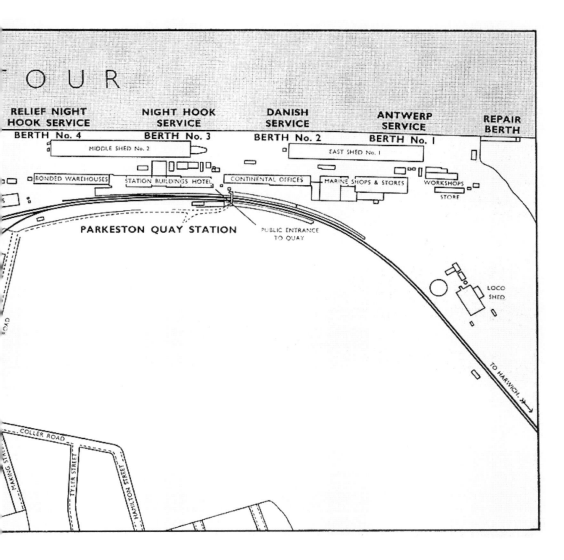

RELIEF NIGHT HOOK SERVICE	NIGHT HOOK SERVICE	DANISH SERVICE	ANTWERP SERVICE	REPAIR BERTH
BERTH No. 4	BERTH No. 3	BERTH No. 2	BERTH No. I	

MIDDLE SHED No. 2

EAST SHED No. I

BONDED WAREHOUSES   STATION BUILDINGS HOTEL   CONTINENTAL OFFICES   MARINE SHOPS & STORES   WORKSHOPS

STORE

PARKESTON QUAY STATION

PUBLIC ENTRANCE TO QUAY

LOCO SHED

TO HARWICH

ROAD

COLLER ROAD

MAKING STREET

TYLER STREET

HAMILTON STREET

on a profile of the passenger ferries and the strength of the activities of the 1958/59 cargo ships. The train ferries down at the town station only got a paragraph. The cover is reproduced (the same image being used on the January 1959 ER magazine). One energetic image inside had tractors suspended in mid-air over a (relatively rare) Hunslet 0–6–0 diesel shunter, later BR Class 05.

The foldout plan in the brochure showed that eight berths were in use plus a repair berth. Nos 1 and 7 were the regular homes for the two BR freight ships *Colchester* and *Isle of Ely* respectively. Two of the berths were in use solely for trooping.

PARKESTON QUAY

BRITISH RAILWAYS

What goes on at

HARWICH

PARKESTON QUAY

Port Series No.1

Sealink

Container Services

Having pioneered in this country the use of containers (originally low-capacity wooden boxes — now high capacity metal boxes of internationally accepted dimensions) British Rail now possess a comprehensive network of freightliner train services. The rail container services of the U.K. are linked with those operated by the railways of Europe via Parkeston Quay. Two container ships "Sea Freightliner I" and "Sea Freightliner II" maintain a twice daily each way service between Parkeston Quay and Zeebrugge. Of cellular construction, these ships were the first of their kind to be built in Britain and each has a capacity of between 130 and 200 (according to length) containers in cells three deep below deck with one layer on deck. Two smaller vessels, British Rail's m.v. "Colchester" and the Zeeland's m.v. "Domburgh" operate a daily service to and from Rotterdam. French Railways also provide a Monday to Friday container service between Parkeston Quay and Dunkerque using m.v. "Transcontainer I". This is a dual purpose container and roll on/roll off ship.

At Parkeston Quay, the Container Terminal basically consists of three cranage areas. At the container berth there are two 30 ton capacity transporter cranes used for loading and unloading the ships. In the adjacent Freightliner Terminal two goliath cranes load and

unload rail-hauled containers — two more goliath type cranes are employed in a new extension to the terminal for handling containers arriving at and departing from the port by road. Transfer of containers between the quayside and the rail and road cranage areas is carried out by a fleet of specially designed internal movement vehicles (tractor-hauled trailers).

The port is served by daily Freightliner trains from London and most major industrial centres throughout the country.

Much of the container traffic imported via Parkeston is consigned through to London, Manchester or Birmingham for inland Customs clearance thus avoiding congestion at the port. A percentage of containers require examination on arrival at the port and there is a special Customs Shed for this purpose located immediately to the rear of the railway station. Adjacent to the Customs Shed is an area especially set aside for dealing with road hauled containers which provides standage and transfer facilities as required. A straddle carrier is employed for container movements in this area.

Ford's Container Train arrives from Halewood

Loading Containers on to m.v. "Sea Freightliner I"

French Railways' RO/RO container ship "Transcontainer I"

Customs checkpoint at the Container Terminal

m.v. "Sea Freightliner I"

Straddle Carrier at the Container Terminal

Transporter Crane, Parkeston Quay

This page and opposite: Doubtless freight and Parkeston Quay has spawned far more publicity than I have found. Another piece known comes from just over a decade later in 1972. *What goes on at Harwich Parkeston Quay Port Series No.1* led off a sought-after · series of port brochures issued by what, since 1969, had become Sealink.

An internal diagram revealed the radical changes just over a decade had made. Two 30-ton transporter cranes serviced a new container berth, and two roll-on roll-off linkspans had been installed for the car ferries. An entirely new build passenger terminal had opened in 1972.

The type of traffic handled by the new container trains included a dedicated service from Ford at Halewood on Merseyside.

This sort of activity was inspirational, one small offshoot perhaps being Matchbox's Container Port playset of 1977. The child could easily imagine this as the new-look Harwich. The straddle crane shown in the leaflet matches Matchbox's model very well. The developments at Harwich would have been prominent in the mind of the 1970's toy designer in Enfield.

European
Container
Service
VIA HARWICH

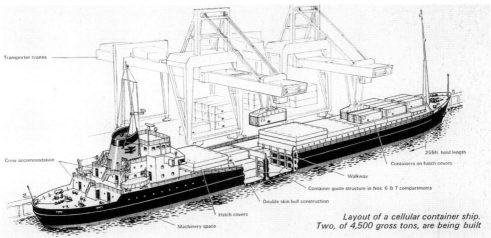

Transporter cranes

Crew accommodation

255ft. hold length

Containers on hatch covers

Walkway

Container guide structure in Nos. 6 & 7 compartments

Double skin hull construction

Hatch covers

Machinery space

Layout of a cellular container ship.
Two, of 4,500 gross tons, are being built

The year for change at Harwich was 1968 with the car ferries and the Freightliner ships and their terminals coming on stream. It all merited a launch by Prince Charles.

European Container Service via Harwich from that year offers an artist's impression of all that activity. The ship in the foreground appeared on the reverse. No name was mentioned but there were two sisters from Readhead's at South Shields: MV *Sea Freightliner 1* and *2*. The service would run to Zeebrugge and the two ships spent their entire lives on the job until disposal in 1987.

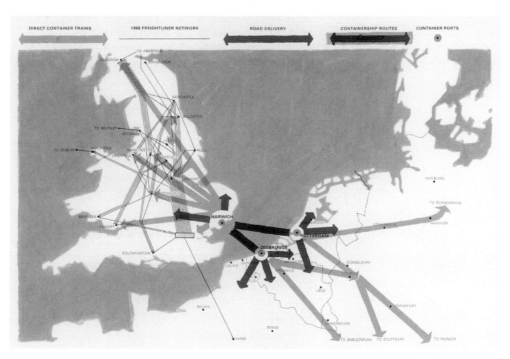

There was a definite flow of literature making the most of this innovation. '*High Capacity Container Services*' was a sixteen-page brochure produced at the new ships' inception. It was dedicated to the whole transit and to the potential customer.

Chapter Three

Beyond the Hook

The previous chapter focused on the activities at Harwich and on the prime railway-owned shipping routes out of the port. British boat trains to the port were covered. Rare, however, was the journey that stopped at the Continental port of arrival. Usually that was just a staging point on the journey and usually the rail traveller's documentation was an inclusive ticket. This desire to project the through journey well beyond the Hook meant that the various British railway administrations went to considerable efforts to publicise journeys beyond the Hook. Dutch and German railway authorities practised the same principle in reverse. All in all, quite a range of potential material for 'Beyond the Hook'.

There were some hardy annuals covering this activity. One example (overleaf) from the LNER was this *Cheap Holiday Tickets* booklet (overleaf) which covered other East Coast services as well (also see Chapter 2). The summer 1938 edition packed fifty-six pages with information. This included a folding map and notice of the introduction of a new summer Saturday-only day service to Zeebrugge, a crossing that was considerably shorter than to the Hook. This was primarily a holidaymaker service and no onward international connections were provided. However, the Belgian Coastal Tramway of the 'Vicinal' was promoted.

Dutch bulbfields are another form of hardy perennial, and a Bulbfield Sunday tour was a bright idea that would continue for decades in various forms. The tickets could be booked from as far afield as Sheffield. Note that these were 'no passport' tours. That's progress and one European homeland for you.

Another little note in the volume suggests the passenger can spend the night before embarkation for Zeeland's Flushing service (Vlissingen) either on board the steamer itself or in the LNER's Parkeston Quay Hotel. There were two railway hotels at Harwich. The Parkeston would close in 1963. The older Harwich Hotel became the town hall in 1951. I wish I had some dedicated ephemera from either to show. A lucky person has a surviving pre-First World War Great Eastern Railway paper bag advertising both. Postcards for both might be a shade easier to find. Alsop's *The Official Railway Postcard Book* records a *few* from both the GER and LNER. Both the GER and LNER issued considerably more postcards for the ships.

CHEAP
HOLIDAY TICKETS
to the
CONTINENT

HOLLAND
BELGIUM
GERMANY

VIA HARWICH
GRIMSBY OR HULL
9th APRIL, 1938 (until further notice)

THIS PUBLICATION CANCELS THE "CHEAP HOLIDAY
TICKETS TO THE CONTINENT" BOOKLET, OCTOBER 1937

Zeeland Steamship Company
London & North Eastern Railway
Associated Humber Lines

No. 42   PRINTED IN GREAT BRITAIN

FROM LONDON AND PROVINCES

BULBFIELDS SUNDAYS IN HOLLAND
Via HARWICH

10th, 17th, 24th APRIL, 1st and 8th MAY

Special trips will be arranged in Holland on the above dates, when it is anticipated the flowers will be at their best.

The itinerary will be approximately as follows :—

SATURDAY (9th, 16th, 23rd and 30th April, and 7th May).

London (Liverpool Street)	dep. 20 30
Harwich (Parkeston Quay)	,, 22 00

SUNDAY (10th, 17th, 24th April also 1st and 8th May).

Hook of Holland (Dutch Time) ... ... arr. 5 30
Breakfast on steamer at Hook of Holland.

8 30 Leave Hook of Holland by motor coach.

9 15 Arrive at The Hague. Sightseeing by coach in The Hague and Scheveningen for 1½ hours.

10 30 Leave The Hague by motor coach for trip through the Bulbfields via Lisse and Hillegom. A stop of half-an-hour will be made at the Cafe-Restaurant "De Nachtigall" near Lisse, a Bulbfields centre, affording passengers an opportunity to purchase flowers and walk through the fields.

13 00 Arrive Haarlem. Lunch at Hotel Restaurant Lion d'Or.

14 00 Leave Haarlem by motor coach for Amsterdam. Sightseeing by coach for 2 hours.

16 10 Tea at Carlton Hotel, Amsterdam. To passengers not returning from Amsterdam by the first train, a 1½ hour motor-boat trip round the Canals and Docks is recommended. Tickets (75 Cents., approx. 1s. 9d.) and information obtainable from Guides.

17 45 Leave Amsterdam (Central Station) by train, arriving Hook of Holland 19.26 or,

21 07 Leave Amsterdam (Central Station), arriving Hook of Holland 22.38. Refreshments obtainable on the steamer.

Hook of Holland (Dutch Time) ... ... dep. 23 00

MONDAY (11th, 18th, 25th April also 2nd and 9th May).

Harwich (Parkeston Quay)	{ arr. 6 15
	{ dep. 7 00
London (Liverpool Street)	arr. 8 38

The fares include the following :—

Return rail and steamer journey to Hook of Holland.
Breakfast on steamer at Hook of Holland.
Motor coach tour in Holland.
Lunch at Haarlem.
Tea at Amsterdam.
Rail journey Amsterdam to Hook of Holland.

A Guide will accompany the party throughout the motor-coach tour in Holland.

INCLUSIVE FARES

From :—	2nd Rail, 1st Steamer	2nd Class throughout
LONDON (Liverpool Street) ...	£3 8 8	£2 18 8
HARWICH (Parkeston Quay) ...	£3 2 2	£2 12 2
Children—4 to 10 years		
From :—		
LONDON (Liverpool Street) ...	£1 19 7	£1 14 7
HARWICH (Parkeston Quay) ...	£1 16 4	£1 11 4

[Fares from Provincial Stations on next page

NO PASSPORTS REQUIRED FOR THESE TOURS

Via HARWICH

26

LONDON—AMSTERDAM

Via HARWICH—HOOK OF HOLLAND

NIGHT SERVICE
(Sundays included)

Miles.	OUTWARDS.		I & 2 Cl. A
—	London (Liverpool Street Station)	dep.	20 00 } THE HOOK
69	Harwich (Parkeston Quay)	{ arr.	21 40 } CONTINENTAL
		{ dep.	22 00
		{ arr.	5 45
190	Hook of Holland		I & 2 & 3 Cl.
		{ dep.	7 40
		{ arr.	8 00
204	Schiedam	dep.	8 03
216	The Hague (H.S.)	{ arr.	8 19
		{ dep.	8 21
225	Leiden	{ arr.	8 33
		{ dep.	8 35
243	Haarlem	{ arr.	8 57
		{ dep.	9 00
254	Amsterdam (C.S.)	arr.	9 16

THROUGH CARRIAGES. ✕—Restaurant Car.
A—London-Harwich (Parkeston Quay), 1 & 2 Cl. and ✕. Hook of Holland-Amsterdam, 1, 2 & 3 Cl.

DAY SERVICE
(Zeeland S.S. Company)
Daily (Sundays included)

Miles.	OUTWARDS.		I & 2 Cl. B
—	London (Liverpool Street Station)	dep.	9 25 } THE DAY
69	Harwich (Parkeston Quay West)	{ arr.	10 58 } CONTINENTAL
		{ dep.	11 30
		{ arr.	18 40
190	Hook of Holland		1, 2 & 3 Cl.
		{ dep.	19 45
		{ arr.	20 05
207	Rotterdam (D.P.)	dep.	20 08
216	Tha Hague (H.S.)	{ arr.	20 26
		{ dep.	20 28
225	Leiden	{ arr.	20 39
		{ dep.	20 40
243	Haarlem	{ arr.	21 00
		{ dep.	21 01
254	Amsterdam (C.S.)	arr.	21 15

THROUGH CARRIAGES. ⌇—Buffet Car.
B—London-Harwich (Parkeston Quay West), 1 & 2 Cl. and ⌇. Hook of Holland-Amsterdam, 1, 2 & 3 Cl.

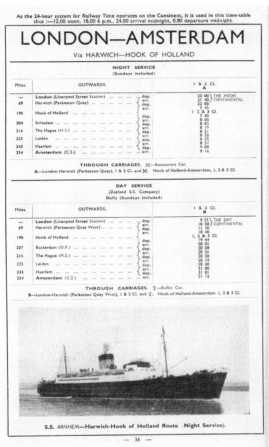

S.S. *ARNHEM*—Harwich-Hook of Holland Route (Night Service).

AMSTERDAM—LONDON

Via HOOK OF HOLLAND—HARWICH

NIGHT SERVICE
(Sundays included)

	INWARDS.		1, 2 & 3 Cl. A
	Amsterdam (C.S.)	dep.	20 30
	Haarlem	{ arr.	20 44
		{ dep.	20 45
	Leiden	{ arr.	21 06
		{ dep.	21 07
	The Hague (H.S.)	{ arr.	21 18
		{ dep.	21 20
	Schiedam	{ arr.	21 35
		{ dep.	21 38
	Hook of Holland	arr.	21 58
			I & 2 Cl.
		dep.	22 50
	Harwich (Parkeston Quay)	{ arr.	6 00
		{ dep.	6a45 } THE HOOK
	London (Liverpool Street Station)	arr.	8a23 } CONTINENTAL

✕—Restaurant Car.
a—Prior to June 18 and from Sept. 17 Harwich (Parkeston Quay) depart 7.15, London (Liverpool Street) arrives 8.55.
A—Amsterdam-Hook of Holland, 1, 2 & 3 Cl. Harwich (Parkeston Quay)-London, 1 & 2 Cl. and ✕.

DAY SERVICE
(Zeeland S.S. Company)
Daily (including Sundays)

	INWARDS.		1, 2 & 3 Cl. B
	Amsterdam (C.S.)	dep.	8 55
	Haarlem	{ arr.	9 09
		{ dep.	9 10
	Leiden	{ arr.	9 30
		{ dep.	9 31
	The Hague (H.S.)	{ arr.	9 42
		{ dep.	9 44
	Rotterdam (D.P.)	{ arr.	10 02
		{ dep.	10 05
	Hook of Holland	arr.	10 27
			I & 2 Cl.
		dep.	11 30
	Harwich (Parkeston Quay West)	{ arr.	18 40
		{ dep.	19 45 } THE DAY
	London (Liverpool Street Station)	arr.	21 20 } CONTINENTAL

✕—Restaurant Car.
B—Amsterdam-Hook of Holland, 1, 2 & 3 Cl. Harwich (Parkeston Quay West)-London, 1 & 2 Cl. and ✕.

H.M. CUSTOMS EXAMINATION—HARWICH SERVICES

PASSENGERS TRAVELLING VIA HARWICH ARE ADVISED THAT THE EXAMINATION BY H.M. CUSTOMS OF **ALL** BAGGAGE (WHETHER ACCOMPANIED OR SENT IN ADVANCE, AND IRRESPECTIVE OF DESTINATION) TAKES PLACE AT **HARWICH (PARKESTON QUAY)** IN BOTH DIRECTIONS, AND PASSENGERS **MUST** BE PRESENT AT THE EXAMINATION.

ALL BAGGAGE SENT IN ADVANCE TO HARWICH (PARKESTON QUAY) SHOULD BEAR A LABEL SHOWING BY WHICH **ROUTE AND SERVICE** THE PASSENGER IS TRAVELLING TO THE CONTINENT, WITH A PARTICULARLY CLEAR INDICATION IF THE HOOK OF HOLLAND **DAY SERVICE** IS TO BE USED.

The important aspect of the *Continental Handbook* (see colour 4) was that it was not primarily a timetable of the ferry services. Instead, the crossings were set in the context of much more extensive journeys. At one point (pp.36–37), this was the London–Amsterdam service which embraced the other two sentinel Dutch cities of Rotterdam and Den Haag. That seems quite simple but there were tables for much more complex journeys, like the Scandinavia table which used the Harwich Esbjerg DFDS service as a springboard for a long train/ship journey to Stockholm which involved sleeping cars on Danish train ferries.

LONDON & AMSTERDAM

Services

and

fares

31st MAY to

3rd OCTOBER

1959 inclusive

BRITISH RAILWAYS

The demand for simple timetables for the London–Amsterdam journey has been considerable and a wide variety have appeared.

This 1950s example has a small and plain cover but unfolds into twelve panels with illustrations. Something like this seems typical of the 1950s.

By 1961 something larger and livelier was being done and continued for years. A feature of these brochures was the detailing of two formerly competing routes via Harwich and via Dover – this was a consequence of nationalisation.

The cover shows a typical Amsterdam waterbus and what is perhaps the Montelbaanstoren. Amsterdam provides some choice in towers overlooking canals.

LONDON

AMSTERDAM

**Services
and
Fares**

1st **OCTOBER 1961** to **26th MAY 1962**

BRITISH RAILWAYS

LONDON AMSTERDAM

by train and ship

Services and Fares

25 SEPTEMBER 1966 TO 27 MAY 1967

British Rail

The previous cover did service in the early 1960s. In the mid-1960s, a photograph of Dam Square with the National Monument and the Koninklijk Paleis was employed. The Harwich route was offering its core day and night service, but a reflection of growing demand was a summer-only additional eastbound service from Liverpool Street at 12.45 – two hours behind the *Day Continental*. Another feature of the volume of traffic was the timetabled provision of relief trains. The overnight *Hook Continental* left Liverpool Street at 20.00. Relief paths were available and publicised for 19.40 and 20.10. A procession of three boat trains for Harwich out of Liverpool Street as late as 1965 is quite a thought.

London
Amsterdam
by train and ship

Amsterdam's waterbuses have made numerous appearances on railway-published publicity. Two successive and different images were used on what was now a year-long timetable issued in 1969/70 and 1970/71. Their significance is due to their broadly similar design, encompassing the change from British Rail to Sealink branding.

Timetable and Fares
1 June 1969 to 30 May 1970

London Liverpool Street   Amsterdam CS

6 April to 27 September, 1980

	London Liverpool Street	Amsterdam CS
	09 30	19 05
🛏	21 16	09b 14

28 September to 25 October, 1980

	09 30	19c 48
🛏	21 16	09b 14

26 October to 21 March, 1981

	09 30	19 05	Not December 25
🛏	21 16	09b 14	Not December 25

22 March to 4 April, 1981

	09 30	19c 48
🛏	21 16	09b 14

5 April to 30 May, 1981

	09 30	19 05
🛏	21 16	09b 14

Notes

🛏 Sleeping accommodation available on ship
b   09 05 Suns.
c   20 07 Suns.

These inter-capital timetables (previous pages) were part of a series, whose design was shared, encompassing Brussels and Paris.

During the 1970s and into the early 1980s, the three Continental cities shared another timetable series. Within the UK, corporate image had produced a standardised series of timetable cards to A7 size. A sub-set appeared for Inter-City Sealink services. I know of five titles, three being for the continental capitals. London–Amsterdam was certainly published 1977–1980.

The information on these cards was very basic and no intermediate times were given. A fascinating question is whether BR (in distinction to NS) may have issued a Dutch language version. A Flemish version from Brussels has come my way and includes Harwich–Hook sailings.

Save a day Service London Brussels Amsterdam

≷ Europe

British Rail and Sealink's overnight service to Brussels and Amsterdam

Save a Day and arrive refreshed and relaxed in the centre of Brussels or Amsterdam. Travelling overnight on our connecting and comfortable rail/sea service, you arrive in good time for business or leisure. Save the cost of hotel accommodation and the stress and expense of city centre to airport transfers. Travelling from London, the evening boat train offers you a choice of an appetising dinner in the restaurant car or a snack and drink in the buffet (except on Sundays when there is a light refreshment service). On the return night service from Holland, take the opportunity to enjoy the Great British Breakfast as you speed from Harwich Parkeston Quay to London Liverpool Street (Monday-Saturday). First class single or double cabins are available with the option of cheaper second class travel and berths.

First Class Comfort
Cost Effective
Convenient Departure and Arrival Times

Valid 1 November 1981 – 30 April 1982

A flimsy variant on the inter-capital timetable is this November 1981 'Save a day service' leaflet, promoting the rail-connected services to both Amsterdam and Brussels using the overnight boats only. There are various editions. This one is just two sides, with bare timetable, map and fare information on the reverse.

Amsterdam Rotterdam by Rail

SUMMER TIMES AND FARES 1992

**GREAT FARES
GREAT VALUE**

≷ British Rail International

The rail/ship London–Amsterdam timetable has made its way through the trauma of privatisation. First it was the ships in 1984 and then the trains in the mid-1990s. The last years of the nationalised railway saw a new brand to handle European travel, now that the ships were no longer railway-owned. This was British Rail International. As in previous decades a group of flimsy 'capital' timetables appeared. *Amsterdam Rotterdam by rail* was the Dutch one. The artwork for this simple two-sider was used on five issues between 1992 and 1994.

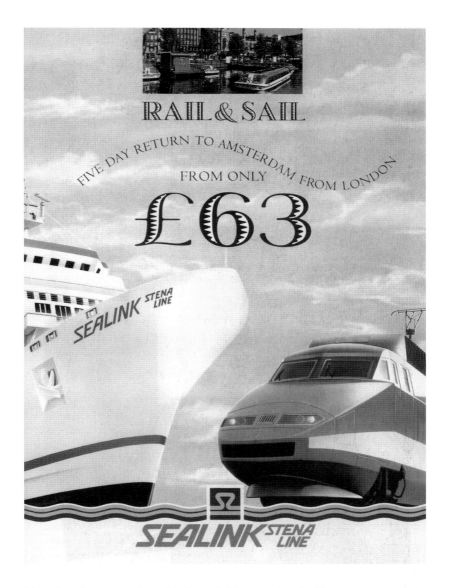

RAIL & SAIL

FIVE DAY RETURN TO AMSTERDAM FROM LONDON

FROM ONLY

£63

SEALINK STENA LINE

SEALINK STENA LINE

Meantime the separation of train and ship operators led to a new phenomenon. Each agency was producing its own publicity for more or less the same product.

For the same summer of 1992, Sealink Stena Line put out this four-side *Rail and Sail* brochure for London–Amsterdam. In as much as there was a justification for this duplication, it revolved around the different locations to which the operators could distribute their publicity. This Sealink Stena Line item was found in a St Andrew's travel agency. While the Amsterdam waterbus was safe territory on the cover, the appearance of a French TGV was totally fanciful and suggests a loosening of editorial grip through the process of fragmentation. This is not difficult to imagine during a time of continual change. The Sealink Stena Line branding was itself only current from 1991–1992.

Amsterdam from London by train

and the new Stena HSS

From just £59 RETURN

Stena Line

2 June – 27 September 97

Anglia
RAILWAYS

A degree of stability was to return to the London–Amsterdam timetable but it would not remove the duplication which continued as this was written in 2004. The stability arose in what became a partnership between Anglia Railways and Stena Line. Anglia Railways was the product of privatisation that took over the London Harwich boat trains. The brand name was launched in 1994 with privatisation following in 1997. Anglia consistently produced a London–Amsterdam timetable following on from the British Rail International one.

At least nine issues appeared before privatisation and five of these featured P. Kooij's waterbuses on the cover, providing some re-assuring element of continuity for the passenger.

What is reproduced here is the first to appear in full privatised Anglia Railways image for the summer of 1997. That development happened to coincide with the appearance of the HSS on the Harwich route. Through this time, the timetable grew up to twelve pages.

Lest everyone get too comfortable, the Anglia franchise was abolished in 2004, and the new Greater Anglia franchise awarded to an entirely different holder who has created the 'One' brand, under which guise the timetable continues.

Stena Line Edition One 2000

Amsterdam Express
from London & Cambridge

Amsterdam from **£49*** return
*See inside for details

Holland by rail and Stena HSS

Accommodation in Amsterdam

New Cambridge to Amsterdam

The world's leading ferry company

Left: The HSS speed up led to the coining of the cover name *Amsterdam Express*. Both Anglia and Stena Line used this from 2000. This is the Stena Line brochure cover. Within the covers, each brochure was individual to its operator. The shipping operator consistently achieves a much wider distribution area and this brochure came from an Aberaeron travel agent.

BRITISH RAILWAYS

LONDON
and
BRUSSELS
via
Dover - Calais
Dover - Ostend
and
Harwich -
Hook of Holland Routes

SERVICES & FARES

APRIL 16th to
MAY 13th, 1950, inclusive.

Right: From the inter-capital series of timetables, the Brussels route issue has relevance to the Harwich story. One example can be squeezed in. It is the earliest British Railways issue I can show, from the third spring of nationalisation. For Brussels, the Hook route was only one of three options. At 303 miles, it was considerably further than the Dover routes. Note the very short validity – less than a month.

There is rather more to the Netherlands than Amsterdam or even points between the Hook and Amsterdam.

The one-volume *Continental Handbook* has already been noted. This was published from 1950 until 1960 when it took a break that lasted until 1974. The tradition of timetable offprints is very well known. The 1950s BR regional timetable and later the All Lines issue spawned all sorts. It appears the *Continental Handbook* did this, only for the children to become the mainstay after the solo volume was abandoned.

These offprints took the form of 'National' timetables. These were booklets and they seem to provide a sequence published by BR from at least the winter of 1954 to the winter of 1973. Thereafter a new version of a single-volume 'International' timetable appeared, with the All Lines timetable which was launched in May 1974. In quantity perhaps some two issues a year for twenty years in a series getting into double figures for titles? The series is particularly well known for the number of artist signed covers used.

Holland had signed covers by Lander and John Cort, in at least three principal designs known to me between 1956 (summer issue shown opposite) and 1968. The cover designs were used with different colours for several issues at a time. It is likely another Lander design exists from earlier 1950s issues.

This Lander cover adopted around 1960 (*above*) took cheese for its subject. The earlier *Holland* issues ignored some of the lesser routes but this edition had a page each for the AHL service from Hull and for the Transport Ferry Service route from Tilbury. Both went to Rotterdam and both were 'nationalised transport' (see also colour 5).

The *Holland* issue was always one of the slimmer members of the series. Sometime in 1969/70, it was decided to combine *Holland* with *Belgium & Luxembourg* to create the *Benelux* volume, which ran to the end of the series. It is very likely that the change was synchronised with the launch of the Sealink brand. The cover design is not signed but I think it entirely possible it came from John Cort. The final few issues abandoned artists in favour of monochromes. After 26 May 1974, a new numbered leaflet series dominated (see p.115).

The Continent via Harwich

HARWICH HOOK OF HOLLAND

BRITISH RAILWAYS

ADVANCE INFORMATION
OF SERVICES
31st May to
3rd October 1959

Timetables for services through the Hook and on into Europe were issued in many shapes and sizes. A summary of the Continental travel options was issued as a folder in many editions. This is the summer of 1959. In addition to two panels purely about the crossing, eight panels looked at the onward possibilities with headings like 'Scandinavia'. Many of these involved famous named trains like the *Holland–Scandinavia Express*. This involved through coaches and train ferries in a journey across four counties to Stockholm. This summary timetable was itself the basis of individual leaflets to the different groups of destinations.

Austria
VIA HARWICH

1st October 1961 to 26th May 1962

BRITISH RAILWAYS

A structure to this is discernable: inter-capital, the handbook, the country offprints, the advance summary and now the long line of individual route leaflet. In our master Harwich file, the group that follows occupies, in all versions, a long section.

This is A for 'Austria' and, like its siblings, is notable in the quality of the artist cover which regularly changed. Full colour on the cover and beyond, this publicity, competing with the infancy of the airlines and private car as a means to go abroad, was hoping to entice the wealthy (mass student travel was still in the future in 1961).

As a winter issue, skiing is to the fore. The previous summer issue had a pair of 'typical' Austrian youths (shorts and braces) skipping through the meadows. The principal train that the leaflet promoted was the *Austria Express*, which left the Hook after the arrival of the day boat and ran overnight to Klagenfurt and Innsbruck.

From the summer of 1963 through to the summer of 1969, colour photo covers appeared and this may be regarded as standard across the series. After 1969, Sealink handled these timetables differently. (See colour section no.7)

Day and night services

Germany

by British Rail and Zeeland S.S. Co.

1st JUNE to 27th SEPTEMBER 1969

Between 1967–1969 (Sealink appearing late in 1969 changed things) this logo combining the BR double arrow and the Zeeland seaman was widely applied to literature covering all aspects of Harwich–Hook shipping. A rather more lively photo was employed for 'Germany' in the summer of 1969. Two panels of the brochure were used for a diagrammatic map. Maps were an important part of all these continental leaflets.

In ethos a bit like the London–Amsterdam summary timetables, this small folder enjoyed a signed 'Blake' cover and focused on the train service from the Hook to Hamburg.

British Rail | Zeeland S.S. Co.

30th **MAY** to 25th **SEPTEMBER** 1965

HOLLAND

Austria and Holland seem to have led the transition to the route logo which was employed in the summer of 1963, one year earlier than for *Germany*. If this seems trivial, the interest lies in the fact that between 1963 and 1965 BR was developing its corporate image in a whole series of moves. Seeing standardised typefaces and logos appearing is part of this process.

We show an example of *Holland* for the summer of 1965 with the route logo employed between the two other versions noted on these pieces: British Rail and Zeeland in text side by side. The clogs and the tulips were certainly Dutch but, like their German equivalents, not exactly motivating. Later *Holland* photo covers have something more energetic.

31st MAY to
26th SEPTEMBER 1964

BRITISH RAILWAYS
HARWICH HOOK

35168/1

POLAND
and the U.S.S.R

These Harwich route leaflets could extend a long way – *Poland & the USSR* is an example. The through cars that worked from the Hook to Warsaw and Moscow, putting Communist Bloc vehicles beside British Railways ships were the inspiration for the leaflet. The Moscow carriages had to change gauge en route at Brest-Litovsk. Inside, a Kremlin monochrome was courtesy of Intourist.

SCANDINAVIA

AND

SWITZERLAND

VIA

HARWICH - HOOK OF HOLLAND

TRAVEL IN COMFORT VIA HARWICH

9th MAY, 1948
until further notice

Printed in Great Britain at the Railway Printing Works, Stratford, London, E.15   2043/48   20,750

My knowledge of how the subject was handled in the early years of BR is limited. It seems likely that the full colour leaflets were not inherited and were developed as a concept by the Eastern Region. Shown is what happened in the first summer of nationalisation – a very plain paper folder whose logic seems alphabetical in putting Scandinavia and Switzerland together. Should we expect an Austria and Germany companion?

Everything smacks of post-war austerity, as does the considerable reference to currency controls, although that phenomenon did not go away in a hurry. It would take until 1979 for all such controls to be removed.

111

Opposite: Scandinavia and Switzerland for the purposes of these timetables spent most of their life in separation. Scandinavia was an exciting subject at Harwich which for the traveller from southern Britain was very much the gateway (Newcastle-upon-Tyne also had a role which we cover later). You either went via the Hook and a long train journey or you said goodbye to British Railways at Harwich and joined another company like DFDS (see next chapter).

Throughout the life of the *Scandinavia* leaflet until its demise after 1969, it focused on the primarily overland route; there was more business in this for the railway despite hosting DFDS at Harwich. When the Sealink map series started in 1974, the DFDS option was integrated into the 'Northern Germany & Scandinavia' leaflet.

The summer of 1959 leaflet with its jigsaw cover and imagery of day and night boats is enticing. The reverse cover map was a regular and shows the two further ferry crossings then required. Inside the tables dealt with the two key named trains. The *North-West Express* from the Hook to Copenhagen connected out of the day boat. The *Holland–Scandinavia* went further and reached Stockholm. Its patrons used the night boat. The entire journey London to Stockholm took over forty hours.

The *North-West Express* had commenced on 14 June 1952. Some launch literature will surely exist but I have not seen it. This Scandinavian provision had not existed before the Second World War.

Prominent on the cover is one of the Dutch day crossing boats. What is noticeable is her post-war profile following their 1946 rebuild which lifted the bridge house up one deck (see colour 8).

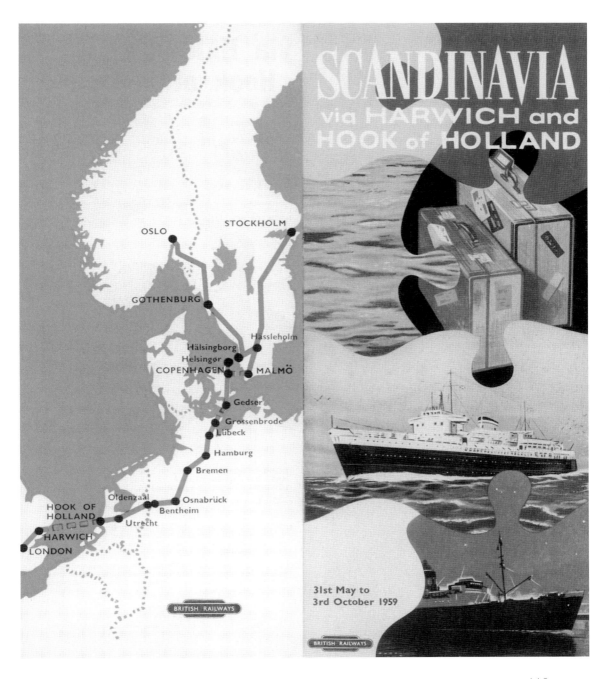

SCANDINAVIA
via HARWICH and
HOOK of HOLLAND

31st May to
3rd October 1959

BRITISH RAILWAYS

Although not shown with the pair shown in colour 9, the leaflets of this time had completely different front and back covers. This feature is shown for the winter of 1961 issue. The mirrored glasses are a lovely touch. The role of the female in these leaflets had a later echo in the Inter City 'See a Friend this Weekend' promotion of 1969. The intriguing truth is that transport advertising reflects a tussle between allowing the vehicle to take centre stage and allowing people to displace the vehicle. Which is the romance of travel?

Such debates took a nosedive for a long time in the 1970s, with marketing that was less 'loaded' either way and was more measured and rational. Sealink had appeared and faced the issue of how to present a unified front for marketing the Continental routes by rail and sea out of Britain.

These map cover leaflets replaced the Harwich route's Continental timetable leaflets. The latter had been largely an Eastern Region product. Sealink had also to interface with the appearance in May 1974 of the BR All Lines timetable which came with a matching International timetable book in the package. That development undermined the country timetable books (just as All Lines replaced the regional books within Great Britain) and so the map cover series was launched at the same time.

Appropriately this is No.1 of the new series' first issue. Integration meant that both former Eastern and Southern Region routes appear together. The design is unadventurous. The most exciting element is the French styling of the SNCF electric by Paul Arzens.

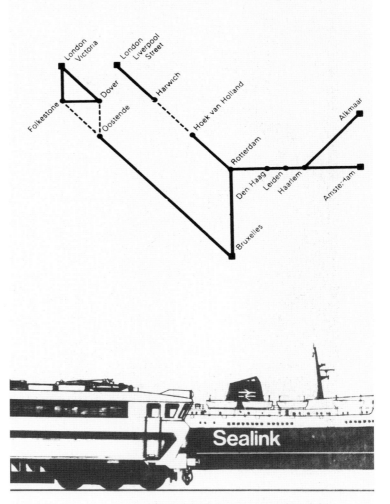

1
LONDON
WEST HOLLAND AND
AMSTERDAM

May 26 to September 28, 1974

Inter-City ⇄ Sealink
Europe made easy

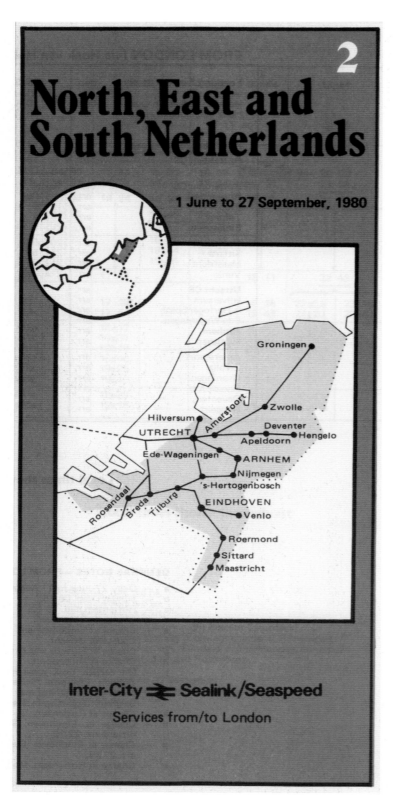

2

North, East and South Netherlands

1 June to 27 September, 1980

Groningen

Zwolle

Hilversum
Amersfoort
UTRECHT
Deventer
Apeldoorn
Hengelo
Ede-Wageningen
ARNHEM
Nijmegen
's-Hertogenbosch
Roosendaal
Breda
Tilburg
EINDHOVEN
Venlo
Roermond
Sittard
Maastricht

Inter-City ⇌ Sealink/Seaspeed

Services from/to London

Initially the series totalled twenty-four leaflets, only a proportion of which covered Harwich. The design slowly changed but remained quiet, the maps gaining strength. This is the summer of 1980.

**29 May to
24 September 1983**

The
Netherlands

The map series was issued through to the winter of 1982. Outside, the winds of change were beginning to blow as Thatcherism took hold. The somewhat bland nature of corporate image that had been the mantra since the mid-1960s was going to be undone. For the little matter of these Continental leaflets, it started in the summer of 1983, as did the reappearance of artist covers, signed 'JPL'. His signed covers were developed for the next four years. Along with them, the series was contracting in size. *The Netherlands* was one title. The windmill was quintessentially Dutch. A map remained important but went inside.

InterCity ⟫ Europe

The Netherlands

29 September 1985 to 31 May 1986

InterCity ⩫ Europe

A theme can be seen for these covers. In summer and winter 1983 it was buildings. In 1984 it was people. In 1985 it was trains. Excitement of excitements, the Dutch 'Dog's Head' DMU of the 1950s which had done the job in 1964 (see colour 6) was back in a new rendition. The leaflets revealed inside the cover that this was an 'Intercity train at Utrecht Centraal Station'.

There was a return to buildings in 1986. For the Netherlands, this produced the Montelbaanstoren in Amsterdam cover. This tower has been met before. Some varied colourwashes were added.

The Netherlands

27 September 1987 to 28 May 1988

 **Europe**

The use of varied colourwashes continued in 1987 when that year's two issue sets featured trains again, but from a new hand. 'AC' is the signature. The 'Dog's Head' DMU remained the favoured subject although newer designs did exist. The choice was slightly updated to use a 'Mat 64' two-car EMU. There was one small but significant change between the summer and winter issues. The word 'Intercity' was dropped. 'Intercity' was now a business sector of BR closely associated with internal routes that had little connection to the ports. The Harwich connections were Intercity-worked and remained so for many years more, but even there, as this timetable pointed out inside, the new buzzword was 'Eurocity'. From the spring of 1988, the country leaflet series was discontinued.

EuroCity

*European
Rail Travel
at its Best*

Eurocity was a rigidly defined European operation whose only British route this 1987 piece detailed. These are the English language and therefore BR productions. The cover train was one of the Dutch Koplopper or Camel electric multiple units. A BR Intercity Class 87 adorned the rear. These had been working to Harwich since 1986.

In the years following Eurocity, which employed EMUs on the boat train to Amsterdam, there was a rundown of the traditional long-distance express connection from the Hook.

CAR-SLEEPER

CAR SLEEPER SERVICES
HOOK OF HOLLAND-SALZBURG-VILLACH

Gateway for **AUSTRIA**
YUGOSLAVIA
AND THE BALKANS

AMSTERDAM - AVIGNON
FOR SOUTHERN FRANCE AND SPAIN
AMSTERDAM - MILAN FOR ITALY

1965 IN CONNECTION WITH THE
HARWICH - HOOK OF HOLLAND ROUTE

Above and opposite: It had not only been passengers that had made the connection at the Hook. Another sequence (probably a small one) of brochures was issued for the Car-Sleeper services that operated. This brochure for the summer of 1965 was issued jointly by BR and NS. It is printed in Holland, but in English and with British Railways Eastern Region branding on the reverse.

That year three services were advertised to Villach in Austria, Avignon and Milan. The day boat was used before an overnight train journey to Austria. Check the small print and it becomes clear that only the Villach train really worked for the ship. The two other services were from Amsterdam Amstel, and this was NS trying to find some more takers. In time, Continental motorway improvements got the better of this idea. This was not before some

122

CAR SLEEPER SERVICES

Amsterdam — Avignon for Southern France and Spain

in connection with the Night Steamer Harwich — Hook of Holland.

Travel by this service presents the opportunity of spending a few hours visiting Holland. Arrival is in the early morning at the Hook of Holland and departure from Amsterdam Amstel-station or 's-Hertogenbosch is in the later afternoon.

TIME TABLE 1965

From Amsterdam/'s-Hertogenbosch every Tuesday from April 6th to September 21st; from Avignon every Sunday from April 11th to September 26th.

1)	2)			3)	4)
17.30	16.40	dep.	Amsterdam Amstel arr. ▲	11.50	10.45
18.37	17.43	dep.	's-Hertogenbosch arr.	10.45	9.37
20.08	19.25	dep.	Maastricht arr.	9.00	8.00
21.00	20.14	dep.	Liège-Bressoux arr.	8.07	7.09
10.42	8.32 ▼	arr.	Avignon Fontcouverte dep.	18.05	18.23

¹) From Holland: Tuesdays from April 6th to May 25th
²) From Holland: Tuesdays from June 1st to September 21st
³) From France: Sundays from April 11th to May 30th
⁴) From France: Sundays from June 6th to September 26th

Conditions under which cars are conveyed

Cars may not exceed
— height: 5' 4" (including luggage racks)
— length: no limitation in dimension
— width: no limitation in dimension.
On the lower deck 3-wheeled cars can also be carried.

Loading and Unloading

Loading only on the day of departure
— at Amsterdam Amstel, April 6th-May 25th, between 15.15 and 16.30 hrs;
— at 's-Hertogenbosch, April 6th-May 25th, between 16.15 and 17.45 hrs;
— at Amsterdam Amstel, June 1st-September 21st, between 14.15 and 15.30 hrs;
— at 's-Hertogenbosch, June 1st-September 21st, between 15.15 and 16.45 hrs;
The times will be endorsed on the confirmation by the Reservation Office Amsterdam.
— at Avignon-Fontcouverte, April 11th-May 30th, between 15.00 and 17.15 hrs;
— at Avignon-Fontcouverte, June 6th-September 26th, between 15.00 and 17.15 hrs.
Unloading immediately after arrival

Restaurant Car

A Restaurant Car runs in this train on the whole section. Passengers are advised to reserve meals at the Application Offices.

For rates and further information ask your travel agent or British Railways.

CAR SLEEPER SERVICES

Amsterdam — Milan for Italy

in connection with the Night Steamer Harwich — Hook of Holland.

This service also presents the opportunity of a few hours' touring in Holland. The car sleeper trains leave in the afternoon from Amsterdam Amstel-station or 's-Hertogenbosch.

TIME TABLE 1965

1)	2)			3)	4)
16.40	16.38	dep.	Amsterdam Amstel arr. ▲	13.15	13.15
17.43	17.43	dep.	's-Hertogenbosch arr.	12.10	12.10
18.45	18.45	dep.	Venlo arr.	11.02	11.02
10.10	10.10 ▼	arr.	Milano Porta Vittoria dep.	19.25	19.25

¹) From Holland: on Fridays April 2nd and April 9th; on Wednesday April 14th and on Fridays from April 23rd to May 28th.
²) From Holland: on Sundays and Wednesdays from May 30th to October 6th.
³) From Italy: on Saturdays April 3rd and April 10th; on Tuesday April 20th and on Saturdays from April 24th to May 29th.
⁴) From Italy: on Mondays and Saturdays from May 31st to October 9th.

Conditions under which cars are conveyed

Cars must not exceed
— height: 5' 10" (including luggage racks)
— length: no limitation in dimension
— width: no limitation in dimension
Also 3-wheeled cars can be carried; the distance of one axle measured between inside of tyres must not exceed 3'.

Loading and Unloading

Loading only on the day of departure
— at Amsterdam Amstel: between 14.30 and 15.45 hrs.
— at 's-Hertogenbosch: between 15.15 and 16.45 hrs.
The times will be endorsed on the confirmation by the Reservation Office Amsterdam.
— at Milano Porta Vittoria: between 15.55 and 17.55 hrs.
Unloading immediately after arrival.

Restaurant Car

A Restaurant Car runs in this train.
— Section Amsterdam — Milan:
between Amsterdam Amstel and Neu Isenburg (± 23.00 hrs);
between Domodossola (± 8.00 hrs) and Milan (open till ± 10.30 hrs);
— Section Milan — Amsterdam:
between Milan and Domodossola (3 series at 18.00, 19.00 and 20.00 hrs);
between Neu Isenburg (± 6.30 hrs) and Amsterdam Amstel.
Passengers are advised to reserve meals at the Booking Offices.

years of growth. The 1965 brochure looks similar to a British Railway's Car-Sleeper (later Motorail) services leaflet of the time. By 1971 BR had opted out of promotion leaving NS to issue an English language brochure entirely alone. At that point the three trains all ran from the Hook and went to Villach, Ljubljana and Biasca.

Dover and Newhaven received BR car-carrying connections from the 1950s. Such services never got nearer Harwich than Cambridge and Ely from 1974. The Motorail brochure that year pushed the benefit for Scottish motorists of using the new Edinburgh–Cambridge Motorail train in the course of their journey to Harwich. In 1974, Harwich remained quite a drive from Cambridge. Edinburgh's Dutch-inclined tourists were unlikely to be tempted to go any further than North Sea Ferries at Hull.

Above left: Definitely in the very attractive slot is this twelve-page brochure, targeting the businessman, from 1984. The rail/sea route was still determined to fight air traffic in this market. *European Executive* in gold is the title. Its stimulus was the advent of *St Nicholas*. Along with an obvious focus on journeys to Amsterdam and Brussels, the centrespread was given over to the conference facilities available on that ship. Partying and lobbying could be conducted in a manner impossible on an aircraft.

Above right: BR's promotion of traffic beyond the Hook embraced the international train journey, car-carrying connections, the businessman and, now, the inclusive tour market. Activities such as visits to Holland's tulips have already been seen in the 1938 LNER brochure.

   See Holland in Springtime (or a similar title) was a BR regular. This 1967 issue operated daily for under a month. Four different tours were operated and quite some space had to be diverted to the differing implications they might have on the visitor's foreign currency allowance.

Sail Away
to Amsterdam and Rotterdam
Summer 1978

The use of a thirty-six or forty-eight-hour excursion ticket to Amsterdam and Rotterdam in the mid-1970s created another string of brochures like this 1978 example. These were issued from a wide spread of Eastern England. The title *Sail Away* is no accident. It plays on the 'away-day' theme British-based BR excursions had adopted.

Sealink

31/5 '81-22/5 '82 (zomer tot/Summer till/Sommer bis 26/9 '81)
(winter van/Winter from/Winter ab 27/9 '81)

Nachtboot aankomst/Night steamer arrival/Nachtboot Ankunft ± 6 15

Trein Train Zug	Vertrek Departure Abfahrt	Spoor Platform Gleis	
4121	6 43	2	Rotterdam CS, stoptrein/stopping train/Nahverkehrszug **1**
D 215*	6 56	6	**Rhein-Expres** Venlo-Mönchengladbach-Köln ('s zomers/in summer/ im Sommer: Bonn-Basel Bad) **2**
4123 ✗	6 59	1	Rotterdam CS, stoptrein/stopping train/Nahverkehrszug **1**
D 231*	7 10	4	**Holland-Scandinavië Expres** Utrecht-Hengelo-Osnabrück-Hamburg ('s zomers/in summer/im Sommer: Puttgarden-København) Hannover-Bad Harzburg-Berlin
4125	7 19	1	Rotterdam CS, stoptrein/stopping train/Nahverkehrszug **1**
140002*	7 30	3	Schiedam-RW, Den Haag HS, Leiden, Haarlem, Amsterdam CS (Boottrein)
4127 ✗	7 35	1	Rotterdam CS, stoptrein/stopping train/Nahverkehrszug **1**
4129	7 49	2	Rotterdam CS, stoptrein/stopping train/Nahverkehrszug **1**

* aanbevolen ontschepingstijd/recommended disembarkation times/empfohlene
  Ausschiffungszeiten: D 215 – 6 15, D 231 – 6 30, 14002 – 6 50

Dagboot aankomst / Day steamer arrival / Tagboot Ankunft 19 00

Trein Train Zug	Vertrek Departure Abfahrt	Dagboot Platform Gleis	
4175	19 15	2	Rotterdam CS, stoptrein/stopping train/Nahverkehrszug **1**
D 317	19 30	4	**Brittania Expres** Venlo-Köln-Stuttgart-Ulm-München Innsbruck-('s zomers/in summer/im Sommer: Bolzano- Merano)-Friedrichshafen-Lindau **2**
14004	19 33	3	Schiedam-RW, Den Haag HS, Leiden, Haarlem, Amsterdam CS (Boottrein)
D 237	19 36	5	**Nord-West Expres** Utrecht-Hengelo-Osnabrück-Hamburg-Puttgarden- København-('s winters/in winter/im Winter: Berlin- Warszawa-Moskwa)
4177	18 48	2	Rotterdam CS, stoptrein/stopping train/Nahverkehrszug **1**
D 1245	20 00	6	**Hoek Warszawa Expres** Utrecht-Bad Bentheim-Hannover-Berlin-Warszawa-Moskwa
4179	20 19	2	Rotterdam CS, stoptrein/stopping train/Nahverkehrszug **1**

✗ Niet zon- en feestdagen/nicht an Sonn- und Feiertagen/daily except Sundays and public
  holidays
1 Maassluis West, Maassluis, Vlaardingen West, Vlaardingen C, Vlaardingen Oost,
  Schiedam Nieuwland, Schiedam-RW, Rotterdam CS, (Antwerpen-Brussel)
2 Antwerpen-Brussel (overstappen / change / umsteigen in / at Rotterdam CS)

This page and opposite: If looking at the impact of the Harwich Hook connection beyond the Hook, it is as well to consider literature from the European railway administrations: what was the view from the Continent?

It is obvious that the NS – Dutch Railways – would produce much relevant literature, even if the British collector may not expect to find it so readily.

The rather bland Hoek van Holland cover reproduced (opposite, bottom) is important. Its title is self evident but what interests me is tucked inside. A train departure style timetable summarises all the connections out of Hoek Van Holland in the summer of 1981. The day boat, as an example, came in at 19.00. Between 19.15 and 20.19 seven connections left, three being named international services. The last page was a diagram of the station, which shows the berths used. Note how each departure is marked against

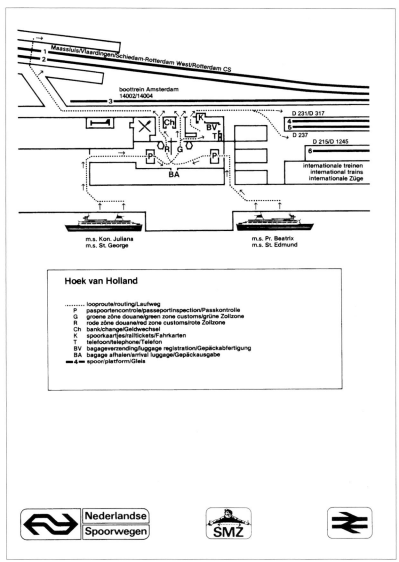

Hoek van Holland

.... looproute/routing/Laufweg
P paspoortencontrole/passeportinspection/Passkontrolle
G groene zône douane/green zone customs/grüne Zollzone
R rode zône douane/red zone customs/rote Zollzone
Ch bank/change/Geldwechsel
K spoorkaartjes/railtickets/Fahrkarten
T telefoon/telephone/Telefon
BV bagageverzending/luggage registration/Gepäckabfertigung
BA bagage afhalen/arrival luggage/Gepäckausgabe
■4■ spoor/platform/Gleis

a platform.

Platforms 1 and 2 were through platforms for the tracks which continued to a final terminal at Hoek Van Holland Strand. For many years Table 11 in the NS timetable book was the Hoek Van Holland Strand to Rotterdam CS service, but incorporating the connections to Harwich and London. Offprints of this were available as a yellow A5 folder in 1981 and other years. I mention this because NS has not published individual route timetables prolifically.

To the railway enthusiast, the international trains were notable for bringing Communist Bloc coaches to the harbour station. On 29 July 1989, the night boat having docked, train D345 is waiting to leave at 08.58. The Mitropa restaurant car is a Deutsche Reischbahn vehicle from East Germany and is running to Berlin. These precise arrangements show some change from the 1981 departure sheet when the equivalent train D231 (the *Holland–Scandinavia*) left at 07.10. The use of Platform 4 for this train to Northern Germany had not changed. Platforms 4–6 at the Hoek were associated with the long-distance connections for many years. The last real international train at the Hoek was the *Hoek–Warszawa Express*, which ran until 7 November 1992.

Opposite: Much time can be spent finding the European ephemera of these international trains. Publicity in Germany and to a lesser extent in the Netherlands is often train based. This winter 1975 item covers the three expresses then working from the Hoek east out of the Netherlands (the *Noordzee* actually started at Rotterdam). Because these trains tended to convey many portions, a page was given over to the times and another page to the consist. For instance, decoding the symbols on the *Nord-West Expres* page shows the Moscow sleeper was a composite coach which ran four nights a week, and that a second-class couchette and a composite sleeper ran nightly to Copenhagen. The train consist is shown as it ran from the Hoek to Bentheim at the German border, where it can then be seen another Moscow sleeper was attached. This one ran daily and had started in Paris. Puttgarden was the terminus for one ordinary seating coach in the consist because this was the German terminal for the train ferry to Denmark. These symbols were standard across European timetables. 'Nord-West' refers to Britain's isolated position!

1 Back at Tilbury a very long-lived operation that continued into the Eastern Region era was the connection with the Batavier Line (see p.23). This was a Thames–Rotterdam service commenced as far back as 1830 – the first successful foreign-owned passenger steamer service to reach London. The first and last such vessel carried the name *Batavier*. At one time the service ran from Gravesend but latterly used Tilbury Landing Stage with a dedicated train connection to London Fenchurch Street. By the time of this 1955 brochure, the service had only three more years to go before boiler problems led to the withdrawal of *Batavier II*. This 1921 vessel was itself a replacement for a First World War loss and a 1939 successor was sunk in 1942. *Batavier II* had first-class cabins only and her 1955 schedule was not intensive. A sailing from Tilbury on a Wednesday and from Rotterdam on a Saturday constituted the entire service.

2 The impressive lines of the 1948 *Royal Sovereign* are evident in this postcard General Steam published from a painting by J. Nicholson (see p.30). She was capable of twenty knots. It will come as no surprise to learn that the postcard was posted in Margate on 31 August 1955 by one of her passengers. After withdrawal, this vessel was, in 1967, converted to the car carrier *Autocarrier*.

and all who sail in her

s.s. **AVALON**
THE NEW BRITISH RAILWAYS SHIP
FOR HARWICH - HOOK OF HOLLAND NIGHT SERVICE

3 Naturally enough the most stunning contrast to an *Avalon* ticket is an *Avalon* poster (see p.49). This one celebrates her arrival. It is unsigned artwork which is a pity. A later version, also set at night, shows her in the double-arrow funnel period and is signed S.A. Walker.

4 (*Opposite*) In Chapter 1 mention is made of the British Railways *Continental Handbook* (see after p.90). Its issues are a key source for Harwich. Something like this would be issued in varied guises as late as 1987 and lesser manifestations of the nationalised railway's interest in Europe continued into the 1990s under the British Railways International brand.

BRITISH RAILWAYS

CONTINENTAL
HANDBOOK

ALL ROUTES Summer 1950

Holland

by train and ship

SERVICES AND FARES

24 September 1967 to 25 May 1968

British Rail

5 The John Cort cover design was adopted in May 1963 and lasted for six years during which time British Rail's corporate image was added (see p.103).

NIGHT AND DAY SERVICES
ADVANCE INFORMATION

6 For a number of issues in the mid-1960s, the advance information leaflet used this cover. It instantly attracts on several counts. The route logo at the top should be noted – these devices in differing forms appeared on several BR shipping routes. The logo (and other variants) was applied to the various European timetables associated with the Harwich route (see later).

The train and ship both resonate even if the quality of the artistry is a bit basic. The train is one of the classic NS 'Dogs-head' electric multiple units. Specifically I think it is one of the '1954 Plan F' trainsets appearing in its original green livery. Most British commentators will more clearly visualise these in NS yellow. The Scharfenberg automatic coupler is very prominent.

The ship is the then new 1963 *Avalon* (see previously). She wears her first British Railways colours prior to the rail blue hull which she carried for most of her BR career (read after p.105).

Germany

via Harwich—
Hook of Holland

29th September 1963 to 30th May 1964

7 'Germany' can be used to show the transition from the artist cover to a colour photo (see pp 106–107). The photo is not as inspirational as the artist's work but was used summer and winter into 1966.

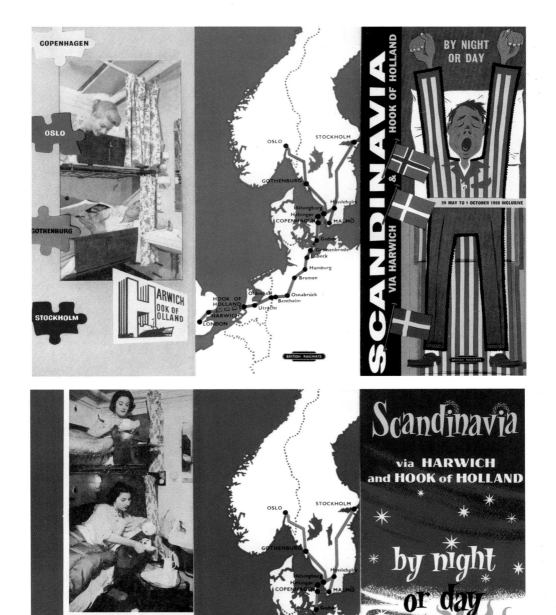

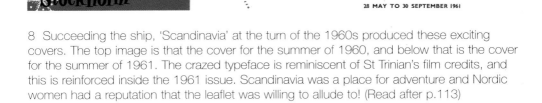

8 Succeeding the ship, 'Scandinavia' at the turn of the 1960s produced these exciting covers. The top image is that the cover for the summer of 1960, and below that is the cover for the summer of 1961. The crazed typeface is reminiscent of St Trinian's film credits, and this is reinforced inside the 1961 issue. Scandinavia was a place for adventure and Nordic women had a reputation that the leaflet was willing to allude to! (Read after p.113)

SWITZERLAND
VIA HARWICH

See centre page
for description
of this scene

BRITISH RAILWAYS

31st May to 3rd October, 1959

9a & 9b (*This page and opposite*) It would be good to know who designed these leaflets (see p.114) at the turn of the 1960s. The crazed or quirky strand was deployed to full extent in 'Switzerland' which, like 'Austria', had summer and winter covers to reflect the changing theme. The fish seem to suggest a varied diet of boredom and excitement. Something makes me think the designer would have loved Monty Python, Hancock and Michael Palin.

SWITZERLAND
VIA HARWICH

BRITISH RAILWAYS

See centre page for
description of this scene

4th October, 1959 to 28th May, 1960

Sealink
GREAT LITTLE ESCAPES
SHORT INCLUSIVE HOLIDAYS
GERMANY
4 NIGHTS FROM £44·50
29 APRIL–28 SEPTEMBER 1976

Sealink Travel Limited

The official travel agency of British Rail Shipping and
International Services Division.

ASSOCIATION OF BRITISH TRAVEL AGENTS

10 Sealink popularised its Mini-breaks or 'Great Little Escapes'. There are many of these Sealink via Harwich holiday leaflets covering Holland, Belgium and Germany. They use a wide range of drawing covers. Dutch windmills are no surprise. This example hardly needs the text to reveal that Germany is the destination for the summer of 1976. Various German towns could be visited by train for two nights with a further two nights on ship. (Read after p.124)

THE CONTINENT
daily

THE CONTINENT
nightly

via
HARWICH - HOOK OF HOLLAND

via
HARWICH - HOOK OF HOLLAND

11 Zeeland would issue literature in several different languages. This is an undated piece but, since the *Koningin Wilhelmina* is trumpeted (that's her on a cover), it is likely to be 1960 or just after. Entirely in English with no route logos, the only clue that it really is Zeeland is 'printed in the Netherlands' and the lack of a BR print code. Clever mirror image design means there is no 'front' cover. 'The Continent nightly' showed off a BR vessel when displayed in that mode. (Read after p.132)

HOEK VAN HOLLAND

SCANDINAVIA-ENGLAND
SUMMER TIMETABLE
29th MAY TO 1st OCTOBER 1960 INCL.

12 Previously it has been seen that British Railways put some effort into their Scandinavia timetable. Any redundancy notwithstanding, Zeeland did likewise with this English language six-side booklet at the same time. This is the summer of 1960 and like the immediately previous item, inside is celebrating the new *Koningin Wilhelmina*, even if one of the pre-war ships is on the cover. The loco is readily identified. It is an American Baldwin-designed but Dutch-erected 1200 Class electric built in the early 1950s and in traffic for over forty years.

hoek van holland harwich ≋

'Zeeland'-reizen 21 maart tot 1 oktober 1975

LONDEN
4-daagse reis v.a. 193.–

ENGELAND!
9-daagse reis v.a. 411.–

13 In addition to timetables a tours or 'Zeeland Reisen' brochure was issued in the square format. Through the mid-1970s, the Zeeland Reisen issue went to a strange not-quite-A4 size. Here is the cover for the summer of 1975. Note the version of the seaman logo for Zeeland's centenary. These brochures are laden with iconic London imagery: red RT buses, the Houses of Parliament and black taxis.

The centenary had another marker in the shape of First Day Covers. *Sealink News* was a very wonderful house magazine. Copies sometimes surface on ebay. Issue 14 dedicated two pages to the centenary and to these covers, available with both British and Dutch stamps. The Dutch Post Office issued a 'Hands across the Sea' logo 35c stamp on 21 May 1975 as well as the covers.

In the late 1970s Zeeland used a Big Ben Tours brand and both the tours and timetable literature appeared in more standardised A4 and A5 formats. (Read after p.135)

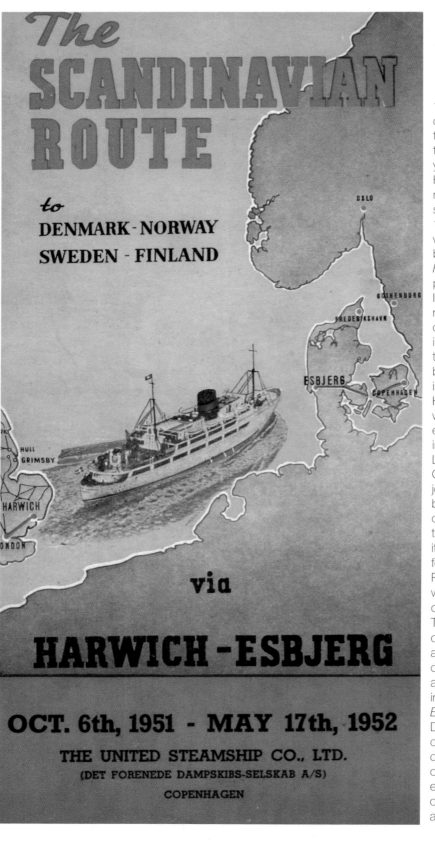

The SCANDINAVIAN ROUTE

to
DENMARK - NORWAY
SWEDEN - FINLAND

via

HARWICH - ESBJERG

OCT. 6th, 1951 - MAY 17th, 1952

THE UNITED STEAMSHIP CO., LTD.
(DET FORENEDE DAMPSKIBS-SELSKAB A/S)
COPENHAGEN

14 With evolving cover design, this item can be traced over many years as the core Harwich–Esbjerg route publicity. As seen in this winter 1951 issue, this was a twelve-page brochure with the *Frederik/Ingrid* pair prominent. Inside there is a nice assortment of text and illustrations. The train connection beyond Esbjerg is promoted. Harwich–Esbjerg was just one element in the inter-capital London–Copenhagen journey. The route beyond Esbjerg can be seen on the cover map and it involved a train ferry. Danish State Railways like DFDS were early users of diesel traction. Thus in 1951 the connection was a special express diesel train called a *Lyntog* with an individual name *Englaenderen*. DFDS put their own stewardesses during the summer on the boat trains either side of the crossing. (Read after p.145)

15 (*Right*) Another of RTM's regulars was their motorist's handbook. Like the standard route leaflets, this 144-page issue for 1968/69 gains in interest through the naming of Harwich–Ostend. The porter is clutching a copy of a brochure which seems to only acknowledge the Dover route. However, this artwork might date back a bit, since Rayber-signed items in our collection tend to come from earlier in the 1960s. (Read after p.175)

16 (*Below*) The other old established Hull operation, Ellerman's Wilson Line, made a real effort to change. This resulted in the 1966 MV *Spero*. She certainly looked the part of a modern vehicle ferry when put on the Hull–Gothenburg run in 1966 and on the cover of this early leaflet. Note the EWL logo, a friendly play, perhaps, on the AHL concern. However, below deck, container-carrying lorries did not have enough headroom. A route to Zeebrugge was introduced but, only a short time after the *Spero* started, the Tor Line competition was biting. EWL plodded on from the Humber until 1978 but the passenger operations and the *Spero* went in 1973. In other hands she stayed in business far from Britain until 2004. (Read after p.229)

BELGIUM 1968/69

Handbook for Motorists

DOVER · OSTEND
AND
HARWICH · OSTEND

Overnight to Europe
HULL - ZEEBRUGGE

ELLERMAN'S WILSON LINE

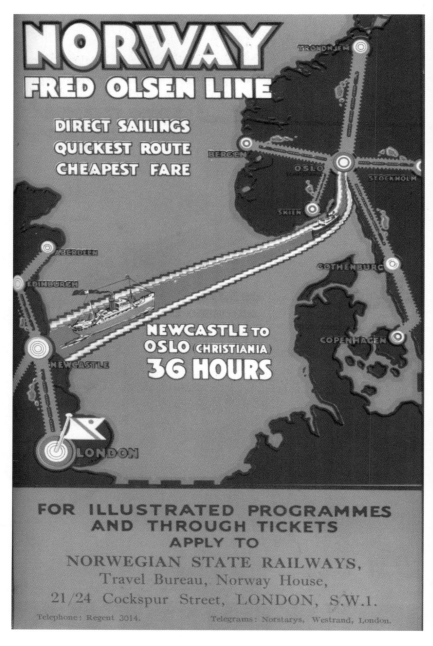

17 Bergen Line had run from the Tyne since 1890. Fred. Olsen offered
sailings from the Tyne from 1906. Like the other Scandinavian operators
Bergen Line and DFDS, Fred. Olsen commissioned motor ships before 1939.
The *Black Watch* and *Black Prince* pair of 1938 were highly regarded. This
earlier map cover brochure is a nice piece of design. The rail connections are
made evident. Inside, the vessels are quoted as the *Bessheim* and *Blenheim*
(these Norwegian operators knew the value of a good name). These were a
1923 pair of vessels. The Olsen route was longer than the sailing to Bergen
but it went direct to the capital and the company tried to ensure their ships
were made more comfortable for the longer crossing. Unfortunately both of
Olsen's 1938 motor ships were destroyed in the Second World War as were
the *Bessheim* and the *Blenheim*. (Read after p.237)

Nord-West Expres (D237/D236)

Dag	D237	D237		D236	D236	Dag
I	....	19 32	V Hoek van Holland Haven . . A	10 44	....	III
	....	19 55	V Schiedam-Rotterdam West . A	10 17	....	
	....	20 44	V Utrecht CS . . . . A	9 25	....	
	....	21 02	V Amersfoort . . . . A	9 03	....	
	....	22 23	V Hengelo . . . . A	7 47	....	
			V Oldenzaal 🚉 . . . A	7 30		
	....	22 45	A Bentheim 🚉 . . . V	7 18	....	
		23 05	A Rheine V	7 01		
		23 39	A Osnabrück Hbf V	6 23		
	D1245	**D233**		**D234**	**D1244**	
II	0 29	0 58	V Osnabrück Hbf . . . . . A	5 32	5 52	
			A Bünde (Westf.) V		5 27	
			A Minden (Westf.) V		5 04	
	1 52		A Hannover Hbf V		4 25	
	D241				**D240**	
	2 52		V Hannover Hbf . . . . . A		4 01	
	3 41		A Braunschweig Hbf V		3 15	
	4 10		A Helmstedt V		2 49	
	D245				**D244**	
	4 20		V Helmstedt 🚉 . . . . . A		1 57	
	4 31		A Mariënborn V		1 49)	
			(Sachs. Anh.) 🚉			
	4 36 (		V Mariënborn 🚉 . . . A		1 44	III
			(Sachs. Anh.)			
	7 23		A Berlin Zoolog. Garten . . V		23 08	
	7 38 (		A Berlin Friedrichstr. V		22 30)	
	8 04)		A Berlin Ostbf. V		22 04 (	
	8 26		V Berlin Ostbf. V		21 42	
	9 20)		A Frankfurt (Oder). V		20 45 (	
	245/241 🍴 a				**240/244** 🍴 a	
	9 30		V Frankfurt (Oder) 🚉 . . A		20 23	
	9 53		A Kunowice V		20 11	
	10 01		V Kunowice . . . . A		20 01	
	12 28		A Poznan Gl. V		17 22 Ⓡ	
	16 35		A Warszawa Gdanska . . . V		13 07 Ⓡ	
	18 03		V Warszawa Gdanska . . . V		12 35	
	21 11		A Terespol V		9 27	
	21 31		V Terespol 🚉 (M.E.T.) . . . V		9 15	
	23 59		A Brest 🚉 (Mos. T.) . . . V		10 55	
	16 🍴				**15** 🍴	
III	1 50		V Brest . . . . A		9 10	II
	14 30		A Moskwa B V		20 50	I
	....	2 01	A Bremen Hbf V	4 28	....	
	....	3 06	A Hamburg Hbf V	3 15	....	
	....	4 04	A Lübeck Hbf V	2 07	....	
	....	5 11	A Puttgarden V	1 02	....	
		🚢🍴		🚢🍴		
	....	5 30	V Puttgarden 🚉 . . . . A	0 35	....	
	....	6 25	A Rødby F. 🚉 V	23 30	....	
		E233		**E234**		
	....	6 55	V Rødby F. . . . . . A	23 02	....	
	....	7 18	A Nykøbing Fl. V	22 39	....	
	....	8 59	A København H. . . . . V 🏛	21 10	....	

a 🍴 Kunowice—Warszawa v.v.

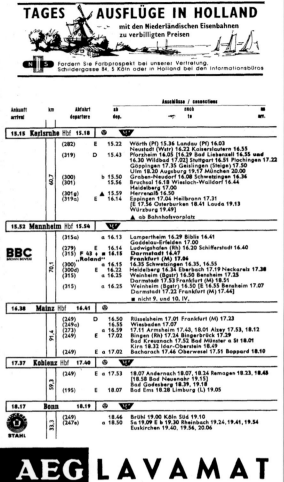

TAGES AUSFLÜGE IN HOLLAND
mit den Niederländischen Eisenbahnen zu verbilligten Preisen

Fordern Sie Farbprospekt bei unserer Vertretung, Schildergasse 84, 5 Köln oder in Holland bei den Informationsbüros

Ankunft arrival	km	Abfahrt departure	ab dep.	Anschlüsse / connections — nach to	an arr.
15.15 Karlsruhe Hbf 15.18					
	60.7	(282)	E 15.22	Wörth (Pf) 15.36 Landau (Pf) 16.03 Neustadt (Wstr) 16.22 Kaiserslautern 16.55	
		(319)	D 15.43	Pforzheim 16.05 [16.29 Bad Liebenzell 16.55 und 16.30 Wildbad 17.02] Stuttgart 16.51 Plochingen 17.22 Göppingen 17.35 Geislingen (Steige) 17.50 Ulm 18.20 Augsburg 19.17 München 20.00	
		(300)	b 15.50	Graben-Neudorf 16.08 Schwetzingen 16.36	
		(301)	15.56	Bruchsal 16.18 Wiesloch-Walldorf 16.44 Heidelberg 17.00	
		(301g)	▲ 15.59	Herrenalb 16.50	
		(319a)	E 16.14	Eppingen 17.04 Heilbronn 17.31 [E 17.56 Osterburken 18.41 Lauda 19.13 Würzburg 19.49]	
				▲ ab Bahnhofsvorplatz	
15.52 Mannheim Hbf 15.54					
BBC BROWN BOVERI	70.1	(315a)	a 16.13	Lampertheim 16.29 Biblis 16.41 Gaddelau-Erfelden 17.00	
		(279)	E 16.14	Ludwigshafen (Rh) 16.20 Schifferstadt 16.40	
		(315) F 43 ♦	■ 16.15 "Roland"	Darmstadt 16.47 Frankfurt (M) 17.06	
		(300)	a 16.15	16.35 Schwetzingen 16.35, 16.55	
		(300d)	E 16.22	Heidelberg 16.34 Eberbach 17.19 Neckarelz 17.38	
		(315)	a 16.25	Weinheim (Bgstr) 16.50 Bensheim 17.25 Darmstadt 17.53 Frankfurt (M) 18.51	
		(315)	a 16.25	Weinheim (Bgstr) 16.50 [E 16.55 Bensheim 17.07 Darmstadt 17.22 Frankfurt (M) 17.44]	
				■ nicht 9. und 10. IV.	
16.38 Mainz Hbf 16.41					
	91.4	(249)	D 16.50	Rüsselsheim 17.01 Frankfurt (M) 17.23	
		(249a)	16.55	Wiesbaden 17.07	
		(273)	a 16.59	17.11 Armsheim 17.43, 18.01 Alzey 17.53, 18.12	
		(249)	E 17.02	Bingen (Rh) 17.24 Bingerbrück 17.29 Bad Kreuznach 17.52 Bad Münster a St 18.01 Kirn 18.32 Idar-Oberstein 18.49	
		(249)	E a 17.02	Bacharach 17.46 Oberwesel 17.51 Boppard 18.10	
17.37 Koblenz Hbf 17.40					
	59.3	(249)	E a 17.53	18.07 Andernach 18.07, 18.24 Remagen 18.23, 18.43 [18.58 Bad Neuenahr 19.15] Bad Godesberg 18.39, 19.18	
		(195)	E 18.07	Bad Ems 18.28 Limburg (L) 19.05	
18.17 Bonn 18.19					
STAHL	33.3	(249)	18.46	Brühl 19.00 Köln Süd 19.10	
		(247e)	a 18.50	Sa 19.09 E b 19.30 Rheinbach 19.24, 19.41, 19.54 Euskirchen 19.40, 19.56, 20.06	

AEG LAVAMAT

The Hook on 29 July 1989 reveals another reason why British enthusiasts find Dutch operations fascinating. Two British loco outlines of the 1950s are sitting together. One is even in BR livery. From the reign of Victoria, the Dutch had bought British steam trains. After the Second World War, the standard British 350hp diesel shunter was bought in quantity by NS. One of these stands against a former Woodhead route BR Class 77. This small class of seven went whole to NS in 1969. Regular service there ceased in 1986 but one of several survivors hauled this *North Country Continental* special in 1989. This was originally BR 27000 *Electra*. The early 1960s livery being worn was immortalised by a contemporary Tri-ang OO-scale model of this engine.

Opposite: German Railways (DB) continues to issue many train-based timetables in 2004. Many, if not all, are now multilingual, and include English versions. No trains now reach the Hoek by through train. Turn back to April 1966 and this DB-issued German and English timetable for F163 *Loreley Express* Basel Hoek Van Holland. The final line of the table on page 4 was the London connection arrival at 09.14 having used the night boat. Basel had been left at 13.00 the day before. Such a train had used the SBB (Switzerland) system for a six-minute journey to the frontier station at Basel Bad Bf. German and Dutch railways provided most mileage but, as the attentive reader will realise, BR's own Switzerland timetable of the period will have covered this train too. That is potentially four administrations issuing publicity.

This little piece with its April 1966 date cannot have had much more than a month's validity. The summer timetables extended the train to/from Chiasso. Separate leaflets were issued for each direction, this is the northbound train. Within Chapter 2 it was noted how BR briefly operated their own train called the *Loreley* in the 1980s.

ZOMERDIENSTREGELING
van 3 juni tot en met 29 september 1956

NEDERLAND-ENGELAND
VIA
HOEK VAN HOLLAND-HARWICH

Zeeland (SMZ), as the partly nationalised Dutch ship operator, was much more separate from NS than was the case for the British-based operation. Which means another issuer of publicity.

This piece for the summer of 1956 is what the Dutch audience would have enjoyed as their 'standard' view of the crossing that year. I cannot say when the seaman logo had appeared but, with small variation, he enjoyed a long currency until at least 1982. Day service and night service, the logo proclaims. Appropriately, one of the Dutch boats is on the cover. The back cover offered BR's *Amsterdam*. The little booklet had twelve pages, and a full suite of rail connections from the Dutch side went as far as London Liverpool Street or Liverpool Central using the 'North Country Train'. Using the 'Dagboottrein' all Dutch connections timetabled would be reached before midnight. Leeuwarden at the end of the table was reached at 23.13, four-and-a-half hours after leaving the Hoek. However an 'Extra Dagboottrein' was in the table for summer Sundays, in which case Leeuwarden was reached two minutes after midnight.

Nach **ENGLAND**

mit Bahn oder Auto

über

HOEK VAN HOLLAND - HARWICH

SOMMERFAHRPLAN
22. MAI BIS 24. SEPTEMBER 1966
AUSGABE SÜD

Whether the previous item was part of a series I do not know. The mid-1960s did see a Zeeland series with this example shown. These can be seen as reverse offerings of the BR Continental country leaflets. 'Nach England' is the common theme when in German, as this example. The Guardsmen and Bearskins appeared in various poses through 1964–66. A version in Italian is known. During their currency the BR double arrow came along to join the Zeeland seaman on the back.

Zeeland issued its own postcards. This one is named for the 1939 pair in their post-war
state with raised bridge house. To be dated from sometime in the 1950s?

hoek van holland
harwich ⇌

m.s. Koningin Juliana
vertrek 11.30 uur

stoomvaart mij zeeland - british rail

hoek van holland
harwich ⇌

m.s. St. George
vertrek 23.15 uur

In the first part of the 1970s Zeeland was notable for a group of square brochures.
Examples appear in English, German and Dutch at least. This item in Dutch is undated
but the two 1968 vessels featured give the period. Sealink appears inside so we may say
around 1970. Note the very simple timetable on the cover ('vertrek' is departure).

A whole category of literature has not yet had any coverage and will only receive this one entry. The onboard tax-free shops produced many catalogues over the years. Collector interest in these might be an acquired taste, but this is a nice example. It is in Zeeland's square format and shows off the 1978 *Prinses Beatrix* in 1982. It is a completely bilingual English/Dutch production. In 1985 this vessel became Brittany Ferries *Duc de Normandie*.

Per trein en boot naar

ENGELAND

Zomer

Dienstregeling

Boottrein

InterCity

Londen Special

Britrail Pass

GELDIG VAN 28 MEI 1989 T/M 23 SEPTEMBER 1989

In 1988 the Dutch Government decided to privatise Zeeland who had, since 1985, traded as Crown Line. In 1989 Stena became the purchaser and a consequence was that Dutch Railways (NS) had to expend more effort in promoting the route.

NS offered in 1989 this item for touring '*Engeland*' which a few years before could have been a Zeeland issue. References inside to 'Crown Line (voorheen SMZ)' told their own story. There was also no reluctance to promote the Olau alternative via Vlissingen to Sheerness. It is a substantial twenty-six-page piece, part of a series covering Europe. Its six timetable pages covered the three available rail connected routes: Hoek, Vlissingen and Oostende. The British Class 90 electric in Intercity livery was running through the Lune Gorge, far, both in distance and ethos, from the Channel ports, but talking about the upland Britain that appeals to many Dutch visitors. This series exists at least from 1989–1992.

Amsterdam - London   *EC*

DAGBOOT *Dayservice*	**Admiraal de Ruyter**	
Aankomst *Arrival*		Vertrek *Departure*
	Amsterdam CS	9 32[2]
9 46	Haarlem	9 48[2]
10 04	Leiden	10 06[2]
10 16	Den Haag HS	10 17[2]
10 30	Schiedam-Rotterdam West	10 35[2]
10 50	Hoek van Holland	11 45[2]
17 45[1]	Harwich PQ	18 40[1)2]
19 57[1]	London Liverpool Street	

[1] Van 27 sept. t/m 24 oct. 1987; 1 uur later
From 27 Sept. until 24 Oct. 1987; 1 hour later
[2] niet op 25 en 26 dec./ *Not on 25 and 26 Dec.*

NACHTBOOT *Nightservice*	**Benjamin Britten**	
Aankomst *Arrival*		Vertrek *Departure*
	Amsterdam CS	20 31[2]
20 45	Haarlem	20 47[2]
21 04	Leiden	21 06[2]
21 17	Den Haag HS	21 21[2]
21 36	Schiedam-Rotterdam West	21 41[2]
21 56	Hoek van Holland	22 45[2]
6 45	Harwich PQ	7 45[1)2]
9 00	London Liverpool Street	

[1] Zondags: 7.25; 25 dec.: per autobus
Sundays: 7.25; 25 Dec.: by coach
[2] niet op 25 en 26 dec./ *Not on 25 and 26 Dec.*

London - Amsterdam   *EC*

DAGBOOT *Dayservice*	**Admiraal de Ruyter**	
Aankomst *Arrival*		Vertrek *Departure*
	London Liverpool Street	9 40[1)2]
10 49	Harwich PQ	11 15[2]
19 00	Hoek van Holland	20 04[2]
20 20	Schiedam-Rotterdam West	20 26[2]
20 39	Den Haag HS	20 40
20 51	Leiden	20 52
21 13	Haarlem	21 15
21 32	Amsterdam CS	

[1] Zondags/*Sundays* 9.20
[2] niet op 25 en 26 dec./ *Not on 25 and 26 Dec.*

NACHTBOOT *Nightservice*	**Benjamin Britten**	
Aankomst *Arrival*		Vertrek *Departure*
	London Liverpool Street	19 50[2]
21 00	Harwich PQ	21 45[2]
6 30	Hoek van Holland	7 32[2]
7 48	Schiedam-Rotterdam West	7 55
8 09	Den Haag HS	8 10
8 21	Leiden	8 22
8 42	Haarlem	8 45
9 02	Amsterdam CS	

[2] niet op 25 en 26 dec./ *Not on 25 and 26 Dec.*

31.5.1987 - 28.5.1988

This tiny item is the NS equivalent of the little BR A7 London–Amsterdam Sealink timetable cards seen previously. Its added interest in 1987 is the presence of the Eurocity EC logo, a subject also examined on British material previously.

Opposite: SNCB or Belgian Railways also had cause to promote the Hoek–Harwich route. In their case, the prime medium for many years was one of their international series of brochure timetables. The principle of a country series is now familiar from the UK and Dutch examples shown. SNCB's relevant title put the Netherlands and Great Britain together over at least fifteen years from the late 1960s (and maybe considerably longer).

Certain quirks of the SNCB issue can be noted. The bilingual nature of Belgium meant that the timetable was issued separately in French and Flemish. This is a French example from May 1970. The fair-minded Belgians, having put the Dutch and British together, then alternated covers to accommodate the two nations. This evidently is a Dutch year.

Harwich did not always feature. It does in this issue and, as the map makes clear, there were five options presented for the Channel crossing. The Eurostar has made this subject history in Belgium.

les Pays-Bas,
la Grande-Bretagne.

Horaires valables
du 31 mai 1970 au 22 mai 1971.

 Chemins de Fer Belges

les Pays-Bas,
la Grande-Bretagne.

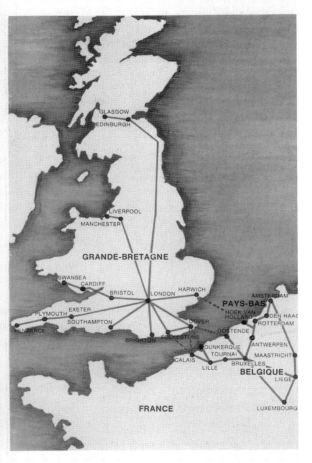

Willkommen auf der modernsten und größten Luxusfähre – der „Koningin Beatrix"!

Fahrplan nach London/Glasgow über:
Venlo/Emmerich - Hoek van Holland - Harwich und zurück

Kabinenpreise (Tarifstand 01. 06. 1986)

Paßangebote innerhalb Großbritanniens

BritRail-Paß

BritRail-Seapaß

Fahrpreisbeispiele nach London über Hoek van Holland – Harwich (Tarifstand 01. 06. 1986)

Above and opposite: Finally, we travel as far as Germany for a DB-issue brochure promoting the crossing. My collection of DB-issued items to the UK is of medium size and reflects the collecting practices of my contributors. It cannot therefore be totally authoritative, but it does appear as if DB put out more material covering either all routes or just the Oostende route. BR/Sealink certainly promoted themselves in Germany over the decades but I have yet to see solely Harwich route BR-issued German language items.

This makes this distinctly impressive brochure from 1986 solely for the Hoek route interesting. What an effective image, expressing the power and purpose of the two modes of transport put together. *Koningin Beatrix* was brand new from 22 April 1986. In the few weeks before, she had managed to disable a Harwich link span for a fortnight and receive media passengers for a short cruise off the first electric passenger train into Parkeston Quay on 21 April. Her SMZ colours were not long-lived, but appear elsewhere in this brochure, which gave her advent a lot of attention. The back cover showed off four logos: DB, NS, BR, SMZ. (Other *Koningin Beatrix* material can be found in Chapter 2).

Matched with the ship is an iconic 125mph DB electric. The Class 103 production series represented here dated from 1970. An almost identical pre-production series of four engines in 1965 means that the role of the class in DB publicity is akin to that of the HST in BR publicity, but with a decade's head start. Remember both are about achieving the 125mph goal. After twenty-one years Class 103 could still express the business. The British HST has managed that too.

Wir machen aus Ihrer Reise nach Großbritannien ein königliches Vergnügen

Sommer 1986

HOLIDAYS IN DENMARK

COPENHAGEN
An Ideal Holiday Centre
via **HARWICH-ESBJERG**

Chapter Four

Not to the Low Countries

Opposite: While the railway ferries focused on the Low Countries for their destinations, another band of operators used Harwich Parkeston Quay.

Largely but not exclusively this is the tale of DFDS or, in expansion and translation from the Danish, the United Steamship Co. DFDS was created in 1866 by a young Danish businessman familiar with Manchester. Esbjerg's new harbour was key and a service to Thameshaven commenced in 1874. This moved in 1880 to Harwich, three years before Parkeston Quay opened. Scope exists therefore for an avalanche of DFDS Harwich material.

Our first publicity insight comes from a forty-page brochure. It is in English but reticent about its publisher and date. The LNER is widely referred to but I cannot promise that it definitely is LNER or DFDS or the Danish Tourist Bureau. All three are named at the back. The design does have an LNER feel to it. Alan Middleton's account of LNER publicity has an itemised list of LNER foreign publications in 1935. This is not listed, although *Cheap Holiday Tickets to the Continent*, seen earlier in its 1938 edition, is present. In 1935 this list could produce fourteen Harwich shipping items.

M/S "Kronprinsesse Ingrid" and M/S "Kronprins Frederik" in Harwich Harbour.

A regular source for DFDS services and one which this volume has examined earlier is in the BR *Continental Handbook*. Another favoured source would be official company-sold postcards. The reverse of the one shown would suggest it is official.

The two vessels shown together in Harwich Harbour are motor ships *Kronprincesse Ingrid* (right) and *Kronprins Frederik* and both represent important stepping stones in the story. DFDS was a pioneer in the use of marine diesels from 1913. From 1925 onwards four motor passenger ships arrived for Harwich services, the first being the significantly named *Parkeston*. No publicity to show her off at Harwich is here (but see the last chapter). *Parkeston* was the only member of this series to survive the ravages of the Second World War. DFDS suffered greatly therein and, after the war, the *Frederik* in 1946 and the *Ingrid* in 1949 were key introductions for the Harwich route.

The card shows something of a DFDS trademark for decades: the light grey hulls displayed the ship's name. The amidships vessel name went right back to the nineteenth century. It would be used into the era of the car ferries that succeeded the 1940s vessels to be shown below.

In the realm of trivia, this item used in August 1954 has some appeal. The outline is that of one of the post-war motor ship pair. The map used makes clear how DFDS saw their 'Scandinavian' route. Recollect that the previous chapter has shown the BR take on that, via northern Germany. There is a slightly different version with the ship redrawn and a wider variety of DFDS routes shown on the map (including Newcastle).

SINGLE AND RETURN FARES

Cost of food not included, see page 12, except on steamer between Copenhagen/Helsingfors.

(Excluding Cabin Supplements—see opposite page.)

From London	1st Class through-out			3rd Class England 1st Class North Sea 1st Class Denmark 2nd Class beyond			3rd Class England 1st Class North Sea 3rd Class Denmark and beyond			3rd Class through-out		
	£	s.	d.	£	s.	d.	£	s.	d.	£	s.	d.
*Aalborg	13	16	6	13	7	0	12	12	1	9	0	7
Return one month	26	5	7	25	16	0	24	9	1	17	6	1
*Aarhus	13	4	2	12	14	8	12	3	9	8	12	3
Return one month	25	3	8	24	14	1	23	14	7	16	11	7
Copenhagen ...	13	18	7	13	9	1	12	13	2	9	1	8
Return one month	26	9	9	26	0	2	24	11	3	17	8	3
Esbjerg	11	11	3	11	1	9	11	1	9	7	10	3
Return one month	22	3	8	21	14	1	21	14	1	14	11	1
*Frederikshavn ...	14	0	10	13	11	4	12	15	1	9	3	7
Return one month	26	13	2	26	3	7	24	14	0	17	11	0
Gothenburg ...	19	5	10	16	2	1	14	9	0	10	17	6
Return one month	37	3	10	31	5	1	28	2	2	20	19	2
Helsingfors (A) ...	26	14	7	26	5	1	21	1	2	17	9	8
Return one month	52	1	9	51	12	2	41	7	3	34	4	3
Helsingor ...	14	0	1	13	10	7	12	14	2	9	2	8
Return one month	26	12	4	26	2	9	24	12	10	17	9	10
Malmo	14	5	0	13	15	7	12	17	6	9	6	0
Return one month	27	2	7	26	13	0	24	19	9	17	16	9
Odense	13	0	7	12	11	1	12	1	2	8	9	8
Return one month	24	17	10	24	8	3	23	9	11	16	6	11
Oslo (A)	18	12	4	18	2	10	15	15	8	12	4	2
Return one month	34	6	0	33	16	5	29	15	6	22	12	6
Oslo	25	3	6	19	0	7	16	4	10	12	13	4
Return one month	48	19	2	37	2	9	31	14	0	24	11	0
Stockholm ...	22	19	8	18	3	3	15	16	0	12	4	6
Return one month	44	11	11	35	7	10	30	16	3	23	13	3

All fares quoted are subject to alteration.

Seat reservation fees between Esbjerg/Copenhagen included, and between Esbjerg/Fredericia for destinations marked *.

Sleeping Car Supplement from Copenhagen to Gothenburg, Oslo or Stockholm—1st class £2 16 2 ; 2nd class £1 8 1 ; 3rd class 16s. 10d.

(A) By sea from Copenhagen. Fares shown in Columns 1/2 cover 1st class between Copenhagen/Helsingfors and Copenhagen/Oslo ; and columns 3/4 Tourist class to Helsingfors and General class with berth to Oslo. An additional 12s. is charged for 1st class bookings to Helsingfors by Finland Line vessels or for "C" deck accommodation on s/s Botnia.

Through Fares quoted to practically all Scandinavian destinations.

Exactly coinciding with the timetable shown in colour 14, the *Railway Magazine* of October 1951 carried a feature about the *Englaenderen*. The 'Englishman' was then a seven-coach articulated 'Lightning' (*Lyntog*) diesel train. It had gained this name in 1937, the express diesels starting in 1935. The *Lyntog* certainly generated publicity and I have little doubt that DSB *Englaenderen* leaflets exist.

COPENHAGEN TO LONDON via ESBJERG — HARWICH	October 8th–October 27th MONDAYS, THURSDAYS m/v Kronprinsesse Ingrid WEDNESDAYS, SATURDAYS m/v Kronprins Frederik	†October 30th to April 19th, 1952 WEDNESDAYS AND SATURDAYS m/v Kronprins Frederik or m/v Kronprinsesse Ingrid	April 21st, 1952, until commencement of Summer season MONDAYS, THURSDAYS m/v Kronprinsesse Ingrid WEDNESDAYS, SATURDAYS m/v Kronprins Frederik
*Dep. COPENHAGEN ... ... "Englænderen"	A12.15	A12.15	A12.15
„ KORSØR	13.38	13.38	13.38
„ ODENSE	15.33	15.33	15.33
Arr. FREDERICIA (see page 6)	16.19	16.19	16.19
Dep. „	16.22	16.22	16.22
Arr. ESBJERG	17.30	17.30	17.30
Dep. „ (England Quay) about	18.00	18.00	18.00
Arr. HARWICH (Parkeston Quay) next day about	C12.30	C12.30	C12.30
Dep. („ „) „ „ „ The "Scandinavian"	13.30	13.30	13.30
Earliest expected arrival LONDON (Liverpool Street Station)	14.58 B15.28	14.58 B15.28	14.58 or B15.25

* For train connections to and from Sweden and Norway—see page 6.
(A) The boat train "Englænderen" is limited to passengers holding seat reservations obtainable at time of booking accommodation on the Ship. Full restaurant service is available on the ferry between Nyborg and Korsør. Passengers not proceeding beyond Korsør should alight on the ferry as the train runs non-stop from the ferry to Copenhagen.
(B) Sundays only. (C) During period of British Summer Time arrive Harwich one hour later and Esbjerg one hour earlier. A corresponding later departure of the "Scandinavian" for London will be available during this period.
† No sailings from Harwich, Tuesday, December 25th, or from Esbjerg, Saturday, December 22nd.

A four-side summary brochure was published in parallel to the larger booklet. This was a very simple affair in 1953–55. Between at least 1958–1963, there was this livelier and continually used design with the *Ingrid*.

A different DFDS source (it might be seen as an early parallel to the full Sealink all routes timetable from the 1970s) is their monthly sailing list. This booklet was likely standard fare for decades, yet I feel fortunate just to have two, such is their probable survival rate. DFDS ran ships worldwide; this document suddenly puts the North Sea routes to the UK into a much wider context.

The
SCANDINAVIAN ROUTE
to
DENMARK · NORWAY · SWEDEN · FINLAND

via
HARWICH - ESBJERG

MAY 1st 1958 - SEPTEMBER 27th 1958

THE UNITED STEAMSHIP COMPANY LIMITED
COPENHAGEN

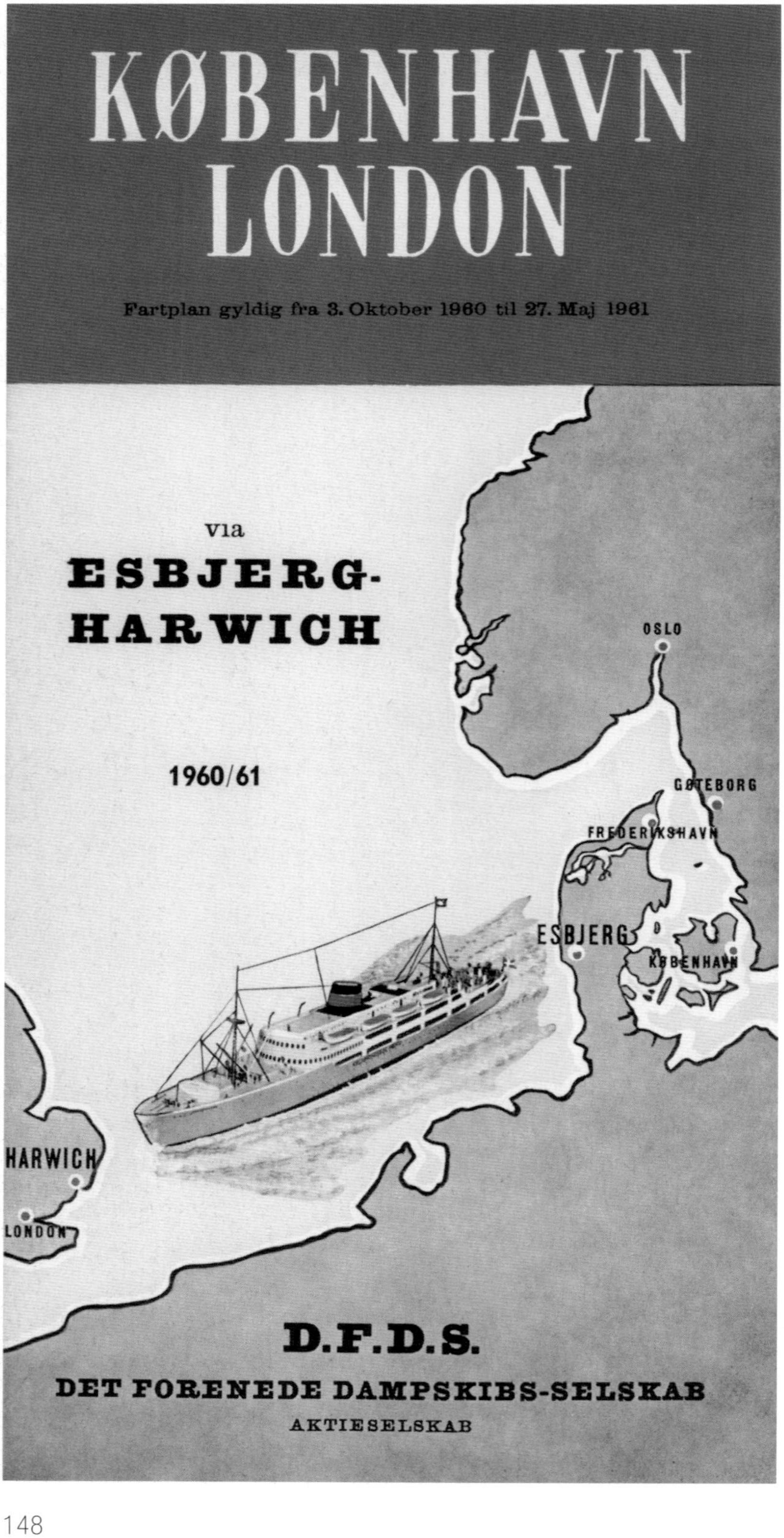

KØBENHAVN
LONDON

Fartplan gyldig fra 3. Oktober 1960 til 27. Maj 1961

via

ESBJERG-
HARWICH

1960/61

OSLO

GØTEBORG

FREDERIKSHAVN

ESBJERG

KØBENHAVN

HARWICH

LONDON

D.F.D.S.
DET FORENEDE DAMPSKIBS-SELSKAB
AKTIESELSKAB

The winter 1960 issue of the main brochure for the Danish market. Observe how the ship is turned about.

148

Another regularly used favourite was a North Sea and Baltic all sailings timetable. Clearly this would be available in Danish (and perhaps other languages). My English run is recognisable from summer 1955 to summer 1964 with this map cover.

These were issued twice yearly, in winter and summer. Winter issue maps continued to show the Newcastle route, although only Harwich functioned through the winter. The map changed. For instance, 1957 showed Leith. Buried in the small print were references to even more routes like Grimsby–Esbjerg and Hull–Copenhagen. These had only limited passenger capacity.

The mainline nature of the Harwich route was apparent from its occupying the first two pages of a twelve-page booklet.

A variant of the map cover design was used on a 'Take Your Car With You' brochure certainly issued by the early 1960s.

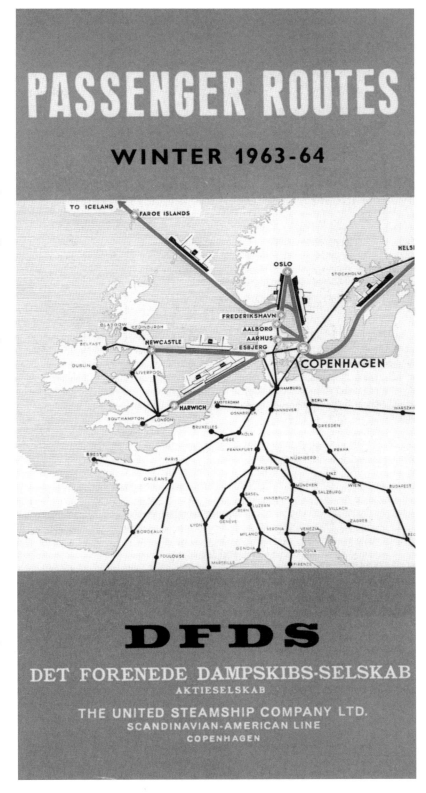

WINTER/SPRING ISSUE

17th September 1967 - 25th May 1968

The SCANDINAVIAN ROUTE

to

DENMARK - NORWAY - SWEDEN - FINLAND

via HARWICH — ESBJERG

D·F·D·S

THE UNITED STEAMSHIP COMPANY LIMITED

COPENHAGEN

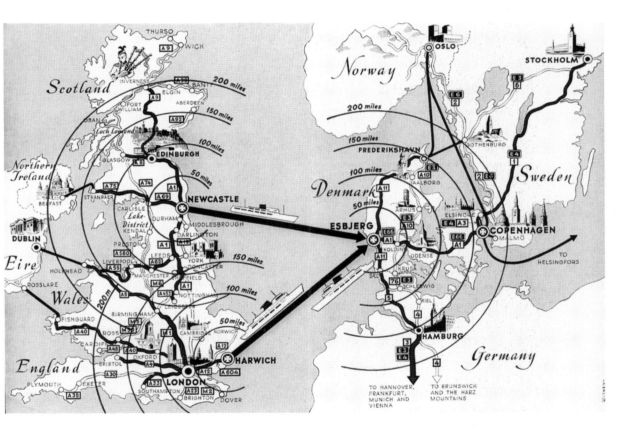

This page and opposite: Change was in the air by the end of the 1950s. Some of the pressure was quite literally in the air, the other pressure came from vehicle users. Artwork changed, as shown in this winter 1967 issue with widespread use of colour photography throughout. The title has survived. Inside, the London–Copenhagen train journey remained prominent. But the vessels had changed and the needs of the motorist clearly affected the design of the map. What was apparent, and would remain so for a long time, was that driving to Harwich from the Midlands and the North was taxing. Two motor vessels had effected the change: the *England* (seen here) and the *Winston Churchill*.

The *England* came first. Her well rounded superstructure was in harmony with the other post-war DFDS ships. Her lines resembled those of a classy packet but she was a car ferry delivered for the Harwich–Esbjerg route in 1964. She was recognised as the first drive-on drive-off car ferry for a North Sea crossing.

DFDS appreciated her significance when she appeared on the cover (top) of their 1966 centenary booklet. This is a most attractive and useful thirty-two pages worth of text, colour imagery and mapping. One assumes at least a Danish language version exists as well? Perhaps the most significant statement in the booklet is: '16 new passenger and cargo vessels being on order for delivery before the end of the 1969'. Six of those were to be roll-on roll-off ferries: the times were a-changing. Another vessel was noted as 'Passenger Liner (*Winston Churchill*) around 10,000 GRT'.

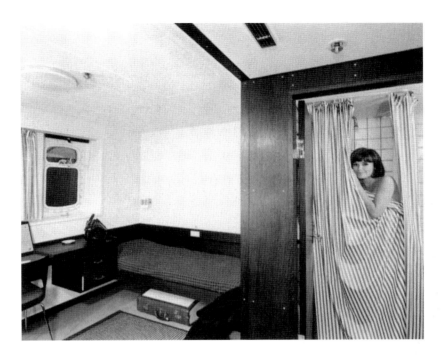

England was really quite a small car ferry. Accessed by side doors, her car deck had to remain exactly that, unable to carry anything larger than a caravan. She could carry 100 cars. Her advent was marked with this impressive brochure (opposite, bottom and above), whose prime image of the ship was spread over six sides. Despite the egalitarian nature of car ownership, *England* was a two-class ship, something the brochure endorsed with eight images of first-class facilities and only one of second.

   England's relatively small size told against her. Part of her role was to undertake off-season cruises. Long before DFDS said goodbye to the *Churchill*, they had passed *England* in 1983 to Cunard for Falklands use. The *Dana Regina* (see below) had replaced her on DFDS Harwich duties. Between 1987 and 2001, she was laid up in Elfsis Bay, Greece. Then, when sold to Pakistani breakers, she managed to sink in the Red Sea.

This page (top) and opposite: England's side doors make an obvious appearance on this period piece from her first season. Her mid-ships name is legible on the original.

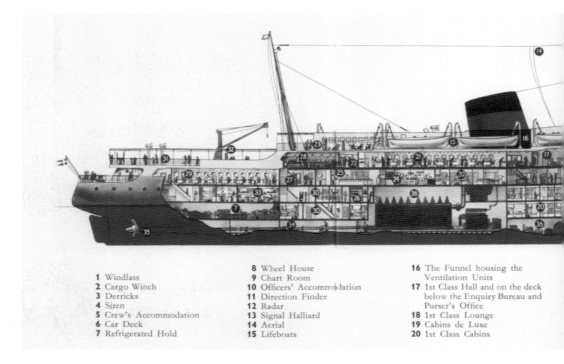

1 Windlass	**8** Wheel House	**16** The Funnel housing the
2 Cargo Winch	**9** Chart Room	Ventilation Units
3 Derricks	**10** Officers' Accommodation	**17** 1st Class Hall and on the deck
4 Siren	**11** Direction Finder	below the Enquiry Bureau and
5 Crew's Accommodation	**12** Radar	Purser's Office
6 Car Deck	**13** Signal Halliard	**18** 1st Class Lounge
7 Refrigerated Hold	**14** Aerial	**19** Cabins de Luxe
	15 Lifeboats	**20** 1st Class Cabins

Above and previous page, bottom: In contrast to the new arrangements, a glance back at how the *Ingrid* and *Frederik* handled cars. This brochure is undated but probably mid-1950s. It was a full colour photo sixteen-panel affair simply elaborating on these two ships. What is of moment is shown in the cutaway diagram and the image to its right. Cars were quite literally stowed away.

Opposite: Winston Churchill with bow and stern doors was intended to handle drive-on and drive-off commercial vehicles. This innovation had arrived for the East Anglian sailings in 1966 with the MV *Suffolk* a pure freight vessel. Her prime cargo was Danish beer. Danish bacon was another cargo that benefited from roll-on roll-off. DFDS had earlier introduced end-door vessels to purely Scandinavian routes.

DFDS knew how to name ships and on 30 June 1967 Churchill's widow named the new vessel on the Thames in a blaze of publicity. The ship instantly became the fleet flagship. Her first commercial crossing took place on the 2 June and one can guess that at these events, folk were clutching copies of a celebration brochure. Probably something more glorious than this item, which was evidently produced some months before. Its one photo shows the ship in build on the foreshore at Riva Trigoso near Genoa.

The Churchill was two-class until 1970 and, with the speed of both the *England* and *Churchill* being in excess of twenty knots, a daily summer service was initiated.

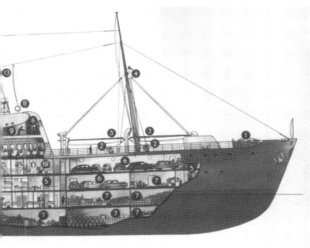

Take your car with you; there is accommodation on board for a considerable number of motor-cars.

1st Class Restaurant	**29** 2nd Class Restaurant
1st Class Promenade Deck	**30** 2nd Class Cabins
1st Class Sun Deck	**31** 2nd Class Sun Deck
Galley	**32** Crane
Pantry	**33** Tweendeck Accommodation
Stores and Provisions	**34** Propeller Shaft
2nd Class Hall	**35** One of the Twin Propellers
2nd Class Lounge	**36** Engine Room

D F D S
THE UNITED STEAMSHIP COMPANY LTD.

DFDS
THE SCANDINAVIAN ROUTE

INTRODUCING THE NEW

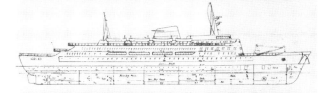

M/V 'WINSTON CHURCHILL'

ENTERING THE HARWICH-ESBJERG SERVICE JUNE 1967

THE UNITED STEAMSHIP COMPANY LTD. COPENHAGEN

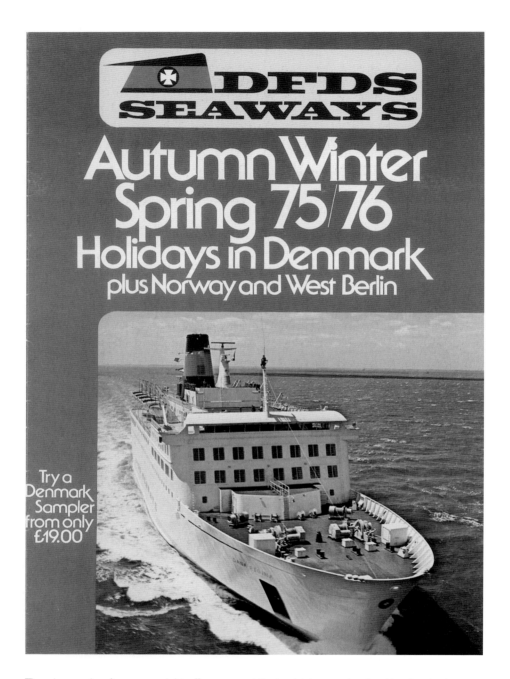

DFDS SEAWAYS

Autumn Winter Spring 75/76

Holidays in Denmark

plus Norway and West Berlin

Try a Denmark Sampler from only £19.00

The demands of commercial traffic ensured that vehicle carrying had to dominate. The *England/Winston Churchill* pairing at Harwich would not be long lived. Angularity would appear in the new designs. Two ships introduced in 1974 and 1978 effected the change.

The 1974 introduction was the *Dana Regina*. Here she is gracing the cover of a 1975 brochure. Other publicity that year billed her as the flagship of DFDS Seaways, an accolade that would not be long lived. She also appears on the ordinary route timetable covers in 1977/78.

DENMARK

Mini Cruise to Esbjerg
Friday 10 March & Friday 7 April

Take a splendid rail-sea break with British Rail and DFD Seaways in the Spring to beautiful Denmark. Get away for a couple of nights in luxurious surroundings. Enjoy excellent food and convivial company on the four star luxury floating hotel, m.s. 'Dana Regina'. Fully air-conditioned and fitted with stabilisers the ship is ideal for a smooth, relaxing 700 miles round trip weekend cruise. It's a delightful bargain at only £27.00.

The cruise starts on Friday   and you return Sunday afternoon with plenty of time to enjoy yourself on board and have about five hours ashore to see something of Denmark. The complete schedule for the entire weekend is featured overleaf.

On board there is just about everything to suit all tastes. For example, try the delicious Scandinavian buffet where you can eat as much as you like from a wide range of hot and cold dishes for under £4. We recommend you do it the Danish way and start with fish and then return with a clean plate and sample the meat and so on. 'Little and often' is the best way. Apart from this there is a large lounge with a live group playing for dancing in the evening, bars, discotheque, shops, cafeteria and childrens playroom.

When you reach Esbjerg a sightseeing tour has been arranged, with afternoon tea included so that you make the best of your visit to Denmark.

The £27.00 inclusive fare per person (no child fares) covers:

Rail travel to Harwich and back from all Western Region stations Oxford to Slough (inc.)

L.T. Underground return from Paddington to Liverpool Street.

700 miles sea cruise Harwich to Esbjerg.

Berth in 4 - berth cabin

Coach tour and afternoon tea.

Cruise fares excludes meals on board ship.

Publicity does not need to be visually exciting to be stimulating. This rather plain four-side leaflet issued by the Western Region was distributed to stations between Oxford and Slough in the early spring of 1978. What it promoted was a special booking on to *Dana Regina*. Including a journey of 700 miles, as well as a Danish coach trip and even the cross London LT fare, it was good value at £27.

DFDS
DANISH SEAWAYS

1 Oct 1979 – 31 Dec 1980
79/80

Timetable and fares

UK – Denmark
UK – Sweden
Denmark – Norway
Denmark – Faroe Islands
Denmark – Sweden (Stena Line)

Issued September 1979

The *Churchill* did not pair the *Regina* for long. Instead 1978 saw a vessel arrive which would stay on station at Harwich with only minimal breaks until 2002. This was *Dana Anglia* whose maiden voyage was on 5 June. Her arrival saw the service become daily. By 1979 the *Anglia* and her massive funnel was on the cover of the English issue timetable. This covered the various European DFDS routes. Note that a Stena Line route is included. The *Anglia* was 2,000 tons larger than the *Regina* and the publicity transferred the flagship epaulet to her. The ships were named against their routes and from this item we find the *England* allocated to the summer Esbjerg–Faroe Islands service.

The *Anglia*, in impressive bow-on colour photo pose, dominated the 1982 DFDS timetable, one that was notable for its combination of brands on the cover: DFDS Danish Seaways, DFDS Prins Ferries and DFDS Tor Line (not to forget Fred. Olsen Bergen Line). Tor and Prins had been acquired during 1981, making 1982 items noteworthy.

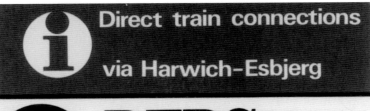

29 May to 24 September 1983

InterCity ⇌ Europe

Although *The Scandinavian* was a named boat train of many years run by BR to connect with the DFDS service, the amount of BR-issued publicity solely associated with the DFDS route was limited compared to the railway-owned services from Harwich. To judge by the fact that only two have so far entered our collection, a 'Direct Train Connection via Harwich–Esbjerg' leaflet is quite unusual. This 1983 example proudly shows off *Dana Anglia*. The core London times were in the DFDS publicity and when this item is opened it turns out to also have times for assorted provincial stations in the UK. A comparable item for 1977 is a very plain one-sider.

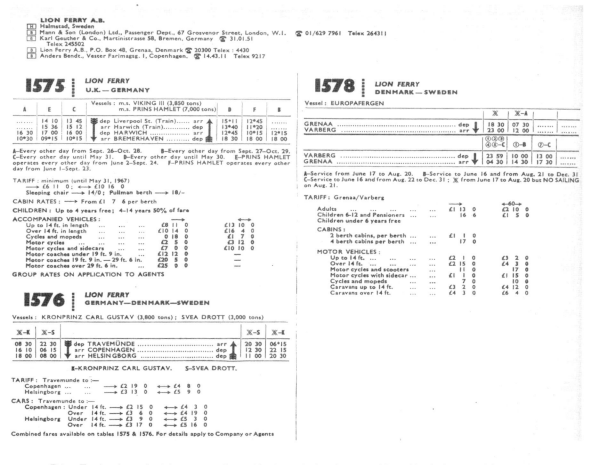

LION FERRY A.B.
H Halmstad, Sweden
B Mann & Son (London) Ltd., Passenger Dept., 67 Grosvenor Street, London, W.1. ☎ 01/629 7961 Telex 264311
G Karl Geuther & Co., Martinistrasse 58, Bremen, Germany ☎ 31.01.51
 Telex 245502
D Lion Ferry A.B., P.O. Box 48, Grenaa, Denmark ☎ 20300 Telex : 4430
B Anders Bendt, Vester Farimagsg. 1, Copenhagen. ☎ 14.43.11 Telex 9217

1575 LION FERRY
U.K. — GERMANY

Vessels : m.s. VIKING III (3,850 tons)
m.s. PRINS HAMLET (7,000 tons)

A	E	C		D	F	B
......	14 10	13 45	dep Liverpool St. (Train)...... arr	15*11	12*45	......
	15 36	15 12	arr Harwich (Train)............ dep	13*40	11*20	
16 30	17 00	16 00	dep HARWICH .... arr	12*45	10*15	12*15
10*30	09*15	10*15	arr BREMERHAVEN .... dep	18 30	18 00	18 00

A—Every other day from Sept. 26–Oct. 28. B—Every other day from Sept. 27–Oct. 29. C—Every other day until May 31. D—Every other day until May 30. E—PRINS HAMLET operates every other day from June 2–Sept. 24. F—PRINS HAMLET operates every other day from June 1–Sept. 23.

TARIFF : minimum (until May 31, 1967)
→ £6 11 0; ←→ £10 16 0
Sleeping chair → 14/0; Pullman berth → 18/-

CABIN RATES : → From £1 7 6 per berth

CHILDREN : Up to 4 years free; 4–14 years 50% of fare

ACCOMPANIED VEHICLES :
				→		←→	
Up to 14 ft. in length	...	...	...	£8 11 0		£13 10 0	
Over 14 ft. in length	...	...	...	£10 14 0		£16 4 0	
Cycles and mopeds	...	...	...	0 18 0		£1 7 0	
Motor cycles	...	...	...	£2 5 0		£3 12 0	
Motor cycles and sidecars	...	...	...	£7 0 0		£10 10 0	
Motor coaches under 19 ft. 9 in.	...	...	...	£12 12 0		—	
Motor coaches 19 ft. 9 in. — 29 ft. 6 in.	...	...	£20 5 0		—	
Motor coaches over 29 ft. 6 in.	...	...	£25 0 0		—	

GROUP RATES ON APPLICATION TO AGENTS

1576 LION FERRY
GERMANY—DENMARK—SWEDEN

Vessels : KRONPRINZ CARL GUSTAV (3,800 tons) ; SVEA DROTT (3,000 tons)

✕–K	✕–S		✕–S	✕–K
08 30	22 30	dep TRAVEMÜNDE .... arr	20 30	06*15
16 10	06 15	arr COPENHAGEN .... dep	12 30	22 15
18 00	08 00	arr HELSINGBORG .... dep	11 00	20 30

K—KRONPRINZ CARL GUSTAV. S—SVEA DROTT.

TARIFF : Travemunde to :—
| Copenhagen ... | ... | → £2 19 0 | ←→ £4 8 0 |
| Helsingborg ... | ... | → £3 13 0 | ←→ £5 9 0 |

CARS : Travemunde to :—
Copenhagen : Under 14 ft.	→ £2 15 0	←→ £4 3 0
Over 14 ft.	→ £3 6 0	←→ £4 19 0
Helsingborg Under 14 ft.	→ £3 9 0	←→ £5 3 0
Over 14 ft.	→ £3 17 0	←→ £5 16 0

Combined fares available on tables 1575 & 1576. For details apply to Company or Agents

1578 LION FERRY
DENMARK — SWEDEN

Vessel : EUROPAFERGEN

		✕	✕–A		
GRENAA .... dep		18 30	07 30	......	......
VARBERG .... arr		23 00	12 00	......	......

		①②③④⑤–C	①–B	②–C	
VARBERG .... dep		23 59	10 00	13 00	......
GRENAA .... arr		04 30	14 30	17 30	......

A—Service from June 17 to Aug. 20. B—Service to June 16 and from Aug. 21 to Dec. 31 C—Service to June 16 and from Aug. 22 to Dec. 31 ; ✕ from June 17 to Aug. 20 but NO SAILING on Aug. 21.

TARIFF : Grenaa/Varberg
			→	←60→	
Adults	£1 13 0		£2 10 0	
Children 6–12 and Pensioners	16 6		£1 5 0	
Children under 6 years free				

CABINS :
| 2 berth cabins, per berth ... ... | £1 1 0 | |
| 4 berth cabins per berth ... ... | 17 0 | |

MOTOR VEHICLES :
Up to 14 ft.	£2 1 0		£3 2 0	
Over 14 ft.	£2 15 0		£4 3 0	
Motor cycles and scooters ...	11 0		17 0	
Motor cycles with sidecar ...	£1 1 0		£1 15 0	
Cycles and mopeds	7 0		10 0	
Caravans up to 14 ft.	£3 2 0		£4 12 0	
Caravans over 14 ft.	£4 3 0		£6 4 0	

Prins Ferries have just been mentioned but must also be considered in their own right before DFDS involvement. The story starts with a new vessel called *Prins Hamlet* built for the Swedish concern Lion Ferry. Between 1966 and 1969, Lion used the No.6 Berth Ro-Ro facility at Parkeston Quay, being one of its earliest customers – a significant matter.

Anyone with relevant publicity items from the 1960s should consider themselves fortunate. The nearest I can offer to a 1960s leaflet is this extract from the *ABC Shipping Guide* for May 1967. Thus far that title has not been referred to as a source but it is another key run of documentation. Produced mainly for the travel trade, despite monthly publication, they are not too common survivors. Presented in alphabetical order of shipping line, the guide offered a swift overview. Here all three Lion Ferry routes on offer can be eyeballed. In 1967 train connections are on offer (see next item).

The operation turned into a German company – Prins Ferries (or Prinzen Linien) – in 1969 and worked independently until 1981.

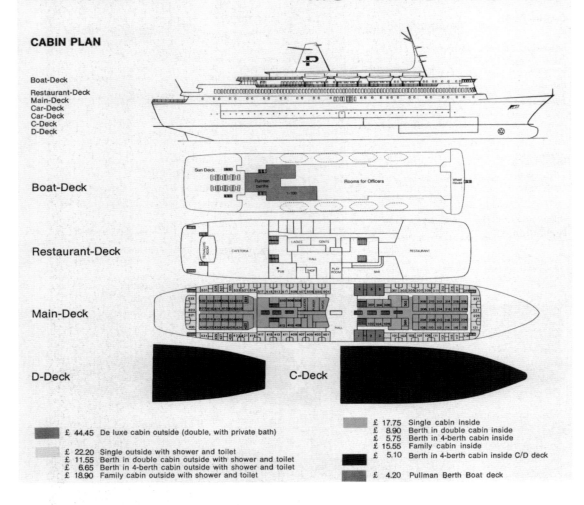

8.000 GRT, length 443 feet, speed 22 knots, built 1970,
stabilizers, 1040 passengers, 250 cars.

MS PRINS OBERON

CABIN PLAN

Boat-Deck
Restaurant-Deck
Main-Deck
Car-Deck
Car-Deck
C-Deck
D-Deck

Boat-Deck

Sun Deck · Pullman berths · 1-100 · Rooms for Officers · Wheel House

Restaurant-Deck

TELEGRAPH ROOM · CAFETERIA · LADIES · GENTS · HALL · PUB · SHOP · PLAY ROOM · BAR · RESTAURANT

Main-Deck

D-Deck · **C-Deck**

£ 44.45	De luxe cabin outside (double, with private bath)

£ 22.20	Single outside with shower and toilet
£ 11.55	Berth in double cabin outside with shower and toilet
£ 6.65	Berth in 4-berth cabin outside with shower and toilet
£ 18.90	Family cabin outside with shower and toilet

£ 17.75	Single cabin inside
£ 8.90	Berth in double cabin inside
£ 5.75	Berth in 4-berth cabin inside
£ 15.55	Family cabin inside
£ 5.10	Berth in 4-berth cabin inside C/D deck
£ 4.20	Pullman Berth Boat deck

Opposite: The service evolved to serve both Bremerhaven (which had a three-hour time advantage) and Hamburg. By 1977 each route had its own ship. The *Prinz Hamlet* (not the 1966 one) went to Hamburg and the 1970 *Prins Oberon* to Bremerhaven. This not too inspirational image is of *Prins Oberon*'s stern door, but it was used more than once. It does show the Prins Ferries funnel colours, which changed to a tailored DFDS version in 1981.

One market for the service was UK military personnel based in northern Germany. In Prins Ferries' publicity the services were clearly targeted at vehicle owners. Their 1977 brochure does not suggest trains reached Harwich at all. This reluctance to push the rail connection is perhaps explained by the fact that between 1969 and 1979 Prins Ferries berthed at Harwich Navyard Wharf, up at the 'Town'. Rail connections of some sort did exist. They were given in the *ABC Shipping Guide* seen above. Reference to daily special trains to Harwich Town is made in the Eastern Region's entry for the service in their May 1971 timetable, but no details are given. The same timetable's Harwich line table shows all the Parkeston Quay boat trains but nothing for the Prins service. This could be explained if the Prins trains were unadvertised to the public.

164

Table U

London—Bremerhaven/Hamburg

Miles			From London 31 May to 2 October		From London 30 May to 3 October				
			May Uneven dates June Even dates July Even dates August Uneven dates September Even dates October Even dates		May Even dates June Uneven dates July Uneven dates August Even dates September Uneven dates October Uneven dates				
			Mons. to Sats.	Suns.	Mons. to Fris.	Suns.	Sats.		
0	London Liverpool Street	d	10 45	10 45	13 42	13 45	13 50	. .	. .
70	Harwich Town	{ a	12 17	12 24	15 17	15 23	15 15	. . . . . .	. . . . . .
		d	b	b	b	b	b	. .	. .
71	Harwich Navyard	{ a	b	b	b	b	b	. . . . . .	. . . . . .
		d	13 00	13 00	16 30	16 30	16 30	. .	. .
427	Bremerhaven	{ a			09 00	09 00	09 00	. . . . . .	. . . . . .
		d			09 15	09 15	09 15	. .	. .
488	Hamburg	a	09 00	09 00	12 10	12 10	12 10	. . . . . .	. . . . . .

For general notes see page 5

b—Special bus connection from Harwich Town to Harwich Navyard.

To clinch this I compared three more sources. The public passenger timetable and the All Lines volume Table 12 for 1976–77 showed the boat trains to Parkeston Quay and none to Harwich Town.

Illumination, though, appeared in the partner International timetable, a separate volume which, along with map and bookmark, constituted the All Lines package. There in Table U was the London–Bremerhaven–Hamburg Prins Ferries service and the proof that direct boat trains did run London to Harwich Town, albeit unadvertised in the main timetable. If seeking a reason for this anomaly, I guess that since the boat trains ran on alternate days, putting them in the public timetable was asking for trouble. Did anyone discover whether they could use these trains for travel only to Harwich Town from London? These connections are shown in 1977 as well, at the time Prins' own literature was so reticent.

LA64

DOWN

	No.	1F24	1F24
Timing Load		D315	DMU
Platform No.		11	
Line		ML	
		Q	
		13 00	. . . . . .
		13 03	. . . . . .
LIVERPOOL STREET dep	1		
Bethnal Green	2		. . . . . .
Bow Junction	3		
Thornton Field C.S.	4	13 07	. .
STRATFORD arr	5		
dep	6		
Maryland	7		. . . . . .
Forest Gate	8		
Forest Gate Jn.	9		
Manor Park	10		
ILFORD arr	11		
dep	12	. .	
Ilford C.S.	13		
Ilford High Road	14		
Seven Kings	15	13 17	. .
Goodmayes	16		
Chadwell Heath	17	. . . . . .	
Romford	18		
GIDEA PARK	19		
Gidea Park Junction	20		
Harold Wood	21		
Brentwood	22	13 24	
SHENFIELD arr	23	. . . . . .	
dep	24		
Billericay	25		
WICKFORD	26		
Rayleigh	27		
Hockley	28		
Rochford	29		
Prittlewell	30	〔1〕	
SOUTHEND VIC. arr	31	13 33	. .
Ingatestone	32	13 41	
CHELMSFORD arr	33		
dep	34	13 47	
Hatfield Peverel	35	〔3〕	
WITHAM	36		
Kelvedon	37		
Mark's Tey	38		
COLCHESTER arr	39	13 54	13 58
dep	40		
St. Botolph's arr	41		
dep	42		
Hythe	43		
Wivenhoe	44		
Alresford	45		
Great Bentley	46		
Weeley	47		
Thorpe-le-Soken arr	48		
dep	49		
CLACTON arr	50		. . . . . .
Kirby Cross arr	51		
dep	52		
Frinton-on-Sea	53		. .
WALTON arr	54		
Manningtree	55	14 02	14 09
Manningtree North Jn.	56		. . . . . .
Mistley	57		
Wrabness	58		
PARKESTON arr	59	14 17	14 23
dep	60		
Dovercourt	61		
HARWICH arr	62	14 22	14 28
Bentley	63	. . . . . .	
IPSWICH arr	64	. .	. .
dep	65	. . . . . .	

Column notes (vertical):
- **D315 / 1F24**: "Applies 30 October to 19 March"; "PRINS FERRIES SERVICE — Alternative path 'B'. See Mandatory Trains Notice"
- **DMU / 1F24**: "PRINS FERRIES SERVICE — Alternative path 'B'. See Mandatory Trains Notice"; "Applies 30 October to 19 March"

To directly set against the International timetable, there is the official Eastern Region working timetable (not for the public). This extract is from the October 1976 issue. This is chapter and verse stuff. Note this is the winter timetable and is not quite the exact partner to Table U, just seen, which is the summer service.

That winter two alternative trains were pathed as 1F24. There was either going to be an as required locomotive hauled train non-stop down from London. Or (low bookings), a DMU would run out from Colchester, where a seven minute connection had been made with a London–Clacton train, non-stop through Manningtree and the other stations and on to Harwich Town. Rollicking through Manningtree Junction on a virtually empty DMU in mid-winter and thence non-stop beside the Stour appeals to me.

Prins' history is very involved. For instance, the *Hamlet* was at times prefixed both with 'Prins' and 'Prinz'! The website http://www.simplonpc.co.uk/Prinz_Ferries.html helped sort me out. This reviews in considerable detail the range of postcards covering the Prins Ferries fleet.

DFDS
PRINS
FERRIES

UK to
Germany

Passenger Information 1983

This six-panel leaflet is quite simple in presentation, being targeted at those who had now bought their tickets. Nonetheless there are several points of interest. Covering the period from January 1983, this is the first DFDS issue after the rationalisation of the former Prins Ferries routes. The ship is the 1973 *Prinz Hamlet*. The DFDS version of the Prins Ferries funnel is in evidence. Inside, after only a few words: 'All travel to Germany with DFDS Prins Ferries is based on our Harwich Hamburg service.' Advice for both rail and car-based travellers is given.

Over the years the German service from Harwich has run round the ports covering Bremerhaven, Hamburg and then, on 2 March 2002, Cuxhaven, which replaced Hamburg.

THREE DAY
SAILWAY
CRUISES
TO DENMARK,
SWEDEN OR
GERMANY
FROM £33
•
PLUS SPECIAL
CELEBRATE
AT SEA CRUISES

Sailway

DFDS SEAWAYS

InterCity ⚡ Europe

SEPT 1986 TO MAY 1987

One consistent market DFDS exploited has retained their link to rail transport. The luxury cruise liner feel of DFDS vessels, developed to compensate for the length of the voyage, and the cosmopolitan nature of their destinations, has aided the popularity of the mini-cruise. This results in a whole tranche of literature given over to them.

In this 1987 example the branding is DFDS Seaways and the constituent names have gone (they did appear on such literature a few years before). By now the former Tor Lines service at Felixstowe was well integrated into the DFDS Harwich operation. So the cover translates into: Denmark (the DFDS core route), Sweden (ex-Tor) and Germany (ex-Prins). Inside the front cover *Tor Britannia* is present in full DFDS Seaways colours. The whole package was integrated into BR connections with add-on fares. For that reason the Intercity Europe brand was added and an Intercity-liveried Class 47 diesel. Slight anachronism there since electric haulage of the boat trains had started earlier in 1986.

Großbritannien erleben –
die HAMBURG genießen.

Die HAMBURG. Das 100.000-Sterne-Hotel nach England.

DFDS Sommerkatalog '88. Gültig: 14.3.88 – 23.10.88

Auf 32 farbenfrohen Seiten laden wir Sie ein, mit uns wieder Spaß in den trüben Alltag zu bringen und zu erfahren, wie England-Urlaub sein muß:

DFDS SEAWAYS
Hamburg – England

This volume has occasionally offered European-issued material – how the Continentals see the Islanders. The ability to read German would heighten the appreciation of this item: the main DFDS brochure issued for summer 1988 for the German market out of Hamburg. Even without the language much can be appreciated.

One level of interest is the ship: the *Hamburg* dominates the brochure. This was her second DFDS season – she had replaced *Prinz Hamlet* in 1987. She would carry this name until 1998, when she was renamed *Admiral of Scandinavia* (having started life as the German built Norwegian-owned *Kronprins Harald* in 1976).

The brochure is laden with examples of British travel ephemera (p.9, 11, 13, 18 and 25). There are the usual British stereotypes, the London suited gent, the black taxi, the red telephone box and the Routemaster bus. Not quite so expected are the PVC-clad punks. All this encompassed by the heading 'Lust auf London'. London does not utterly take over, though I wonder just how many of the *Hamburg*'s patrons made it to Staithes on the North Yorkshire coast, which received a generous picture, along with an adjacent Yorkshire lady carrying bacon and eggs.

170

Having fully integrated Tor and Prins into their operation by 1987/88, DFDS then took a break. The company carried on of course but they decided to re-brand all the North Sea operations as Scandinavian Seaways.

Material from 1989–1999 carries this branding. The example shown comes from 1989. This is a full English issue timetable and can be compared with the same effort from 1963 already seen. What remains consistent is the very wide spread of DFDS operations, otherwise the size of the vessels and of the brochures is in a different league. Harwich sailings (to Esbjerg, Gothenburg and Hamburg) continued to come first and the cover vessel from there was the 1975 *Tor Britannia*. It says something for her positive reputation that this once Felixstowe-based ship could take pride of place after fourteen years. She remained with DFDS until 2003. In 1989, the Scandinavian Seaways fleet was reviewed in an illustrated fleet list just inside, with all the well established favourites shown, including *Dana Anglia*, *Dana Regina* and *Winston Churchill*.

The Tor Line/DFDS service to Gothenburg has been the prime link to Sweden and Norway from the haven ports. Two previous attempts had each been thwarted by World War. A third attempt had more success, and this 1967 brochure is from its inaugural season. The destination was Kristiansand in Norway.

Since shortly after 1900, the Fred. Olsen name had been familiar around the North Sea. The main British route dating back to that time went to the Tyne. Olsens moved in the mid-1960s to operate end-loading car ferries. One interesting result was the 1966 MV *Venus/Black Prince*. She alternated names summer and winter depending on her work. Her summer job in 1967 inaugurated this new link which, with various vessels, worked until 1981. From the outset, Harwich's new linkspan at the East Portal berth was used.

Although *Black Prince*'s role as a Harwich ferry was a bit limited, as a cruise vessel she has become enormously popular, including Harwich calls. After thirty-seven years, she remained an active member in Fred. Olsen's 2005 brochures (also see the last chapter).

Fred. Olsen continued to try to develop a Norway–Harwich ferry link again in the mid-1980s. They had a Hirtshals (Denmark) to Oslo route and between 1984 and 1988 some sailings extended to Harwich. This is the 1988 brochure cover and the ship is the *Braemar*, which was a favourite Olsen name. This *Braemar* started in 1985, when the 1980 built *Viking Song* car ferry was obtained. There was a Fred. Olsen boat train for these sailings.

In the different climate of 2004, boat trains continued to operate. The way to find them is the internet. The Port of Harwich has a good website: it passes my first test of port websites, offering an up-to-date shipping movements page. When I compared both, the Port of Tyne did not. Added to this, there was a list of the special boat trains operated by First Great Eastern to connect with visiting cruise ships! First Great Eastern was then about to metamorphose into One.

After 1966 it seemed as if operators with car ferries were queuing up to use Harwich's new facilities. RTM, or the Belgian Marine Administration, were primarily interested in the Oostende to Dover route but, between 1968 and 1973, their literature added Harwich–Ostend to the cover. The service only ran once a day and did not prove a success, although the journey was only eighteen miles longer than that to Dover.

The item shown here is unusual. Its design is a modification of the main 1969 English brochure. That had a colour cover and named both the Dover and Harwich routes. The purpose of this item was to detail the availability of Shell fuels on the Continent for vehicle drivers newly landed at Ostend. A voucher was included to exchange at five named service stations for a road map of Europe and two postcards.

174

New Harwich-Ostend car ferry service

direct to the motorways of Europe

The only car ferry service between Harwich and Ostend is ours. Surprising when you consider the advantages. Harwich is so convenient for people living east and north of London. And Ostend is the start of the fast motorways into Europe.

So tell everybody about our regular daily service—leaving Harwich at 15.30 and Ostend at 09.25. Tell them about our Minitours, party rates and cheap summer rates for trailers and caravans — everyone likes to save money! Tell them we take passengers without cars too — bus or train connections are provided. And tell them they'll get the same stabilised, comfortable ferries and high standard that they'd enjoy on our Dover — Ostend route.

Get all our brochures and timetables so you can tell them everything about "our European freeway". Tell them and it'll sell itself.

Write or phone now for more information.

DOVER/HARWICH-OSTEND LINES

66 HAYMARKET · LONDON W 1 · TELEPHONE: 01-839 1553

An example of advertising the route to the travel trade is this full page advert placed in the 1970 edition of the *Travel Agency Car Ferry Guide*. Matchbox cars are delightfully prominent; if only arranging real life was so easy.

M/S *Stella Polaris*

5 Cruises in SCANDINAVIA
SUMMER 1966

MEDITERRANEAN Cruise
AUTUMN 1966

CLIPPER LINE

Harwich continues to be a regular port of call for cruise ships. Back in the 1960s, it was not just the BR cruises that used the port. Some very colourful brochures came out from Clipper Line for their ship *Stella Polaris*, whose lines had the definite feel of a yacht. This is the 1966 brochure which had five cruises using Harwich.

Her calls at Parkeston Quay went back a long time. She was a regular caller as a Bergen Line cruise vessel to Norway from 1927 to the war. She was very luxurious for a small vessel at that time, offering a swimming pool, as well as a bath for each cabin. Her calls re-started in 1948 although Bergen Line sold her in 1951 to Clipper Line. They were a Swedish concern and she stayed with them until 1969. While a Bergen Line vessel, she had played a notable role in the opening of the new facilities at Tyne Commission Quay North Shields in 1928.

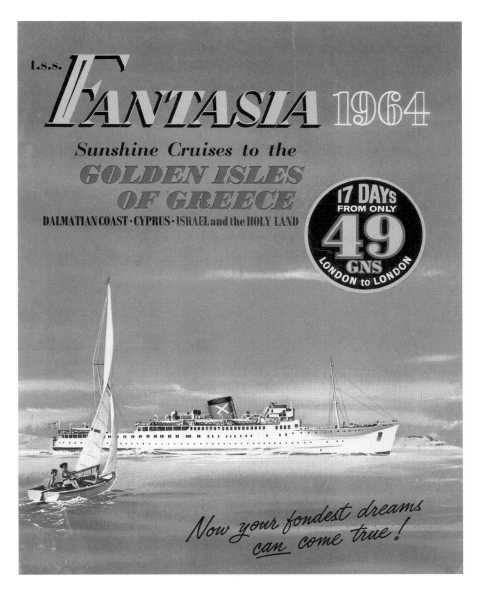

t.s.s. **FANTASIA** 1964

Sunshine Cruises to the

GOLDEN ISLES OF GREECE

DALMATIAN COAST · CYPRUS · ISRAEL and the HOLY LAND

17 DAYS FROM ONLY 49 GNS LONDON to LONDON

Now your fondest dreams can come true!

Far, far, beyond the Hook now. A collecting category not previously examined would be publicity for Harwich veterans in their afterlives. This *Fantasia* leaflet is one splendid example.

Back in Chapter 2, the post-war allocation of the 1935 built LMS ship *Duke of York* to Harwich was encountered. Her Harwich career lasted from 1948–63. *Avalon* displaced her and *Duke of York* became Chandris Cruises' *Fantasia*. There is nothing strange really about that pattern, but it is rewarding to be able to close this chapter with Chandris' 1964 UK issue brochure cover showing her. The journey to Venice for British tour patrons was an epic. Coach from London Euston to Southend Airport, flight to Ostend, thence Pullman motor coach to Venice. Pay more and patrons could fly all the way.

This was *Fantasia*'s first Chandris season. Truly, she had gone far beyond the Low Countries sailing out of Venice to the Eastern Mediterranean. Scrapping eventually followed in 1976.

HARWICH   FELIXSTOWE
SHOTLEY
PASSENGER FERRY SERVICE

17th SEPTEMBER 1956
to 16th JUNE 1957
or until further notice
(weather and other circumstances permitting)

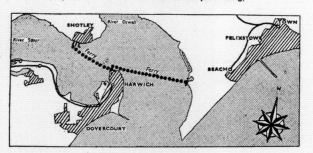

	WEEKDAYS (except Wednesday, **26th December, 1956** and Good Friday, **19th April, 1957**) No services Christmas Day		SUNDAYS (also Wednesday, **26th December** and Good Friday, **19th April** 1957)
HARWICH TO FELIXSTOWE (Dock)	{ 8.0, 9.55, 11.55 a.m. { 2.10, 2.55, 5.25 p.m.		10.55 a.m. 2†15, 3.30, 4†50 p.m. † via Shotley
FELIXSTOWE (Dock) TO HARWICH	{ 8.25, 10.30 a.m. { 12.30, 2.35, 3.30, 5.45 p.m.		11.30 a.m. 3.0, 4.0, 5.30 p.m.
HARWICH TO SHOTLEY	{ 7.40, 9.0, 11.0 a.m. { 1.45, 4.0, 5.0 p.m.		10.0 a.m. 12.45, 2.15, 4.50 p.m.
SHOTLEY TO HARWICH	{ 7.50, 9.15, 11.15 a.m. { 2.0, 4.15, 5.15 p.m.		10.15 a.m. 1.0, 2‡30, 5‡15 p.m. ‡ via Felixstowe

FOR PARTICULARS OF FARES AND RAIL SERVICES—IPSWICH, FELIXSTOWE,
HARWICH PIER—SEE REVERSE

Eastern National Omnibus services connect with the ferry boats at Harwich Quay

CONDITIONS OF ISSUE

Tickets are issued subject to the Bye-Laws, Regulations and Conditions of the British Transport Commission
contained in the Book of General Time Tables and Book of Regulations relating to traffic by Passenger Train,
copies of which can be inspected at any station

Published by British Railways (Eastern Region)   Printed in Great Britain   Stafford & Co., Ltd., Netherfield, Nottingham
PP/401/15

Chapter 5

The Haven Ports — Felixstowe

Opposite: After so much time at Harwich, the haven must be crossed to the twin port of Felixstowe. Nowadays the vast majority of journeys between the two will be a 35 mile trek around the estuaries by car or train. For many years, the obvious connection was a railway-owned ferry.

The Great Eastern Railway service across the haven had opened in 1912 (certain sources suggest it could be much older and that you might find a GER handbill for such sailings as far back as 1887). When nationalised in 1948, it employed four small motor craft. During the 1950s, it appears highly likely that the standard publicity was a typical Eastern Region handbill like this example for the winter of 1956. Note that the Shotley service is operational. At least one printed authority claims this did not operate post-war.

BRITISH RAIL (Shipping & International Services Division)
TILBURY · GRAVESEND FERRY SERVICE
Will run as under, weather and other circumstances permitting.

TILBURY - GRAVESEND (West Street Ferry Terminal)

Mondays to Fridays			Saturdays		Sundays		
0525	then at	1850	0525	1010	0630	1350	2110
0605	10	1905	0605	1030	0650	then at	2130
0622	30	1920	0625	1050	then at	10	2150
0637	50	1935	0645	then at	10	30	2210
0652	minutes	1952	0705	10	30	50	2230
0707	past	2010	0725	30	50	minutes	2250
0722	each hour	2030	0745	50	minutes	past	2310
0737	until	2050	0805	minutes	past	each hour	2330
0752	1650	2110	0825	past	each hour	until	2350
0807	1705	2130	0845	each hour	until	1930	
0822	1720	2150	0910	until	1230	2005	
0837	1735	2210	0930	2310	1305	2030	
0852	1750	2230	0950	2330	1330	2050	
0910	1805	2250		2359			
0930	1820	2310					
0950	1835	2330					
		2350					

GRAVESEND (West Street Ferry Terminal) - TILBURY

Mondays to Fridays			Saturdays		Sundays		
0515	then at	1842	0515	1000	0620	1340	2100
0545	00	1857	0545	1020	0640	then at	2120
0615	20	1912	0615	1040	then at	00	2140
0630	40	1927	0635	then at	00	20	2200
0645	minutes	1942	0655	00	20	40	2220
0700	past	2000	0715	20	40	minutes	2240
0715	each hour	2020	0735	40	minutes	past	2300
0730	until	2040	0755	minutes	past	each hour	2320
0745	1640	2100	0815	past	each hour	until	2340
0800	1657	2120	0835	each hour	until	1940	
0815	1712	2140	0855	until	1240	2012	
0830	1727	2200	0920	2340	1312	2040	
0845	1742	2220	0940				
0900	1757	2240					
0920	1812	2300					
0940	1827	2320					
		2340					

311

ORWELL & HARWICH NAVIGATION CO., LTD.   The Quay, Harwich.
HARWICH · FELIXSTOWE FERRY SERVICE
PASSENGER FERRY SERVICES

Daily—Until 26th September, 1971 and from Spring Bank Holiday, 1972.

HARWICH (Pier) - FELIXSTOWE (Dock)		FELIXSTOWE (Dock) - HARWICH (Pier)	
0900 NSSu	1500	0930 NSSu	1530
1000	1600	1030	1630
1100 NSSu	1700	1130 NSSu	1730
1200	1800	1230	1830
1400		1430	

Mondays to Fridays—From 27th September, 1971 to Spring Bank Holiday, 1972

HARWICH (Pier) - FELIXSTOWE (Dock)		FELIXSTOWE (Dock) - HARWICH (Pier)	
0815	1715	0830	1730

5/9/71

Crossing Time 15 minutes (approx.)
No responsibility can be accepted for other operators times shown above.

NSSu—Not Saturdays or Sundays.

One would expect the haven ferry to have its own entry in the Eastern Region timetable. It certainly did: in the summer of 1954 it had Table 29 all to itself. The two local bus companies, themselves arms of the British Transport Commission, also featured the operation. Eastern National and Eastern Counties materials thereby have relevance.

Studying 1970 Eastern Counties and 1971 Eastern National issues duly obliged. The extract is from the 1971 example. Added value, the other railway-owned ferry in Eastern National's area at Tilbury is included. These were the only shipping services in the timetable, each at the extremity of this company's operations north and south.

RIVERS ORWELL and STOUR CRUISES BOAT TRIPS HARWICH HARBOUR FERRIES

from
HARWICH PIER and FELIXSTOWE DOCK
1972 PROGRAMME—FARES AND SAILING TIMES

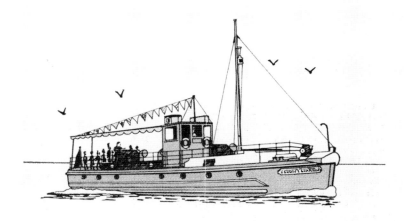

REFRESHMENTS AND LICENSED BAR ON ALL CRUISES

TO AVOID DISAPPOINTMENT
PLEASE STUDY DAYS AND TIMES CAREFULLY
and
BOOK EARLY

ORWELL AND HARWICH NAVIGATION COMPANY LTD.
THE QUAY, HARWICH, ESSEX
Telephones: Harwich 2004 and Wix 296 (night)

Fishing Parties taken during winter months—enquiries welcomed

By the time of these bus timetables, an early fit of privatisation meant that the haven ferry was no longer a railway one. In 1962 the Orwell & Harwich Navigation Company took over the service and the LNER built *Brightlingsea*. She is on the cover of this 1972 leaflet. A programme of cruises included Ipswich.

In 1979 the Felixstowe Dock & Railway Co. bought the ferry company with the result that it became a small cog of European Ferries. The ferry's role declined further with the opening of the Orwell Bridge around 1983.

Thereafter various operators have continued to try to keep the ferry running. I was surprised to visit Harwich on 28 July 1989 and find *Brightlingsea* still operating. She continued to do this until the loss of her berth at Felixstowe Dock around 1992. She was by then one of the oldest railway-built ships still working on her original route (not the oldest, the Lakes can claim that).

The up-to-date picture of cruising on the Orwell is online at: http://www.orwellrivercruises. co.uk/. The ferry operation is separate and is detailed at http://www.harwich.net/ferry.htm. In 2004 it appeared primarily to be a tourist facility and not a worker's connection. A welcome development in 2006 was the revival of the *Brightlingsea* herself, detailed at http://www. msbrightlingsea.com .

Clearly the vast majority of approaches to Felixstowe have come either from the sea or from the Ipswich direction, which leads to the provision of railway links. The community at Harwich was ancient and centred on sea trade. At Felixstowe in the mid-nineteenth century, there was just a small seaside village. Then, as now, the centre of habitation faced the sea and was some way from the banks of the estuary. One man set about changing everything. This was Colonel Tomline of Orwell Park. He bought up much of the Felixstowe area in the 1860s with a twin vision: create a seaside resort and a rival port to Harwich. The first objective happened quite quickly, the second took a lot longer to realise. His vehicle for the undertaking was the creation in 1875 of what through the twentieth century was the Felixstowe Dock and Railway Co. It is useful to remember that this is what makes Felixstowe a railway port, but one whose quirks of ownership kept it in private hands.

Colonel Tomline had rivals, which is why when 'his' railway arrived in 1877, the Felixstowe station was neither near the established community, nor even at the infant dock, but in between, at Felixstowe Beach station, on his own land. Felixstowe Town opened in 1889 and Beach was to close to passengers in 1967. Thirty years afterwards the wooden structure of Beach station survived.

In the end Felixstowe Dock has become so successful, that there seems little prospect of the line through Beach ever being pulled up, which is not how it looked around 1950 just before the Suffolk businessman Henry Gordon Parker bought the dock company. The dock had opened in 1887. Traffic came and went but it was only after 1959 that Felixstowe Dock began to make headlines. It was from the dock of the 1930s that Arthur Ransome had his heroic children set sail in *We Didn't Mean to Go to Sea*. In due course the growth favoured new riverside berths. In 1959, the dock handled 214,000 tons. Ten years later it was 2,019,000 tons, and that more than doubled in another seven years.

One event made the difference: the start, in July 1967, of ISO container traffic. Initially there was just one Paceco Vickers Portainer Crane in use. Even before this, a Ro-Ro berth had opened in 1965. These made the modern history of Felixstowe's shipping. The railway has made money not from bringing passengers to Felixstowe's ships, but from containers. That makes this view of locomotive 56095 handling a train of empty container flats on the branch at Trimley on 24 June 1996 just typical.

The single track behind the engine has been a constant thorn in recent decades' operations. In 2005, Hutchison Ports UK, the dock's owners since 1991, were planning to fund the doubling of this length of the national network.

From the Felixstowe Dock & Railway Co., the Great Eastern Railway had obtained three 2–4–0Ts, with which the branch opened. That was back in the 1880s. The dock company did not own another railway engine until 1968.

What was once a standard BR shunter, No.D3489, was purchased to help handle the container traffic. It is seen here inside the dock complex on 31 March 1985. This was never an easy 'spot' but our party had just left a ferry. The engine was given a name commemorating the company's founder. *Colonel Tomline* in this livery received some more exposure when it became the subject of a Lima OO-scale model train in 1983. Even that has become a rare beast with the passage of time.

The Port of FELIXSTOWE

THE FELIXSTOWE DOCK & RAILWAY CO

1975 Handbook

Opposite: One can be sure that specific publicity relating to the growth of Freightliner traffic at Felixstowe existed and equally sure that most has been destroyed. I have none, but something that does portray the port as growth took off is this official Port of Felixstowe 1975 handbook. This was the year before the dock was sold to European Ferries. The combined dock and railway crest of arms has pride of place in the cover design. Expansion was constant in those years, and in 1986 Princess Anne opened a third container terminal. At that time a new 1-mile link line was being built so that trains could work in a circle back to Trimley.

Next pages: Harwich may have hosted the North Sea's first car ferry in 1964 (DFDS's *England*) but Felixstowe won the race to install a proper Ro-Ro berth. This enabled Atlantic Steam Navigation, otherwise called the Transport Ferry Service, to serve Felixstowe from July 1965. The technology was not new. ASN had been doing it in the Irish Sea since 1948. A Continental service from Tilbury had started right back in 1946 but initially for military traffic. Felixstowe's great appeal was that it halved the voyage time to Rotterdam and offered better labour relations.

From January 1966 an Antwerp service was added. Many of the TFS publicity items were all routes brochures (one reason for showing nothing for Tilbury) but this brochure for March 1968 is exclusively for the Felixstowe–Rotterdam route. Although not prominently noted for their rail connections, the ASN/TFS fleet were part of the nationalised British Transport Commission from 1954.

The brochure seems stimulated by the advent in October 1967 of the *Europic Ferry*. She was the pride of the TFS fleet when Swan Hunter's delivered her and brought the crossing to Rotterdam down to six hours.

This vessel had a long life. She lasted with what had become P&O Ferries until withdrawn from Cairnryan in 1993.

THE TRANSPORT FERRY SERVICE

(ATLANTIC STEAM NAVIGATION CO. LTD.)

Car and Passenger Service (drive on/drive off)
FELIXSTOWE to ROTTERDAM (Europoort)

The service is maintained by the m.v. "Europic Ferry" (4190 tons gross), launched in October 1967, stabilised to provide a smoother crossing and equipped with all latest navigational aids.

44 first class passengers are carried in exceptional comfort, with excellent cabin accommodation, Lounge and Dining Room and ample deck space. Service and meals on board are of the highest standard.

| The luxurious Cabin-de-Luxe, with two beds, private bath-room and toilet. | A spacious four-berth cabin, with wardrobes, drawer space and hot and cold running water. | Excellent meals with first class service are enjoyed in the Dining Room. | The Lounge/Bar, for refreshments or simply to relax. |

SAILINGS:

Daily except Saturday		Daily except Sunday	
Night Crossing		*Day Crossing*	
Felixstowe report	20.00 hrs	Europoort report	11.00 hrs
Felixstowe depart	23.30 hrs	Europoort depart	12.00 hrs
Europoort arrive	06.00 hrs (next day)	Felixstowe arrive	18.30 hrs
disembark	08.00 hrs	disembark on arrival	

For Reservations or further information, ask your travel agent.
or motoring organisation, or write to

THE TRANSPORT FERRY SERVICE,
25 WHITEHALL, LONDON, SW1
Telephone: WHitehall 2363

PASSENGER FARE SCHEDULE AND ACCOMPANIED VEHICLE TARIFF

EFFECTIVE FROM 1st MARCH 1968

Cancelling all previous issues

FIRST CLASS ONLY		Night Crossing Off Season 1st Oct.-30th Apr. £ s d	Night Crossing Summer Season 1st May-30th Sep. £ s d	Day Crossing Off Season 1st Oct.-30th Apr. £ s d	Day Crossing Summer Season 1st May-30th Sep. £ s d
		(per person)		(per person)	
Cabin de Luxe with bath & toilet	2 beds	9.10.0	10.10.0	9. 0.0	10. 0.0
	Sole use	12.10.0	13.10.0	12. 0.0	13. 0.0
Special Cabin with bath & toilet	2 beds	8. 0.0	9. 0.0	7.10.0	8.10.0
	Sole use	10. 0.0	11. 0.0	9.10.0	10.10.0
Single Cabin		9.10.0	10.10.0	9. 0.0	10. 0.0
Berth in 2-berth Cabin		6.10.0	7.10.0	6. 0.0	7. 0.0
Berth in 3-berth Cabin		6. 0.0	6.10.0	5.10.0	6. 0.0
Berth in 4-berth Cabin		5.10.0	6. 0.0	5. 0.0	5.10.0

Fares are for a single journey and include meals en route

CHILDREN (All services)

Under 1 year ...   . FREE
(Separate Berth not guaranteed, but cots are normally provided for children up to 3 years of age.)
1 and under 3 years ...   QUARTER FARE
3 and under 14 years..   ... HALF FARE

BAGGAGE

Free allowance   ...   . 112 lbs
(carried in the Cabin only)

Children pro rata according to fare paid

Excess Baggage   ...   1/- per cubic foot
(for Hold stowage only)

Transportation is available by arrangement between Europoort and Rotterdam Central Station (39 km.) or vice versa for passengers without cars, at a fare of D.fl. 4.00.

ACCOMPANIED CARS, CARAVANS AND BAGGAGE TRAILERS

	Single £ s d	Return £ s d
Not exceeding		
11' (3.35m)	7.0.0	10.10.0
12'6'' (3.81m)	9.0.0	13.10.0
14' (4.27m)	11.0.0	16.10.0
15'6'' (4.72m)	13.0.0	19.10.0
Vehicles exceeding 15'6'' per additional ft. (31cm)	1.0.0	1.10.0

NOTE. Vehicles are carried only at owners risk. Wharfage and landing charges are included.

Petrol tanks can remain full throughout the crossing. Cars are not accessible during the voyage to anyone other than the deck officer on duty, who carries out routine inspections, thus eliminating risk of damage or pilfering. Cars are driven on and off the ship.

CYCLES, MOTOR CYCLES AND SIDECARS

					Single £ s d	Return £ s d
Pedal Cycles and power assisted Pedal Cycles	...	...	...	...	2.10.0	3.15.0
Solo Motor Cycles and Scooters (irrespective of weight)		... ..	...		3.10.0	5. 5.0
Motor Cycle with Sidecar	...	...	...	...	4.10.0	6.15.0

CONDITIONS

Passengers, Accompanied Cars, Baggage, Dogs, etc., are carried subject to the Company's Conditions printed on Passenger Tickets, Accompanied Vehicle Tickets, or other relevant transportation documents issued. These conditions can be seen on demand at any of the Company's Offices. All fares, timings and arrangements quoted herein are subject to alteration or cancellation without notice.

I could drive a 32 ton artic across the North Sea with my eyes shut.

You'd expect the people who pioneered the concept of roll-on/roll-off to make life as easy for the driver as they do for the vehicle.

It's not just that the driver's crossing is free. It's the fact that he's treated to a standard of service throughout which is higher than fare-paying passengers can expect on other lines.

Club-room with television. Excellent menu. Specially reserved cabins so that he can rest or sleep.

And he can sleep easy.

Because the requirements of roll-on/roll-off have influenced every aspect of the TFS operation.

The lower deck of each vessel, for instance, has been designed and custom-built specifically to carry wheeled traffic.

From marshalling yard layout and handling equipment to personnel, TFS have done everything to streamline throughout and avoid delays at each of their terminals.

Then there's the speed of the crossing ($6\frac{1}{2}$ hours to Europoort). And the frequency. Three sailings daily between Felixstowe and Europoort. Frequent daily sailings between Felixstowe and Zeebrugge, Cairnryan and Larne.

TFS. Think of us as wheels across the water.

The Transport Ferry Service, The Docks, Felixstowe, Suffolk IP11 8TB. Tel: Felixstowe 3165. Telex 98236.

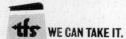 **tfs WE CAN TAKE IT.**

The TFS route was open to all comers but the target audience was truck drivers, something which this advert in the Port of Felixstowe 1975 handbook emphasises.

The Transport Ferry Service ships became part of private enterprise Townsend Thoresen in 1971, itself part of the European Ferries group. In 1976 European Ferries bought the Felixstowe Dock & Railway Co. and two years later celebrated fifty years (since the start of Stuart Townsend's first Channel service). As this brochure makes clear the company were pushing their new route Felixstowe–Rotterdam for the 1978 season. But what was new about this?

The distinction lay in the primarily trucking nature of the TFS operation. Townsend Thoresen had started a fully fledged passenger operation targeting motorists from Felixstowe in 1974 with their Zeebrugge route. This brochure was the start of a parallel operation to the Netherlands.

Note there were no train connections: Felixstowe Pier station had been closed from the 2 July 1951. There have been no European boat trains down the Felixstowe branch. Instead this 1978 brochure offered a connecting coach service from London with National Travel and Grey Green.

P&O

European Ferries

CLIPPER LINE

SHORT TRIPS TO THE CONTINENT

SHORT
TRIPS
TO
BELGIUM
FROM
£11

JANUARY
TO
DECEMBER
1994

FELIXSTOWE –
ZEEBRUGGE

In recent times the worst accident near the Haven involved a Townsend Thoresen vessel when, on 19 December 1982, the *European Gateway* sank after a collision. Then, in 1987, P&O Ferries took over Townsend Thoresen and from 1988 onwards, the new name was in evidence in the brochures.

P&O European Ferries material solely produced for the Felixstowe–Zeebrugge route has proved somewhat thin on the ground because the weight of its marketing lay with the annual all routes brochure. A colourful run of brochures for short trips and days away exist from the 1990s solely for the route. This artwork cover is typical of the quality but the Clipper Line brand is unusual. The brand was a 1994 innovation but it did not stop P&O Ferries closing the route.

The P&O Ferries primarily car and passenger sailings from Felixstowe ceased on 22 October 1995, leaving the trucking operations, the TFS inheritance, to continue.

The year after, on 24 June 1996, one of the commercial vehicle ferries MV *European Tideway* of 1977, is seen bound for Europoort. P&O even pulled out of this in 2002, when Felixstowe operations were sold to Stena Line and moved to Harwich. Remember that for a while from 1987–1991 P&O's interest in the Port of Felixstowe had extended to its complete ownership.

TFS, Townsend Thoresen, and a third passenger operator were vying to use Felixstowe in the first half of the 1970s. That third name was Tor Line. Tor Line arrived in the UK in 1966 at Immingham (see next chapter). Their first move into Felixstowe is shown in this advert from the 1975 port handbook.

The advert probably appeared before the service started, which was on 2 June 1975. It illustrates a freight ferry. Two new sister ships were introduced. First to arrive was *Tor Britannia*, a vessel which would become one of the most successful North Sea ferries through the rest of the twentieth century. In her guise as DFDS's *Prince of Scandinavia* this volume has already met her.

The initial 1975 brochure eulogised her in a cutaway profile. For the time, her 15,500 tons and twenty-four-and-a-half-knot speed made her an instant hit. She could reach Gothenburg in under twenty-four hours. A TV soap opera came aboard. This was *Triangle* with Kate O'Mara, remembered by few, and purgatory to make according to a website in 2005.

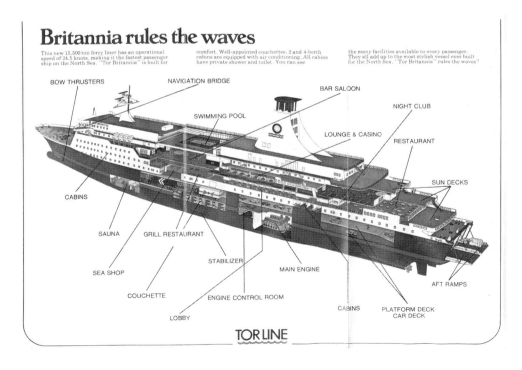

Britannia rules the waves

This new 15,500 ton ferry liner has an operational speed of 24.5 knots, making it the fastest passenger ship on the North Sea. "Tor Britannia" is built for comfort. Well-appointed couchettes, 2 and 4-berth cabins are equipped with air conditioning. All cabins have private shower and toilet. You can see the many facilities available to every passenger. They all add up to the most stylish vessel ever built for the North Sea. "Tor Britannia" rules the waves.

By the winter 1975 timetable, the new ship could be shown with a colour photograph. The competition was finished off by these sisters and Swedish Lloyd withdrew their old established Tilbury–Gothenburg service in 1976.

Tor Scandinavia arrived in 1976. Relatively few postcards have been showcased in this volume. They are a well known subject and publicity has been the prime driver of this book. This Vita Nova brand card showing the two sisters passing was officially sold on the ships in the late 1970s. The vessels were sufficiently luxurious that off-season cruising could be undertaken. As *Princess of Scandinavia*, DFDS sold her in 2006 when they withdrew her after closing the North Shields-Gothenburg service on 1 November 2006.

Felixstowe Gothenburg

m.s. *Tor Scandinavia*
m.s. *Tor Britannia*
or another ship

UK-Sweden
Felixstowe-Gothenburg

DFDS TOR LINE

Timetable

1 Jan-2 Mar 1983

Felixstowe	dep.	Wed 11.30	Fri 15.30	Sun 20.00
Gothenburg	arr.	Thur 11.30	Sat 15.30	Mon 20.30
Gothenburg	dep.	Tues 10.30	Thur 14.30	Sat 18.30
Felixstowe	arr.	Wed 08.30	Fri 12.30	Sun 17.00

3 Mar-24 May & 12-30 Sept

Felixstowe	dep.	Fri 13.30	Sun 19.00	Mon 21.00
Gothenburg	arr.	Sat 14.00	Mon 19.30	Tues 22.00
Gothenburg	dep.	Thur 11.00	Sat 17.00	Sun 18.30
Felixstowe	arr.	Fri 10.30	Sun 16.00	Mon 18.00

25 May-11 Sept

Felixstowe	dep.	Mon 21.00	Thur 13.30	Fri 13.30	Sun 19.00
Gothenburg	arr.	Tues 22.00	Fri 13.30	Mon 13.30	Mon 19.30
Gothenburg	dep.	Sun 16.30	Wed 11.00	Thur 12.30	Sat 16.30
Felixstowe	arr.	Mon 18.00	Thur 10.30	Fri 10.30	Sun 16.00

Berth
Felixstowe: Tor Line Terminal, number 2 gate.
Gothenburg: Skandiahamn.

Embarkation
From 90 minutes before departure. Passengers should be at the quayside at least 60 minutes before departure.

Coach connection
There is a special coach service in connection with DFDS Tor Line departures from Felixstowe, departing Victoria Coach Station, bay 25, 4½ hours before sailing. For further information please contact the DFDS Tor Line Terminal at Felixstowe.

Train connections
For passengers who wish to travel by train there is a rail service from London (Liverpool Street Station) to Ipswich with onward travel from Ipswich to Felixstowe by connecting coach. For details please contact the DFDS Tor Line Terminal at Felixstowe.

Vehicles must be at the quayside at least 90 minutes, and coaches 2 hours, before departure.

Felixstowe

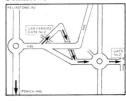

Gothenburg

Fares

single journey

Passengers per person	1 Jan-24 Mar	25 Mar-9 June	10 June-21 Aug	22 Aug-30 Sept
4-berth economy cabin	£44.00	£52.00	£62.00	£52.00
3-berth economy cabin	£49.00	£58.00	£68.00	£58.00
2-berth economy cabin	£54.00	£64.00	£74.00	£64.00
4-berth cabin with shower/toilet	£54.00	£64.00	£74.00	£64.00
3-berth cabin with shower/toilet	£59.00	£69.00	£79.00	£69.00
2-berth cabin with shower/toilet	£64.00	£75.00	£85.00	£75.00
Single cabin with shower/toilet	£84.00	£98.00	£108.00	£98.00

Child fare (4-16 years) is 50% of the above 4-berth economy cabin fare.

Accompanied motor vehicles single journey
These rates do not apply in connection with the transport of commercial goods. Further details on application.

	1 Jan-24 Mar		25 Mar-30 Sept	
Car, minibus or motorised caravans (up to 6m in length)	Up to 2.00m high	Over 2.00m high	Up to 2.00m high	Over 2.00m high
With 1 paying passenger	£25.00	£30.00	£26.00	£32.00
With 2 paying passengers	£25.00	£30.00	£26.00	£32.00
With 3 paying passengers	£25.00	£30.00	£26.00	£32.00
With 4 or more paying passengers	Free	Free	Free	Free
Caravans, Trailers etc. Per metre	£16.00		£17.00	
Coaches (driver free)* With 10-24 paying passengers per metre	£16.00		£19.00	
With 25 or more paying passengers	Free		Free	

*Coaches must be accompanied by a minimum of 10 paying passengers. If less than 10, freight rates will be charged.

Other vehicles		
Motorcycles with sidecar/ motorcycles and scooters	£14.00	£15.00
Mopeds and pedal cycles	£3.00	£3.00

Booking office, Felixstowe. Telephone (03942) 73131

From the customer's viewpoint Tor Line was an out-and-out success. For the owners however, the profit margin on the investment was low. A solution had been sought for some time before the 1981 decision to sell the Tor Line passenger ferries to DFDS. Operations were not moved to Harwich Parkeston Quay until 1 May 1983. For a time the sisters were branded as DFDS Tor Line. This is how it appeared in the DFDS main January 1983 brochure with a rare appearance for Felixstowe in the DFDS literature. Connections to London used either a through coach from London Victoria Coach Station, or a cack-handed arrangement of a coach to and from Ipswich railway station.

Chapter Six

Onwards to Hull

Next pages: The next centre of railway-owned shipping up the East Coast was the Humber. That is a long haul from the Orwell Haven ports but not without any railway-owned ports in-between. The Great Eastern Railway ended up owning the port at Lowestoft and with great influence at King's Lynn with the result that they lineally passed through the London & North Eastern Railway, then via British Transport Docks to their current owner Associated British Ports. Plenty of publicity was generated by these owners for just these two ports.

The example shown is one from a series produced by British Transport Docks Board covering their harbours. The date is 1972, eleven years prior to privatisation as Associated British Ports. The sense of shared ownership in the use of generic symbols and typefaces with other arms of the nationalised transport industry is clear. It feels like a family item. Melbury House, the London headquarters, was also the headquarters of the British Waterways Board. Whereas an item of passenger publicity to have much effect would probably need a five-figure print run, this sort of item, targeted at the specialist user, was produced in much smaller quantities. This one has a print run of 3,000. If I remember correctly they would be given away to a party of visiting schoolchildren. Lowestoft was best known as home to a great fishing fleet but a wide variety of general cargo was handled through the swing bridge in the inner harbour towards Lake Lothing. A nice diagram (p.201) is typical of this series and would show the railway links. At Lowestoft dockside rail sidings remained in 2005 in occasional use.

The railway involvement at Lowestoft went right back into the 1840s and the activities of Samuel Peto. This railway contractor welded together the failing Norwich & Lowestoft Navigation Co. which had spent much money to little commercial effect, with a new railway line towards Norwich and efficient development of the harbour. Back in those early years, passenger-carrying steam packets ran to Rotterdam, Hamburg, and even St Petersburg.

Lowestoft Harbour

Further information from:
Docks Manager
British Transport Docks Board, Custom House,
Lowestoft.   Tel : **2286 (STD : 0502)**

or from Marketing Manager,
British Transport Docks Board, Melbury House,
Melbury Terrace, London NW1 6JY.
Tel : 01-486 6621

British Transport Docks Board

Lowestoft

Part of a nationwide ports service operated by the **British Transport Docks Board**, a publicly owned undertaking, and comprising : **HUMBER:** HULL, GRIMSBY, IMMINGHAM, GOOLE. **EAST COAST :** KING'S LYNN, LOWESTOFT. **SOUTH COAST:** SOUTHAMPTON, PLYMOUTH. **SOUTH WALES:** NEWPORT, CARDIFF, BARRY, PORT TALBOT, SWANSEA. **WEST COAST:** GARSTON, FLEETWOOD, BARROW, SILLOTH. **SCOTLAND:** AYR, TROON.
Printed in England, by Hodgkins Millar Ltd., at Leicester.
LTI/3m/172/80164

④ & ⑤ Aerial views of Lowestoft Harbour looking East.

S2 Dock Plan

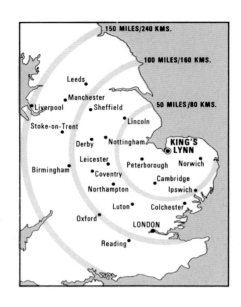

King's Lynn was once a great mediaeval port, the fourth port of the kingdom. But between 1550 and 1853, there was next to no port development, while the coastline and the river channels changed immensely. The railway arrived in Lynn in 1847. A grand scheme awaited the 1865 King's Lynn Dock and Railways Act. Ultimately this created the enclosed Alexandra Dock in 1869, followed by the Bentinck Dock in 1883. These primarily continue to be the harbour of today.

Our selection is another of the BTDB port series. It is undated but likely to be mid-1970s. The two panels (of the twelve) showing the dock plan are reproduced opposite. Over the years, all sorts of primarily freight steamship services had run regularly from Lynn. Individual publicity for all would have been needed. This genre is very hard to find, even harder than any form of port guide. Enclosed in this leaflet was a flyer announcing the start of a service to the Mediterranean by Mercandia-Med Line. Since this was the mid-1970s, it was very late in the day to try to establish a general cargo liner service in the face of containers and trucking.

A rail connection remains at Kings Lynn in 2005 but, like Lowestoft, is little used.

King's Lynn Docks

◖◗ Dock plan

The plan below shows the two connected Docks with the entrance through the lock from the River Great Ouse into Alexandra Dock, and passage through the two swing bridges into the larger Bentinck Dock. All berths are road and rail connected, the principal routes being shown on the plan.

INDUSTRIAL SITES. The King's Lynn district of Norfolk is included in the national "over-spill" scheme and new industries are being developed and encouraged in the area. Very suitable sites are available on the Docks Estate for light industry, storage and service installations, all provided with good road, rail and shipping facilities. Our modernisation programme has been planned to deal with the expanding trade which will inevitably follow these new industries.

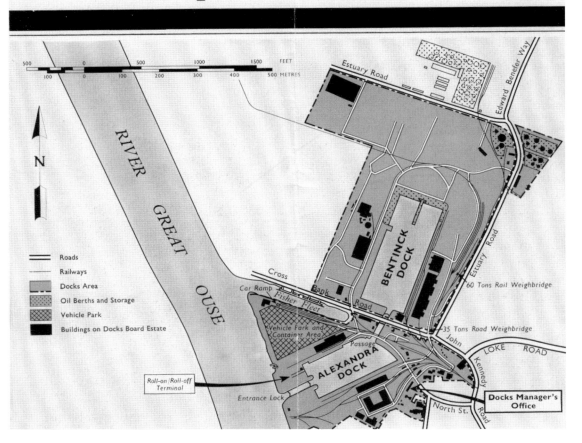

══	Roads
—	Railways
▨	Docks Area
▨	Oil Berths and Storage
▨	Vehicle Park
■	Buildings on Docks Board Estate

Above left: Across the Wash and a few miles up the river Witham, the Port of Boston was, in 1204, the second most important English port. The export of Lincolnshire wool was of critical importance. Yet from 1400–1800, Boston was of little importance as a port. Nineteenth-century revival came as the corporation improved the channel to the sea. Railway communication followed in 1848 and the enclosed dock (another corporation initiative) opened in 1884.

The Great Northern Railway (later LNER/BR) did not directly invest in the dock but did ensure direct railway connections existed. In the last 130 years Boston has been an important regional port with valued railway connections, which were even refurbished around 2000 for the handling of steel traffic.

The item shown dates to around 1960 and was a member of another series of leaflets, all sharing this cover design. The full extent of the series is not known, although two possible pointers come from the fact that it is Eastern Region published, and that BR addresses across Britain are provided.

Above right: Another example is shown from Grimsby and Immingham (but there were surely many more). By this device we enter the Humber, the second largest focus for railway-owned shipping on the East Coast.

Next page: Whether the Humber divides rather than unifies is a subject to excite debate. What is certain is that until the railway grouping of 1923, the two banks were entirely partisan. The North Eastern Railway served Hull while the Great Central Railway and its predecessors colonised the south bank. In 1852, the railway-owned Royal Dock at Grimsby was opened and thereby Grimsby became a railway port which today is part of Associated British Ports. The Great Central Railway was never short of ambition, and nor was Grimsby, in that pre-First World War era, short of fish.

Even prior to activities at Grimsby the railways developed New Holland (from 1848) and between 1901–12, the Great Central Railway created the enormous wet dock complex at Immingham. This was not with fish in mind – the demands of the coal and steel trades dominated then, and remain important today.

Majesty aboard a Great Central Humber paddler opened Immingham Dock amidst a welter of printed publicity now very difficult to source, but with examples on view in A.J. Ludlam's book (see Bibliography).

All three ports retain rail connections although, with regard to its railway business, Immingham remains of central importance, and that is entirely with freight traffic. Associated British Ports produces most attractive publicity currently for the Humber ports.

The second piece from Immingham comes from that past age. It shows some of the fourteen hydraulic luffing cranes installed on No.1 and No.2 Quays for general cargo. It unfolds into twenty-four panels with large plan and illustrations. The plan carries a date of July 1947 and the prime address is given as: 'The Port Master British Railways Grimsby Docks'.

That is the interest in this item from the moment of nationalisation in 1948. Apart from the one mention of British Railways and another mention of 'The Docks and Overseas Trade Office', the item is staggeringly reticent about ownership. The telegraphic address of the 'Trade Office' is Nerdocks. That suggests the office is (logically) a former LNER dock's headquarters.

The Docks & Inland Waterways Executive (later to be British Transport Docks), although created on 1 January 1948, took some time to have all its assets transferred to its portfolio. Among the railway-owned docks and piers, there was some debate about which would pass from BR control. Those like New Holland and Harwich, whose trade was overwhelmingly in support of the railway business and its ships, remained railway ports and in the main would many years later become Sealink ports. There was little doubt that most of the Humber ports would pass to the new body, although exactly when it happened I cannot say. One would conclude that in the first few months of nationalisation Immingham, which had previously been an LNER port, was briefly a British Railways port and, in that short interval, this undated brochure was produced.

IMMINGHAM

The Port
Free From
Tidal
Restrictions

Map shewing location of
IMMINGHAM DOCK
in relation to industrial centres of
Great Britain

TOR LINE

vaarschema, tarieven en algemene inlichtingen geldig van 16 sept. 1969 t/m 31 aug. 1970

varen naar Zweden en Engeland

Grimsby and Immingham have both been associated with modern North Sea vehicle ferry services but the glue never quite sticks for car/passenger services. In the longer term Hull has taken that role in the Humber. An exception was the appearance of Tor Line at Immingham in 1966.

The name Tor Line comes from Trans-Oil and Rex Shipping, its two founding partners. Their idea was to take on the existing Humber operators with modern twenty-two-knot vehicle ferries, having a cruise liner feel. That concept is very well expressed in this 1969 Dutch issue leaflet's cover. Other leaflets were more conformist, offering views of the purpose built MV *Tor Anglia* and *Tor Hollandia*.

A triangular Immingham–Netherlands–Gothenburg service was operated. Direct rail connections never featured at Immingham. A coach connection to Grimsby Town station was provided. In Amsterdam the vessels used the Noordzee Canal to dock in the Coenhaven only 3 miles from the city centre.

Opposite: A rather more classical image shows *Tor Hollandia* ploughing her furrow through the North Sea. Its source is a bit offbeat. It is a copy of a Tor Line advertisement itself, reproduced in a travel industry magazine supplement. The magazine was the *Travel Agent*, whose January 1970 issue contained a thirty-page supplement: 'Car Ferry Guide 1970'. This looks like an annual affair, although I have no idea how over many years it was produced. It gave brief details, on a country by country basis, of routes and operators. The operator's own adverts make a considerable impression as 1970 was perhaps five years into the frantic car ferry revolution.

As this volume has already examined, Tor's passenger focus moved on from Immingham to Felixstowe in 1975. The first pair of ships were sold to the Mediterranean in 1976. Freight services continued from Immingham and the Tor Line branding now presented as DFDS Tor Line was prominent in 2004 when ABP got the go ahead to create a £35 million five-berth tidal terminal at Immingham, so saving vessels the effort of locking in. Two Tor Line freight vessels from the early 1970s were still used by DFDS from Immingham in 2005.

209

The Humber was home to one car ferry service for many decades, which moves the story a few miles upstream from Immingham to another Great Central Railway/LNER/BR operation: New Holland.

It was the direct ancestor of the Great Central called the Manchester, Sheffield & Lincolnshire Railway, which really developed New Holland. Even they had not started the steam paddle ferry service from there, which goes back to around 1832. The railway bought the steamer service and opened its line from Grimsby in 1848 allowing comparatively rapid communication between the two major Humberside towns. The rail/ferry link would remain important until 1981 and the opening of the Humber Bridge, whereupon it was abandoned. Cars were welcomed aboard. Over 2,400 vehicles were carried in 1923. This increased twenty-four-fold by 1955. For many decades the railway operated a lighterage service for goods as well.

The Hull terminal at Victoria Pier was quite straightforward, although it offered the anomaly of a BR terminus with no trains in sight (shades of Dartmouth). The pier was owned by Hull Corporation and, through almost the entire life of the railway ferry, 7 Nelson Street, just across the road, was the railway-owned booking office.

At New Holland, a pier 1,500ft in length existed to reach deep water and, in another notable parallel (this time with Ryde), the mainline trains worked along the pier between New Holland Town and Pier stations.

On a dull 14 March 1981 the pier was laden with 'atmosphere'. One constituent of this was a full selection of Eastern Region blue enamel signs which evidently were not worth modernising. The platforms between the two stations were continuous, providing a walkway on one side and a road on the other, with the railway between. Driving a car required nerve even before getting to the vessel.

The GCR and the LNER had both invested in modern paddle steamers. The three LNER examples gained real fame as they became very late survivors of the genre. All three survived the millennium. *Lincoln Castle*, which was the last built and the last in service (until 1978, despite quoted dates which vary from 1973 to 1981), spent a while in the shadow of the Humber Bridge on the foreshore at Hessle. She is now resident at Grimsby Dock.

Tattershall Castle become one of London's hospitality ships. She looked quite authentic when photographed on 30 December 1985, with Charing Cross Railway Bridge in the background. A refit in 2004 radically changed her appearance for the worse.

Wingfield Castle has fared best in that she is a thoroughly restored museum ship back at Hartlepool, where she was built in 1934.

In its last few years the route was notable by being worked by a former Southern Railway/ Region Solent paddler. This was a diesel electric paddle car ferry dating from 1947 called *Farringford*. She closed the route on 24 June 1981. A special commemorative ticket for the final three sailings was issued. This shot of her was taken on 14 March 1981.

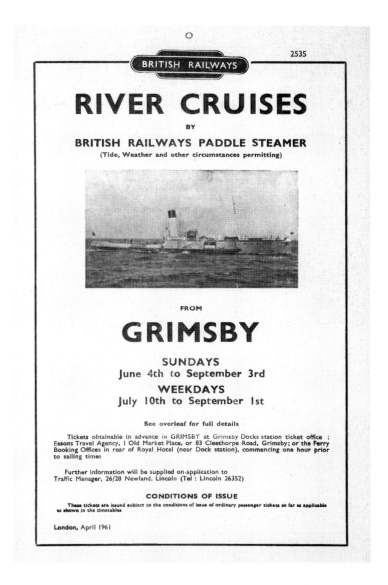

The Humber paddlers provoked plenty of publicity, although it probably had a limited geographical circulation. Very straightforward classic handbills provided the timetable between at least 1948 and the issue of April 1966 (which had adopted the double arrow).

In their heyday, the vessels did not restrict themselves to the New Holland crossing and a variety of cruises were offered. This is the two-sided programme for the 1961 season when summer non-landing cruises were offered to Spurn Point. In this context note that this is the Grimsby programme. Another bill might cover the same sailings ex-Hull, and it looks as if in rather limited circumstances a direct Grimsby–Hull ticket could be procured.

A later example of this cruise took place in 1971 when the Paddle Steamer Preservation Society themselves promoted a Spurn cruise on 15 August. BR had abandoned the cruise programme after 1967. That year a private company called Humber Hovercraft announced they were starting a hover ferry in 1968. Services started but were short-lived. What publicity could they offer?

Instead of a hovercraft, the Humber vessels were re-branded as Sealink around 1970 (when I believe eleven or twelve years of AHL management ceased). In their final years, some quite distinctive publicity existed.

For the four years 1970–1974, the probability is that four issues resembling the 1971 item appeared, a Sealink version of BR's most ordinary white card corporate image A7 folder.

For the last seven years the blue, whale embellished, folder was issued. This combined Sealink and Humberail. The latter was a marketing brand BR had introduced on both sides of the estuary.

Lincoln Castle had a panel all to herself inside 1976, the issue illustrated. It said: 'The PS *Lincoln Castle* is the last coal-fired paddle steamer in regular use in Britain.'

Tickets, while not precisely publicity, are a form of printed ephemera with a following. Occasional examples have appeared earlier. The Transport Ticket Society has been the vehicle whereby various Humber Ferry issues have survived. A wide range of the classic Edmondson card existed. These had to cover not only pure passenger and vehicle requirements on the ferry themselves, but there were numerous tickets for through journeys further afield.

The long distance ticket shown is for Grimsby Town to Whitby, marked for the coast route via Scarborough, which closed north of that town in 1965. The first single from Barton on Humber to Hull is a British Transport Commission pre-decimal issue (probably late 1950s). Much more recent is an Ultimatic roll ticket purely for the crossing from Hull Corporation Pier. Such roll tickets were used for the most popular bookings.

A detailed article on the ticketing practice from the Transport Ticket Society is noted in the Bibliography. It appears that, although Sealink were responsible for the last decade of the ferry, Sealink-headed tickets were never ordered.

To indicate the potential interest, the TTS article illustrated a three-part ticket to Skegness Butlin's, from Hull on the ferry, rail to Skegness and Lincolnshire Roadcar coach thereon. This facility must have had its own publicity and hits four collecting themes! It probably ceased with the closure in 1970 of the line south of Grimsby. Some tickets headed Kingston-upon-Hull corporation were printed purely to cover admission to Victoria Pier.

Opposite: Through the middle years of the twentieth century, British passenger shipping out of the Humber was dominated by two concerns: Associated Humber Lines and Ellerman's Wilson Line. In the transition to Ro-Ro both reacted too late, enabling newcomers to topple them. In the event only the arrival of North Sea Ferries proved of long-lasting consequence.

Prior to the railway grouping in 1923, railway-owned steamer services from the Humber were offered by the Great Central, Lancashire & Yorkshire and North Eastern Railway. Nor did grouping provide one owner, and the situation was the stimulus for the creation of Associated Humber Lines in 1935. It grouped five concerns and would last until 1971.

Our first view is through the medium of the BR Eastern Region magazine of July 1951 and an opportunity to pay tribute to a wartime veteran with a reminder of the outstanding service so many of these cross-channel vessels had to offer.

Note that this vessel, although built for the Humber trade, had ended her railway service at Harwich.

A LADY OF THE SEA

WHEN the s.s. *Accrington* recently towed out of Harwich harbour another old Railway-owned ship was bound for the breaker's yard after a long period of varied service afloat.

Built in 1910 for the Great Central Railway by Earle's of Hull, she was 265 feet long, 36 feet beam, 1,680 tons burthen and of a speed of 14 knots obtained from triple expansion reciprocating engines. Accommodation was provided for nearly 150 passengers and the holds afforded space for several hundred tons of cargo. Together with sister ships of the same period—*Bury, Dewsbury* and *Stockport*—she was included in the descriptive phrase: "these magnificent new ships for the Grimsby-Hamburg service". Surely Kipling could not have had any smarter craft in mind when he wrote "The liner she's a lady".

Details of the *Accrington's* service in the First World War are unfortunately not to hand, but the writer has heard it said that she was at one time a special service training and experimental ship with the Royal Navy and that she was also connected with Boom Defence.

Between the wars, and on the formation of the Associated Humber Lines, she was variously employed on the Continental Services from the Humber ports until Europe was over-run in 1940. Being at this time thirty years of age she was then requisitioned by the Government, stripped of portable fittings and kept ready for use as a blockship in the event of invasion by the enemy.

Early in 1942, however, the Authorities sent her to the shipbuilder's for refitting and she soon resumed active sea-going service as a Rescue vessel with the convoys in the Battle of the Atlantic. For this new work, extensive structural alterations were made internally and externally. Bunker capacity was increased, ballast and buoyage were provided to maintain seaworthiness in the apparently unending Atlantic gales, and to prolong the period of floatation in case of mishap.

Accommodation was rearranged to take a greatly augmented crew and space was reserved for survivors rescued from the sea. A Naval surgeon had charge of an up-to-date hospital and operating theatre. Ingenious rescue apparatus was developed and placed at hand around the decks. Outfits of clothes and accessories (down to the proverbial toothbrush) were put on board by the British Sailors Society for issue to survivors.

Occasionally the *Accrington* called at Gibraltar, but more usually the voyages took her to Halifax, Nova Scotia. At the latter port she, like the other Rescue vessels, soon became known in shipping circles and her crew received many small but kind and friendly attentions from the Canadians.

Seemingly blessed by Providence, or bearing a special charm of her own, it was seldom that a convoy she accompanied was seriously attacked by the enemy. The rigours endured by the crew were rather more often those of the elements. The climatic conditions varied from the tropical with blue sky and smooth sea to the near-arctic, with ice, snow and bounding billows.

Inevitably there were some calls for actual rescue work. Once, during the long darkness of a foul winter's night of heavy seas and driving snow squalls, a straggler was heavily torpedoed some distance astern of the convoy. The *Accrington* was occupied for many hours attempting to pick up survivors from boat, rafts and the wreck itself. Much of the success obtained was due to the gallant action of two seamen who jumped overside on to the rafts and secured ropes to the numbed and helpless survivors. The Rescue boat's crew of volunteers finally took a solitary survivor from the burning wreck. In all, a total of 27 lives were saved on this occasion.

A number of decorations to officers and men of the ship's company were later given for this and for other work with the convoys.

As soon as possible after the war ended the *Accrington* was reconditioned and, with her sister-ship *Dewsbury*, operated the Harwich-Antwerp Passenger and Cargo service until that service was suspended in February 1950. She continued to ply as a cargo vessel for nearly a year, when her usefulness was deemed to have ended, as she could no longer go *forward* efficiently.

Many of us are glad to have known such a robust and charming old lady. May her successors soon appear to continue a worthy tradition into the years of peace and prosperity for which we hope and strive.

A.G.

ASSOCIATED HUMBER LINES LTD

(GOOLE STEAM SHIPPING)

REGULAR LINER SERVICES

Serving SCANDINAVIA AND EUROPE from
GOOLE

AMSTERDAM	SATURDAY
ANTWERP .. WEDNESDAY and SATURDAY
BREMEN	WEEKLY
COPENHAGEN FRIDAY and alternate WEDNESDAYS
DUNKIRK	Alternate SATURDAYS
HAMBURG	3 Sailings per fortnight
ROTTERDAM	SATURDAY

from HULL

ANTWERP	SATURDAY
GHENT	SATURDAY
ROTTERDAM	
Winter .. .. WEDNESDAY and SATURDAY
Spring and Autumn MON., WED. and SATURDAY
Summer MON., TUES., WED., THURS. and SAT.

For rates of freight and passenger information apply to
Port Agents.

GOOLE: ASSOCIATED HUMBER LINES LTD.

(GOOLE STEAM SHIPPING)
Telephone : 1103

HULL: ELLERMAN'S WILSON LINE LTD.

Telephone : 26081

A good idea of the spread of the railway-associated trade from the Humber just prior to the radical changes of the 1960s can be seen from this advert. Its source is *Goole: The Official Handbook of the Town and Port*. I believe it to be the 1962 edition, and its particular title shows how intertwined the two activities were at Goole. Goole owed a great deal – though not everything – to the activities of the North Eastern Railway and Lancashire & Yorkshire, the latter of which relied on developing the port for its eastern terminal.

The fact that sea-going vessels could berth so far inland and the presence of other navigations heading still further inland had all helped Goole thrive. Indeed in 1939 over 2 million tons of cargo were handled, and the Ocean Lock opened. War destroyed more than half of Goole's business. It was not until 1950 that the railway-owned elements of Goole Docks passed to the Docks & Inland Waterways Executive, which had already inherited the Aire & Calder Navigation.

Investment followed in the 1950s. The vessel illustrated is the *Kirkham Abbey*. She came from Austin & Pickersgill in 1956. Her attractive lines could not inoculate her from the changes about to overwhelm the trade. She was designed with refrigerated holds for the 'Copenhagen Beer & Butter' trade. She left the Humber in 1970 and was broken up in 1983.

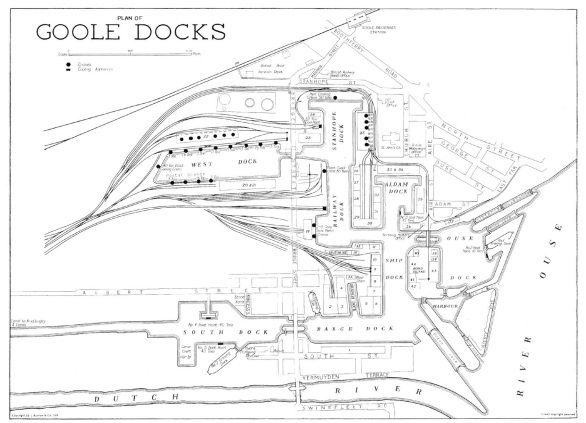

Goole Official Handbook, published by Ed. J. Burrow & Co. Ltd., Cheltenham and London

The fascination of this extract comes from the ability to see the various nationalised transport industry partners plotted. The advert from British Transport Docks faces the plan. A British Road Services depot (advert elsewhere), British Waterways Office, a BR Goods Office, Goole Passenger Station and the Dock Office itself could have promised rich pickings to the brave publicity collector willing to explain himself in 1962.

The individual cranes are denoted as are the canal-promoted Tom Pudding coal pan hoists which were unique to Goole. Apart from a preserved example, that trade has gone, but Goole retains significant rail-connected trade in 2005.

The advantageous situation of Goole Docks in relation to
industrial centres of Great Britain

Opposite: Previously the medium of the *British Railways Magazine* was used to eyeball one of the oldest vessels the region inherited in 1948. This extract from the North Eastern Region edition of December 1958 looks the other way. It was celebrating the launch in Lowestoft at Brooke Marine on 16 October 1958 of the *Melrose Abbey* and made the point that, since 1954, ten new vessels had been ordered for AHL. In 1971 she took the final AHL sailing from Hull to Rotterdam. Less than a decade later she was scrapped after some Mediterranean service. Essentially the AHL modernisation was money wasted.

'Melrose Abbey' and 'Harrogate' launched

Running parallel with the great drive forward in rail modernisation in the North Eastern Region is the attention being paid to our shipping traffic in the near Continental Trades through the medium of Associated Humber Lines Ltd.

Soon, AHL, as we in the NE know it, will have a completely modern fleet of ten new vessels all put into service since 1954.

Two steps forward in this achievement have resulted from the recent launchings of m.v. *Melrose Abbey* at Lowestoft and m.v. *Harrogate* on the Clyde.

A striking view of the " Melrose Abbey "

The *Melrose Abbey* built by Brooke Marine Ltd was launched on 16 October by Mrs G. E. van Walsum-Quispel, wife of the Burgomaster of Rotterdam.

Offering comfortable accommodation for eighty passengers in single and two berth cabins, carefully planned with all modern facilities for an overnight crossing, she is expected to be in service about the end of the year, to join her sister ship the m v *Bolton Abbey* on the Hull-Rotterdam run.

At the launching the Chairman of Associated Humber Lines and General Manager, North Eastern Region (Mr H. A. Short), paid tribute to Mrs van Walsum-Quispel and her husband. He said that their presence was evidence of the interest which Rotterdam was showing in the improved service which the *Melrose Abbey* in conjunction with the *Bolton Abbey* would enable AHL to maintain.

Mr Short referred to the approaching completion of the reconstructed Riverside Quay at Hull, which would enable regular scheduled timings for departure to be maintained. He also expressed high appreciation of all that had been done by the Rotterdam port authorities to help ship owners, not only in the port itself but also in its approaches.

The mv *Harrogate* (a sister ship to the mv *Darlington* launched last

Mrs G. E. van Walsum-Quispel launches the Melrose Abbey. Included in this picture on the left are Sir Daril Watson (Member of the Shipping and International Services Sub-Commission, BTC) and Lady Watson. Behind Mrs van Walsum-Quispel are Mr E. D. Russell (Managing Director, Brooke Marine), Mr H. A. Short (Chairman), of Associated Humber Lines and General Manager, North Eastern Region) and Mr G. M. Leach (International Traffic Officer, BTC).

24-HOUR SYSTEM FOR RAILWAY TIME.

All the countries on the Continent of Europe have adopted the 24-hour system (reckoning the hours from midnight to midnight) for Railway time, and it is used for all the time-table information in this Handbook, thus : 12.00 noon, 18.00 6.0 p.m., 24.00 arrival midnight, 0.00 departure midnight.

DIFFERENCE OF TIME.

The following diagrams indicate the times in various Continental countries when it is 12.00 Greenwich Mean Time :—

Greenwich Mean Time	British Single Summer Time, French Time, Belgian Time and Central European Time.	Eastern European Time.	Turkish Summer Time (one hour in advance of Eastern European Time).
Portugal (from Oct. 1).	Gt. Britain, France, Belgium, Luxembourg, Spain, Portugal (until Sept. 30), Holland, Italy, Germany, Denmark, Norway, Sweden, Switzerland, Austria, Hungary, Czechoslovakia, Yugoslavia and Poland.	Bulgaria, Greece, Roumania and Finland.	Turkey.

In order to signify the difference in time in certain Continental countries, the following indications appear in some of the time-table pages of this Handbook :—

    C.E.T.—Central European Time (coincides with British, French and Belgian Time).
    E.E.T.—Eastern European Time (one hour in advance of Central European Time).
    T.S.T.—Turkish Summer Time (one hour in advance of Eastern European Time).

ALTERATIONS TO SERVICES IN OCTOBER, 1950.

Single Summer Time (one hour in advance of Greenwich Mean Time) is now in force in Great Britain.

The Winter Services on the Continent will operate on and from Sunday, October 8, 1950, and train and steamer times after October 7, 1950, should, therefore, be confirmed beforehand with the Continental Enquiry Office, British Railways (Southern Region), Victoria Station, London, S.W.1 (Hudson's Place ; adjacent to Platform No. 1). In the case of services on the Continent in connection with steamers on the Harwich routes, enquiry should be made of the Continental Ticket and Information Bureau, British Railways (Eastern Region), Liverpool Street Station, London, E.C.2, or British Railways' Ticket and Information Bureau, 71, Regent Street, London, W.1.

EARLY DEPARTURE OF STEAMERS.

Passengers joining the Steamers at the Ports should be on board at least 15 minutes before the advertised times, as the sailings take place as soon as the passengers, baggage, etc., arriving by connecting trains have been embarked.

EXPLANATION OF SIGNS.

Certain features have been introduced throughout the time-table pages which it is hoped will be of assistance in choosing suitable trains, itineraries, etc. The following are details :—

    Through Carriages, Sleeping Cars, etc., from the French, Belgian and Dutch Ports to destinations on the Continent (also Sleeping Cars from London) have been indicated by dotted lines.

    Indicates connection between certain points by Motor Service.

    Indicates Sleeping Car attached to a train during the whole or part of its running as indicated in " Through Carriage " notes.

    Indicates Restaurant Car attached to a train as indicated in " Through Carriage " notes.

    Indicates Buffet Car attached to a train as indicated in " Through Carriage " notes.

    Frontier Station where passports, hand-baggage and registered baggage are examined. (See special regulations concerning examination of hand-baggage and registered baggage.)

Autor.   Certain services in France are maintained by Autorail trains. These Autorails have limited accommodation, and some do not convey heavy baggage. It should be noted that advance reservation of seats is necessary in the case of certain Autorails.

    Indicates that connection may also be made with the train in adjoining column, according to direction of line.

Fête Days   Certain trains in this time-table are shown as running " Daily (except Sundays and Fête Days)." For information, the principal Fête Days in France, Belgium and Holland are as follows :—

    FRANCE.—January 1, Easter Monday, Ascension Day, Whit Monday, July 14 (Fête Nationale), August 15 (Assumption), November 1 (All Saints), November 11 and Christmas Day.

    BELGIUM.—January 1, Easter Monday, Ascension Day, Whit Monday, July 21 (Fête Nationale), August 15 (Assumption), November 1 (All Saints) and Christmas Day.

    HOLLAND.—January 1, Easter Monday, Ascension Day, Whit Monday, Christmas Day and December 26.

This page and opposite: That *vade mecum*, the BR *Continental Handbook*, provides a useful summary of the range of AHL services and the nature of the partnership. The extract is from the summer 1950 issue. An unusual item that precedes it is an Eastern Region-issued Harwich–Hull and Newcastle sailings timetable book. I know of this from 1948. Clearly it grew out of an all-LNER publication and was issued by the Eastern Region only before the larger *Continental Handbook* became established. It was not evidently thought worthwhile to split out the 'North Eastern Region' content. This volume has the expected ER blue cover, so no tangerine dreams (the NER of BR colour).

ASSOCIATED HUMBER LINES

COMPRISING

The Railway Executive (Humber Services) : Hull & Netherlands Steam Ship Co., Ltd., Hull: Wilson's & North Eastern Railway Shipping Co., Ltd., Hull.

HULL—ROTTERDAM SERVICE
(S.S. *Melrose Abbey* & S.S. *Bury*)

Sailings :—

From Hull (Humber Dock)	Wednesdays* and Saturdays.
From Rotterdam (Parkhaven)	Tuesdays and Saturdays.*

*—The Wednesday sailings from Hull and the Saturday sailings from Rotterdam operate between May 31st and September 30th, only.

Departures from Hull are governed by the state of the tide and intending passengers will be advised of the time they should arrive on board. Departures from Rotterdam will also be at times to be advised. The average duration of the passage is 19 hours.

HULL—HAMBURG SERVICE
(S.S. *Dewsbury* and Cargo Boat)

Sailings :—
Saloon Class—No 3rd Class accommodation.

From Hull	Thursdays.
From Hamburg	Thursdays.

HULL—BREMEN SERVICE
(Cargo Boat)

Sailings (Outwards only) :—
Saloon Class—No 3rd Class accommodation.

From Hull	Fridays.

> Attention is directed to the Information on Page 168 relating to Military Visas.

HULL—ANTWERP SERVICE
(Cargo Boat)

Sailings :—
Saloon Class—No 3rd Class accommodation.

From Hull	Saturdays.
From Antwerp	Tuesdays.

GOOLE—AMSTERDAM SERVICE
(Cargo Boat)

Sailings :—
Saloon Class—No 3rd Class accommodation.

From Goole	Wednesdays.
From Amsterdam	Saturdays.

GOOLE—ROTTERDAM SERVICE
(Cargo Boat)

Sailings :—
Saloon Class—No 3rd Class accommodation.

From Goole	Wednesdays.
From Rotterdam	Mondays.

GOOLE—ANTWERP SERVICE
(Cargo Boat)

Sailings :—
Saloon Class—No 3rd Class accommodation.

From Goole	Wednesdays and Saturdays (a).
From Antwerp	Wednesdays and Saturdays.

(a)—Outwards on Saturdays via Ghent.

GOOLE—GHENT SERVICE
(Cargo Boat)

Sailings (Outwards only) :—
Saloon Class—No 3rd Class accommodation.

From Goole	Saturdays.

GOOLE—HAMBURG SERVICE
(Cargo Boat)

Sailings :—
Saloon Class—No 3rd Class accommodation.

From Goole	Thursdays.
From Hamburg	Wednesdays.

GOOLE—BREMEN SERVICE
(Cargo Boat)

Sailings (Outward only) :—
Saloon Class—No 3rd Class accommodation.

From Goole	Thursdays.

> Attention is directed to the Information on Page 168 relating to Military Visas.

GOOLE—COPENHAGEN SERVICE
(Cargo Boat)

Sailings :—
Saloon Class—No 3rd Class accommodation.

From Goole	Saturdays.
From Copenhagen	Saturdays.

Further particulars may be obtained from the Port Agents named below, to whom applications for tickets and accommodation on the above services should be addressed :—

HULL Services :
Ellerman's Wilson Line, Ltd., Hull.
Telegrams : " Wilsons Hull."　　　　　　　　Telephone : Hull Central 16180.

GOOLE Services :
Goole Steam Shipping (The Railway Executive), Goole.
Telegrams : " Despatch Goole."　　　　　　　Telephone : Goole 360.

AHL most definitely issued its own publicity and this is a good example from the summer of 1959. The presence of the house flag is nice. Within its own pages, there was no evidence whatsoever that this was a nationalised concern.

HOLLAND
Land of Windmills and Tulips

A regular link between HULL and ROTTERDAM is maintained by our new motor vessels—"BOLTON ABBEY" and "MELROSE ABBEY." Each ship has accommodation for 80 first-class passengers comprising a two-berth cabin-de-luxe with private shower and toilet, 12 single and 33 double berth cabins situated on A & B decks.

DEPARTURES

HULL		ROTTERDAM	
(RIVERSIDE QUAY)		(PARKHAVEN)	
MONDAYS	⎫ Embark - 5.0 p.m.	MONDAYS	⎫ Embark - 4.0 p.m.
WEDNESDAYS	⎬ Arrival	WEDNESDAYS	⎬ Arrival
SATURDAYS	⎭ Rotterdam 8.30 a.m.	SATURDAYS	⎭ Hull - - 8.0 a.m.

FARES (inclusive of meals)

1st April to 30th Sept. 1959
(dates inclusive)

REDUCED RATES

1st Oct. 1959 to 31st Mar. 1960

PER BERTH

	Single £ s. d.	Return £ s. d.	Single	Return
Two-Berth Cabins - -	6 10 0	13 0 0	£5	£ 9
Single-Berth Cabins - -	7 10 0	15 0 0	£6	£11
Two-Berth Cabin-De-Luxe	8 0 0	16 0 0	£7	£12

(Children under 14 years of age, half fare, or free if under 1 year of age and not requiring separate accommodation)

Passengers wishing to stay on board the vessel at Rotterdam may do so by making prior arrangements with the Passenger Department.

Charge including breakfast £1 per night   (Children under 14) 10/- per night

WEEKEND TICKETS. During the period 1st October, 1959, to 31st March, 1960, Weekend Tickets are available at an inclusive cost of **£10 10s. 0d.** for any type of accommodation, leaving Hull on Saturday night, with an arrival back at Hull on Tuesday Morning. The ticket includes all meals at sea and dinner, bed and breakfast on board at Rotterdam.

Considerable care has been directed to the provision of a bright and pleasant dining saloon with a first-class cuisine

DINING SALOON
m.v. "Bolton Abbey"

By 1959, the fleet seemed fit for the future and the pride felt was expressed. This is evidenced by this extract from p.2 for the main Hull–Rotterdam service. The mini-cruise is nothing new. A £10 weekend ticket existed.

Opposite: Another recommended source, although not always easy to find, is *Transport Age*. This was very different from the *British Railways Magazine*. The latter was primarily a staff magazine. *Transport Age* was erudite and glossy. It employed colour widely. It was a printed version of a British Transport film. Respectable artists signed its covers. In the more aggressive era of the 1960s it sank. It covered the whole realm of the British Transport Commission, showcasing many innovations destined for a short life.

Between 1957 and 1965 thirty-three issues appeared. I do not think it lasted long after that. Our extract looks at No.17 from April 1961 and the start of a feature on Hull Docks. Despite its upbeat presentation and mention of many new industries in town, it did not foresee the container and roll-on/roll-off revolution about to arrive. Imagery showed new transit sheds being built at King George Dock when what the new technology would demand was acres of hard standing for vehicles and containers. AHL's new Riverside Quay was shown off.

Oftentimes it is said inherent conservatism did for the nationalised transport industry, and reading *Transport Age*, one is at once grabbed by its romantic style, while realising that perhaps this was blinding itself. Hull Docks inherited huge amounts of tradition. One author wrote of its late-Victorian owner (the North Eastern Railway) that they were the 'principal dock owning railway company in Britain'. Our extract itself starts: 'A port like Hull, with seven centuries of individual tradition cannot be modernised according to a set formula.' Wasn't upstart Felixstowe (and even Parkeston Quay, then less than a century old) lucky?

New Look
for Hull Docks

Harry Miller

A PORT like Hull, with seven centuries of individual tradition, cannot be modernised according to a set formula: innovations must fit in with the character of the place. The massive reconstruction scheme now under way at the port reflects this individuality. While careful of local idiosyncrasies, it is quietly introducing to the docks and quays of Britain's third port a range of equipment as modern as any in Europe.

The Second World War made this process easier to initiate. Port and city, interdependent to an uncommon degree, were shattered in the same assault. Streets crumbled beyond recognition. In the docks, sturdy timber structures that had resisted the salt water of the Humber for a generation burned to a cinder. Now, for many years, a new city centre has been rising, with broad shopping streets and gay gardens in place of the

Cargo for Sweden: an 83-ton roller being loaded by floating crane at Albert Dock, Hull. Ties with Scandinavia are particularly close

SPRING and AUTUMN ROUND VOYAGES 1963

HULL - ROTTERDAM

by

ASSOCIATED HUMBER LINES LTD.

AHL issued their own mini-cruise literature, not that the phrase was used. This is a 1963 piece and, inside, one of the drawings showed off *Bolton Abbey* and text detailed how to make the best of her as a hotel while in port.

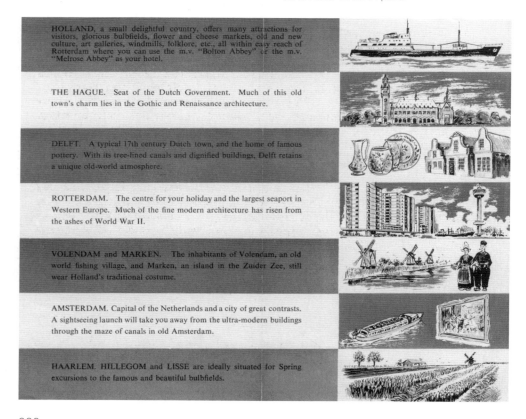

HOLLAND, a small delightful country, offers many attractions for visitors, glorious bulbfields, flower and cheese markets, old and new culture, art galleries, windmills, folklore, etc., all within easy reach of Rotterdam where you can use the m.v. "Bolton Abbey" or the m.v. "Melrose Abbey" as your hotel.

THE HAGUE. Seat of the Dutch Government. Much of this old town's charm lies in the Gothic and Renaissance architecture.

DELFT. A typical 17th century Dutch town, and the home of famous pottery. With its tree-lined canals and dignified buildings, Delft retains a unique old-world atmosphere.

ROTTERDAM. The centre for your holiday and the largest seaport in Western Europe. Much of the fine modern architecture has risen from the ashes of World War II.

VOLENDAM and MARKEN. The inhabitants of Volendam, an old world fishing village, and Marken, an island in the Zuider Zee, still wear Holland's traditional costume.

AMSTERDAM. Capital of the Netherlands and a city of great contrasts. A sightseeing launch will take you away from the ultra-modern buildings through the maze of canals in old Amsterdam.

HAARLEM, HILLEGOM and LISSE are ideally situated for Spring excursions to the famous and beautiful bulbfields.

III.—THE NORTH OF ENGLAND TO HOLLAND.

Via Hull and Rotterdam.

An improved service, with new and fast steamers, was established by this route between England and the Continent on July 1, 1908. Through fares are now in operation between the principal English railway stations and Rotterdam, and *vice versâ* ; also from the principal North Eastern Railway stations to the chief places in Holland and Germany, and to Bâle in Switzerland. This route is the *cheapest* between the *North of England* and the Continent ; and special boat-trains in connection with the departure of each steamer are run to the new North Eastern Railway Riverside Quay Station at Hull. The service is maintained by a fleet of five up-to-date steamers, named respectively *Jervaulx Abbey, Kirkham Abbey, Rievaulx Abbey, Selby Abbey,* and *Whitby Abbey.* On each boat the saloons and state-rooms are situated amidships, and the accommodation offers every comfort and convenience for passengers. The vessels are lighted throughout by electricity. The sailings have been so arranged that dinner is served whilst in smooth water. Other refreshments at a moderate tariff are always obtainable (except during the serving of dinner). The boats sail from Hull every weekday at 6.15 P.M., and from Rotterdam every weekday at 8 P.M. (Dutch time). The boats arrive at Rotterdam at 10.30 A.M. the following morning, and at Hull at 11.30 A.M.

The idea that an *Abbey* vessel formed the Hull–Netherlands link was then in its last decade. The *Abbey* tradition went back to 1908 and to close this group we eyeball the presentation of those steamers at their inception through a paragraph in Black's guidebook to Holland (1908 edition).

north
sea
ferries

H U L L — R O T T E R D A M

HULL

ROTTERDAM

The operation that changed the Humber more than any other was North Sea Ferries. This was a partnership venture which ultimately P&O has come to dominate (1996 was the last 'independent' NSF brochure). They in turn would bury the North Sea Ferries name in 2003. Not that the evolution of branding does anything to downplay the success of the venture which has seen ever larger vessels built, usually in pairs, for the route.

Vehicle carriage is the mainstay and luxury passenger facilities. As such the connection to rail traffic is limited. A large file could fill with North Sea Ferries items but in our context the selection is just of the first year brochure when the *Norwave/Norwind* pair were introduced to the route. There was no rail side connection at either terminal. Bus links to the town railway stations were advertised in the brochures. A print code helpfully reveals that there were 75,000 of these brochures in June 1965.

Over the years my guess is that those passengers who have made their way to Hull using public transport for a North Sea Ferry connection have more than likely used coach connections. Advertised coach links from Scotland and elsewhere to the ferry terminal have been in existence for many years and have produced their own National Express leaflets.

The example is from the last couple of years of North Sea Ferries' independence and their logo graces the leaflet which, in the main, is a standard National Express production. Scottish Citylink have also issued publicity which allowed North Sea Ferries on to the cover. Detailed information about this ferry link service is also in the full National Express timetable and, if you can find any, a fascinating subset called the *International Express Guide*. There were certainly at least six editions of this between 1986 and 1988 and it is a goldmine of information for the ferry enthusiast.

Service 794 / 382

HULL DOCKS

NORTH SEA FERRIES *First in Ferries!*

from
North Wales, North West, North East & Scotland

HULL TO BANGOR — FROM £23.00 RETURN

HULL TO GLASGOW — FROM £24.50 RETURN

HULL TO LIVERPOOL — FROM £13.50 RETURN

HULL TO INVERNESS — FROM £37.50 RETURN

16 May 1994 - 30 October 1994

NATIONAL EXPRESS ≫

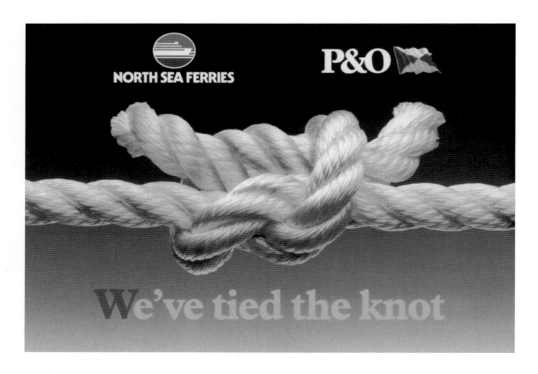

The year of amalgamation with P&O was 1996 and this marriage brochure marks the moment. It is now a very long way from the time when railway companies and train connections were the essential component of Humber passenger shipping.

Chapter 7

To Tyne Commission Quay

At Hartlepool on 24 March 2001 the dredger *Goole Bight* offered a link back to railway shipping. She had been built in 1958 for British Transport Docks so, while not quite a railway ship, she was certainly in the lineage and was definitely a British Transport Commission ship. She left Goole and ABP on 31 March 2000. After undertaking some work at Hartlepool, she was sold again and became the *Abigail H*. That name intrigues. Her owners had become Humber Work Boats. Is it only coincidence that it rhymes with the famous Harker's vessels, the ...*dale H* series?

Hartlepool was North Eastern Railway-owned from 1857 and vitally associated with the north-east coal trade. It retains rail-connected facilities in 2005.

Table 58

Newcastle and Tyne Commission Quay
(Bergen Line and Fred Olsen Line Boat Trains)

Weekdays

Miles			B		SO		A								
—	8 LONDON KING'S CROSS .. .. d		09 00	..	09 00	..	11 00	..	..	..	..	..	..	..
— 8¼	NEWCASTLE .... d TYNE COMMISSION QUAY .. a		14 10 14 45	....	14 10 14 45	.. ..	15 45 16 20	....	....	..	..	..	..	....

Weekdays | **Sundays**

Miles			G			L SO	H				K		
— 8¼	TYNE COMMISSION QUAY .. d NEWCASTLE .... a		08 35 09 10	.. ....	.. ..	11 23 11 52	13 15 13 50	.. ....	.. ..	.. ..	14 50 15 25	.. ....	..
—	8 LONDON KING'S CROSS .. a		14 16	..	..	17 49	19 30	..		..	..	20 11	..	..

A Mondays 6, 13, May, 16, 23 and 30 September, Thursdays 9, 16 May and 6 June to 26 September, Saturdays 11 May, and 1 June to 21 September

B Mondays 20 May to 16 September, 31 March and 7 April, Tuesdays 7, 14 May, 24 September to 5 November and 10 December to 29 April (except 24 December, 1 and 8 April), Wednesdays 22 May to 18 September and 2, 9 April

G Mondays, Wednesdays and Fridays 17 June to 6 September

H Mondays 6, 13 May, 16 and 23 September, Thursdays 9, 16 May, and 6 June to 8 June to 21 September

K 29 September only

L 1 June only

Heavy figures denote through carriages
For general notes see page 2

For full particulars of sailings from and to
Tyne Commission Quay see pages 54 to 56

In reaching Newcastle and the Tyne, this voyage is coming to its end. It is also the chapter whose Eastern Region of British Railways connection is most tenuous. Neither the passenger facilities on the Tyne nor the ferries from the river were railway-owned. Despite this, the importance of the Scandinavian connections from Tyne Commission Quay ensured that railway-issued timetables covered the services and that a special station with its own trains was created.

Tyne Commission Quay station at North Shields opened as Albert Edward Dock in February 1900. It became a public station in 1928, following a major rebuild of the facilities, and was closed from 4 May 1970. It was firmly within the North Eastern Railway, later LNER, umbrella. The vagaries of BR organisation mean that only three issues of the official Eastern Region timetable contained it, after the abolition of the North Eastern Region in 1967.

Here it is with its own timetable in the public volume for May 1968. The run-down was swift. Through carriages from London were being worked down to the quay in this timetable. The ER timetables for both May 1969 and May 1970 contained the quay table but now only diesel multiple unit connections operated. The presence of the trains in the May 1970 issue was a great anomaly. The usual notice of closure never appeared in the public timetable, but none of the trains shown operated. Instead a bus link from Newcastle Central station was introduced, which has run ever since.

Above left: Tyne Commission Quay and its associated services becomes what drives this chapter. The location is, in 2004, the river's central hub for the European ferries. Proper cruise ships are even calling. In days gone, however, not all the services used Tyne Commission Quay.

An informative and often attractive source of information is the *Port of Tyne* handbook. This is the cover of the 1957 edition when the authority was the Tyne Improvement Commission.

It is this volume which reveals that, in 1956, 126,000 passengers went through the river mouth, mainly to/from Scandinavian destinations. At the time the three core passenger operators were Bergen Line, Fred. Olsen Line and DFDS.

Despite the cover's signed artwork – 'DHL' – no information was provided about the ship entering the river.

Above right: In 1993, the quayside at Newcastle still displayed this entirely outdated Tyne-Tees sign. One of the destinations was London (the Tyne to the Thames by passenger steamer). New ships had been built for this as late as 1923 when the *Bernicia* and *Hadrian* were completed. The depression, coupled to the motor coach, closed this ancient route to passengers in 1936. Freighter sailings by the company continued until 1976. They had been part of the Coast Lines group since the Second World War.

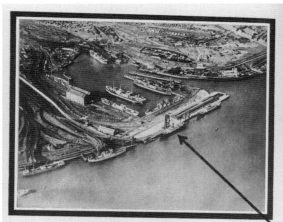

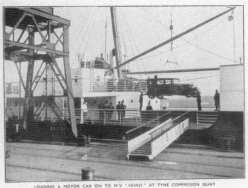

LOADING A MOTOR CAR ON TO M.V "VENUS" AT TYNE COMMISSION QUAY

It is nice to be reminded that taking one's car abroad was a subject for the sales pitch in the 1930s. Surviving advertising materials from that time will be limited. Several of the following items survived due to the foresight of some unknown individual back then who bound them together. These extracts show the cover and the first two pages of a brochure issued at the outset of the car-touring revolution. 'B&N Line' is another term for Bergen line and a good aerial view of Tyne Commission Quay is afforded.

Where the coaling staithes are located (left) is today's main passenger terminal, Tyne Commission Quay and station are indicated by the arrow. The image dates from soon after the 1928 development. The quay was still there in 2004 and accommodates cruise liners. The station has gone and the whole of the enclosed Albert Edward Dock is redeveloped as a marina and for housing. One of its occupants is the *Earl of Zetland*, a former Shetland ferry of 1939.

At this time there was nothing approaching a car ferry to use. The two Bergen Line ships berthed in the aerial photo would have been the 1915 *Jupiter* (behind) and the 1920 *Leda* (forward). These were to be well used names.

B & N LINE ROYAL MAIL

ENGLAND TO NORWAY
IN LESS THAN A DAY

LARGEST AND FASTEST SHIP
ENGLAND TO SCANDINAVIA

ENGLAND TO NORWAY
IN LESS THAN A DAY

WORLD'S FASTEST *Venus* MOTOR VESSEL
7000 tons displacement

TUESDAYS and SATURDAYS
at 8 p.m. from
NEWCASTLE-ON-TYNE
TO

BERGEN
21 HOURS

OSLO
35 HOURS

STOCKHOLM
49 HOURS

TRONDHJEM
48 HOURS

connecting services with all
Scandinavian destinations
QUICKEST ROUTE
SHORTEST SEA PASSAGE

Reserve berths and obtain tickets from the Agents :
THE NORWEGIAN STATE RAILWAYS,
Norway House, 21/24 Cockspur Street, London, S.W. 1.

The car-touring brochure's image of a car being craned aboard refers to MV *Venus*. This 1931 vessel was the fastest motor ship anywhere when built, capable of more than twenty knots. This sense of speed is conveyed by the cover and contents of this Bergen Line brochure issued at the start of her service. She would continue to visit the Tyne until 1966 despite a wartime record that included being sunk at Hamburg during an Allied air raid.

ENGLAND to NORWAY *in* less than a day

NEW MOTOR SHIP "VENUS" WORLD'S FASTEST.
LARGEST VESSEL BETWEEN ENGLAND AND THE CONTINENT.

THE introduction in May, 1931, of the new twin-screw Motor Ship, "VENUS," in regular passenger service between England and Norway, marks an epoch in travel.

"England to Norway in less than a day" is a slogan which will be a continuous reminder that Nature's Wonderland is brought many hours nearer to England. The B. & N. Line Royal Mail (Bergenske Steamship Co., Bergen) vessels have maintained for many years the most frequent regular passenger service—three sailings each week—between England (Newcastle-on-Tyne) and Norway (Bergen), and by the shortest sea route. The new ship, "VENUS," will sail twice each week—Tuesdays

— 3 —

That *vade mecum*, the *British Railways Continental Handbook*, for the summer of 1950 offers value on several counts. Here is its presentation of the Bergen Line route. The table is an inter-capital one: London to Oslo. The named boat train connection – *The Norseman* – is in evidence, as are supplementary workings down to the Tyne Commission Quay.

The Norseman was a new train for the 1950 timetable and only ran for three months a year, otherwise the connection was made by through carriages. As a special boat train it was made up of ten coaches and ran the 188 miles from London to York non-stop in 201 minutes. The headboard of *The Norseman* re-appeared on the final diesel multiple unit working in 1970 and I do not doubt it is still in existence.

The exact ships are named against their sailings. *Astrea* was a Finnish motor ship that the company managed to secretly buy in the Second World War. *Venus* was the 1931 ship back in full fettle. *Jupiter* was the 1915 steamer still in traffic until 1955. The Fred. Olsen ships were itemised likewise as the SS *Bali* and the MV *Bretagne*. *Bali* had been Tyne-Tees's 1929 *Alnwick*. *Bretagne* was a 1937 motor ship which survived the war. Her Newcastle appearances were as a prolonged stopgap pending the arrival of the early 1950s *Blenheim* and *Braemar* pair. The 1950 timetable was therefore an interim statement reflecting post-war conditions in which the new boat train was the promise of better things.

As the 24-hour system for Railway Time operates on the Continent, it is used in this time-table thus :—12.00 noon, 18.00 6 p.m., 24.00 arrival midnight, 0.00 departure midnight.

LONDON — NORWAY
STAVANGER—OSLO—BERGEN
NEWCASTLE—BERGEN ROUTE
(BERGEN LINE.)

MAY 14 to SEPTEMBER 30.

OUTWARDS.		SAILINGS OF M.S. VENUS.		SAILINGS OF M.S. ASTREA AND S.S. JUPITER.		
		May 27 to June 3.	June 7 to Sept. 30.	May 14 to May 30. (Sats. excepted)	May 20 only	June 6 to Sept. 30.
		A	B	A	A	A
London (King's Cross) ... ... dep.		9 30	9c10	10 05	12 20	12c00
York ... ... dep.		13 25	12c34	14 05	16 14	15c47
Newcastle (Central) ... ... arr.		15 07	14c04	15 51	17 55	17c31
Newcastle (Central) ... ... dep.		15 25	14c12	16 20	18 12	17c48
Tyne Commission Quay ... ... arr.		15 55	14c47	16 55	18 47	18c23
Tyne Commission Quay... ... ... dep.		16 30			19 00	
Stavanger ... ... arr.					19a00	
Stavanger (Rail) ... ... dep.					20a05d	
Oslo ... ... arr.					7b30d	
Stavanger ... ... dep.					21a30	
Haugesund ... ... arr.		15a00			0b30	
Bergen ... ... arr.					6b00	

		Until June 9. R S	From June 10. R S	Until June 9. R	From June 10. R	June 10 to Aug. 27. R
Bergen (Rail) ... ... dep.		19a30	19a50	7b30	7b50	9b00
Oslo ... ... arr.		7b00	7b00	19b50	19b50	20b50

a—Second day. b—Third day. c—After Sept. 24 these timings are subject to alteration d—Commences June 13. Note "S" will also apply.

THROUGH CARRIAGES. ✕—Restaurant Car.

A—King's Cross—Tyne Commission Quay, 1 & 3 Cl. King's Cross—Newcastle (Central), ✕.
B—*THE NORSEMAN* Boat train, King's Cross—Tyne Commission Quay, 1 & 3 Cl. and ✕,
R—✕ for whole or part of journey.
S—Conveys 2nd and 3rd Class Sleeping Cars. 3rd Class only for non-Sleeping Car passengers.

SPECIAL BOAT TRAINS FOR PASSENGERS FROM PROVINCIAL STATIONS TO TYNE COMMISSION QUAY.

Passengers from stations not served by the trains from London (King's Cross) and local passengers travel on the under-mentioned special boat trains from Newcastle (Central) to Tyne Commission Quay :—

	Passengers for M.S. VENUS	Passengers for M.S. ASTREA or S.S. JUPITER
Newcastle (Central)	15.00	16.20
Tyne Commission Quay	15.35	16.50

SAILINGS—NEWCASTLE TO BERGEN.

Mon. May 15	Astrea*	Wed. July 5	Jupiter*	Wed. Aug. 16	Venus
Wed. ,, 17	Jupiter*	Sat. ,, 8	Venus	Wed. ,, 16	Jupiter*
Sat. ,, 20	Astrea*	Sat. ,, 8	Astrea*	Sat. ,, 19	Venus
Mon. ,, 22	Jupiter*	Mon. ,, 10	Jupiter*	Sat. ,, 19	Astrea*
Wed. ,, 24	Astrea*	Wed. ,, 12	Venus	Mon. ,, 21	Jupiter*
Sat. ,, 27	Venus	Wed. ,, 12	Astrea*	Wed. ,, 23	Venus
Tue. ,, 30	Astrea*	Sat. ,, 15	Venus	Wed. ,, 23	Astrea*
Wed. ,, 31	Venus	Sat. ,, 15	Jupiter*	Sat. ,, 26	Venus
Sat. June 3	Venus	Mon. ,, 17	Astrea*	Sat. ,, 26	Jupiter*
Tue. ,, 6	Jupiter*	Wed. ,, 19	Venus	Mon. ,, 28	Astrea*
Wed. ,, 7	Venus	Wed. ,, 19	Jupiter*	Wed. ,, 30	Venus
Sat. ,, 10	Venus	Sat. ,, 22	Venus	Wed. ,, 30	Jupiter*
Mon. ,, 12	Jupiter*	Sat. ,, 22	Astrea*	Sat. Sept. 2	Venus
Wed. ,, 14	Venus	Mon. ,, 24	Jupiter*	Sat. ,, 2	Astrea*
Wed. ,, 14	Astrea*	Wed. ,, 26	Venus	Mon. ,, 4	Jupiter*
Sat. ,, 17	Venus	Wed. ,, 26	Astrea*	Wed. ,, 6	Venus
Sat. ,, 17	Jupiter*	Sat. ,, 29	Venus	Wed. ,, 6	Astrea*
Mon. ,, 19	Astrea*	Sat. ,, 29	Jupiter*	Sat. ,, 9	Venus
Wed. ,, 21	Venus	Mon. ,, 31	Astrea*	Sat. ,, 9	Jupiter*
Wed. ,, 21	Jupiter*	Wed. Aug. 2	Venus	Tue. ,, 12	Astrea*
Sat. ,, 24	Venus	Wed. ,, 2	Jupiter*	Wed. ,, 13	Venus
Sat. ,, 24	Astrea*	Sat. ,, 5	Venus	Sat. ,, 16	Venus
Mon. ,, 26	Jupiter*	Sat. ,, 5	Astrea*	Tue. ,, 19	Astrea*
Wed. ,, 28	Venus	Mon. ,, 7	Jupiter*	Wed. ,, 20	Venus
Wed. ,, 28	Venus	Wed. ,, 9	Venus	Sat. ,, 23	Venus
Sat. July 1	Venus	Wed. ,, 9	Astrea*	Tue. ,, 26	Astrea*
Sat. ,, 1	Jupiter*	Sat. ,, 12	Venus	Wed. ,, 27	Venus
Mon. ,, 3	Astrea*	Sat. ,, 12	Jupiter*	Sat. ,, 30	Venus
Wed. ,, 5	Venus	Mon. ,, 14	Astrea*		

*—Via Stavanger and Haugesund.

For further information respecting the above Services to and from Norway apply to :—
BERGEN STEAMSHIP COMPANY, LTD.
NORWAY HOUSE, 21-24, COCKSPUR STREET, LONDON, S.W.1,
OR
BRITISH RAILWAYS' TICKET AND INFORMATION BUREAU,
71, REGENT STREET, LONDON, W.1,
AND PRINCIPAL TRAVEL AGENCIES.

TYNE COMMISSION QUAY TO NEWCASTLE

WEEKDAYS — Empty trains from Tyne Commission Quay to Heaton Carriage Sidings may convey passengers to Walker Gate when required and will then be signalled Class A — **SUNDAYS**

UP

Mileage M C			A 4435	A 4433		A (To King's Cross) 73		A (To King's Cross) 4471	A 4479	A 4481	A (To King's Cross) 75	C (ECS) 4455	C (ECS) 4475	A 4483
				MO		ThO		FO	ThO	FO	SO	Q TWX	WFX	
0	0	TYNE COMM. QUAY .. dep	am 8 6	am 8 35	..	am 9 10	..	am 10 35	am 10 40	am 11 10	am 12 20	PM 2†35	PM 3†0	PM 3 0
1	79	Percy Main North .... arr	8 16	8 45	..	9 20	..	10 45	11 50	11 20	12 30	2 45	3 10	3 10
		.... dep	8 26	8 55	..	9 25	..	10 50	11 0	11 30	12 35	2 55	3 20	3 20
		Heaton Carriage Sidings arr	..	..	..	..	..	..	..	..	..	3†10	3†35	..
8	19	NEWCASTLE .. .. .. arr	8 43	9 10	..	9 40	..	11 5	11 15	11 45	12 50	..	..	3 35

Column footnotes:

- 4433 (MO): Until 8th June inclusive. Also runs Thursdays until 30th April inclusive except 28th December, Fridays until 1st May inclusive except 28th December
- 73 (ThO): From 9th to 23rd October inclusive. Also runs Monday 19th September
- 4471 (FO): Runs 19th September only
- 4479 (ThO): Runs 25th September and 2nd October only
- 4481 (FO): Runs 19th September only
- 75 (SO): Runs 26th September only
- 4455 (TWX): Until 2nd May inclusive, except 23rd, 25th, 27th December. Also runs Friday 19th September
- 4483 (Sundays): From 28th September to 26th April inclusive

This is the Tyne Commission Quay service in the winter of 1958 as shown in the North Eastern Region working timetable. Access to the quay was complicated. Approaching from Newcastle a train would turn north before Percy Main station and join the Blyth & Tyne Railway. Then it reversed before descending steeply under the Coast Circle along which it had arrived, and dropped down to river level at the quay. This explains the ten minutes at Percy Main North signal box during which the train reversed. The timetable includes an option enabling passengers to return to Walker Gate on an empty coaching stock train. This perhaps enabled friends and relatives and others left behind at the quay to have a route back to normality. Walker Gate was a station on the electrified Coast Circle with a frequent service back into Newcastle.

CONTINENTAL
SERVICES

BY
RAIL
AND
SEA

BRITISH RAILWAYS

FROM NEWCASTLE,
HULL AND GOOLE
1962

This brochure is included partly for the artwork of a foreshortened Class 40 diesel and partly because I know of no others in series with it. It is specifically a North Eastern Region shipping item from 1962. It has interest in just that regional focus.

the *daytime*

ANGLO-SCOTTISH CAR CARRIER

EDINBURGH ●

NEWCASTLE ● ⇨ **Norway link** to Bergen and Oslo

LONDON ●

WEEKDAYS, 30th MAY to 1st OCTOBER 1960

BRITISH RAILWAYS

Not for the first time Motorail services enter the account. This time the British target station was realistically near. Several of *the Daytime Anglo-Scottish Car Carrier* leaflets of the period used artwork which made the potential link with the sailings from the Tyne explicit. This is the summer 1960 issue. Inside, a diagram showed the motorist how to drive from Newcastle Central to Tyne Commission Quay. Summer 1960 was the first time this service ran, and a handbill for its launch made the shipping link as well.

Olsen's 1938 motor ships *Black Prince* and *Black Watch* carried the most British of bow figureheads. The Highlander on the bow of *Black Watch* must have irked the Germans when they seized the vessel. The names carry power. In 2004, Olsen's cruising fleet was *Black Prince*, *Black Watch* and *Braemar*. In between times, those names have been re-used several times and, to utterly confuse, Olsen's also got into the habit of changing names during the season with a cruising and a ferry name!

To replace the 1938 ships, the *Blenheim*, in 1951, and the *Braemar*, in 1953, were commissioned. In 1961, at the time of this leaflet showing the *Braemar*, they were well established. The 'crystal palace' is visible – a special sun lounge, streamlined like the rest of the ship. The leaflet called the two vessels 'motor-liners' and it featured the train connections, including the new car-carrier, in detail. *Braemar* was to manage twenty-two years on the Newcastle–Oslo run. She became the last passenger-only vessel running out of Newcastle.

BERGEN LINE
Summer Service

ENGLAND-NORWAY

May to September

1955

BERGEN LINE
ENGLAND-NORWAY
WINTER SERVICE
OCTOBER 3 1960
to APRIL 30 1961

Bergen Line, like Olsen, was producing a generous assortment of English language brochures. They had many distinct products including the direct Norway ferry from Newcastle, coastal cruising around Norway, and cruises much further afield. They had commissioned the *Meteor* in 1955 primarily for cruising. On the run to the Tyne the *Venus* and the *Leda* dominated. The *Venus* was an oft-repeated name. The second use was on the 1931 vessel which after many adventures lasted well into the post-war period. Bergen's first new post-war ferry for the Tyne was launched in 1952 at Swan Hunter's on the Tyne. This was the speedy turbine-powered *Leda*, rumoured to have made twenty-seven knots. It is her profile that graces these 1955 and 1960 leaflets. She lasted with Bergen until 1974. *Venus* and *Jupiter*, which were established Bergen Line names, were next used after 1966, when, in a joint twenty-year arrangement with Olsen, the rather extraordinary ritual of swapping names and duties commenced on the introduction of car ferries.

LONDON—NEWCASTLE—OSLO

VIA KRISTIANSAND

(FRED. OLSEN NORWAY LINE)

The sister ships BLENHEIM and BRAEMAR (Motor Vessels) will sail according to the following schedule:

Miles	OUTWARDS	Mondays May 27 to June 10	June 17 to Sept. 2	Wednesdays May 29 to June 12	June 19 to Sept. 4	Saturdays June 1 to June 15	June 22 to Sept. 7
—	London (King's Cross) ... ... dep	9 00	9 30	9 00	9 30	9 05	9 30
268	Newcastle ... ... dep	14 04	14 24	14 04	14 24	14 32	14 30
275	Newcastle (Tyne Commission Quay) arr	14 39	15 00	14 39	15 00	15 02	15 05
	Newcastle (Tyne Commission Quay) dep	16 30		16 30		16 30	
698	Kristiansand ... ... { arr			17a00		17a00	
				17a30		17a30	
880	Oslo (Vippetangen) ... ... arr	7b00		7b00		7b00	

a—Second day   b—Third day

	INWARDS	Mondays	Wednesdays	Saturdays
	Oslo (Vippetangen) ... ... dep	16 00	16 00	16 00
	Kristiansand ... ... { arr		2a15	2a15
	{ dep		3a00	3a00
	Newcastle (Tyne Commission Quay) ... arr	7b00	7b00	7b00

		May 29 to June 12	June 19 to Sept. 2	May 31 to June 14	June 21 to Sept. 6	May 27 to June 10	June 17 to Sept. 2
	Newcastle (Tyne Commission Quay) ... dep	8b35	8b35	8b35	8b35	8b35	8b35
	Newcastle ... ... arr	9b08	9b08	9b08	9b08	9b08	9b08
	London (King's Cross) ... ... arr	14b21	14b10	14b21	14b10	14b21	14b10

a—Second day   b—Third day

THROUGH CARRIAGES Restaurant car ✕.
King's Cross-Tyne Commission Quay & vice versa 1 & 2 Cl.   King's Cross-Newcastle & vice versa ✕.
(Services from Sept. 9 will be quoted upon application)

On certain days a limited train for the conveyance of private cars and accompanying passengers runs between London (Holloway Car Loading Bay, Caledonian Road, London, N.7) and Newcastle. Full particulars from Traffic Manager, Car Sleeper Office, British Railways, Eastern Region, Great Northern House, 79/81 Euston Road, London, N.W.1

Tickets and reservations may be obtained from principal travel agencies

General Passenger Agents in the United Kingdom:
NORWEGIAN STATE RAILWAYS,   P. H. Matthiessen & Co., Ltd.,
21/24, Cockspur Street, London, S.W.1   54, Pilgrim Street, Newcastle-on-Tyne, I
Telephone: WHI 6666 Telegrams: NORSTARYS   Telephone: 26171 Telegrams: NORSK

For further information apply to:
FRED. OLSEN LINES PASSENGER LIAISON SERVICE
33/34, Bury Street, London, E.C.3
Telephone: AVEnue 4699

ASSOCIATED HUMBER LINES LTD.

GOOLE—COPENHAGEN SERVICE
(Limited accommodation for passengers)

Sailings:
From Goole ... ... Fridays
From Copenhagen ... ... Fridays

Further particulars may be obtained from the Port Agents named below to whom applications for tickets and accommodation on the above services should be addressed:

Associated Humber Lines Ltd. (Goole Steam Shipping), Goole
Telegrams: "Despatch, Goole" Telephone: Goole 1103

DET FORENEDE DAMPSKIBS—SELSKAB,
COPENHAGEN
UNITED STEAMSHIP CO. LTD.

NEWCASTLE—COPENHAGEN via ESBJERG

M.V. PARKESTON with 1st and 2nd class accommodation

Miles	OUTWARDS		June 15 to Sept. 14 Tues. and Sats.
—	Newcastle ... ... dep		13A30
341	Esbjerg ... ... (next day) arr. abt.		14 00
	Esbjerg Station ... ... dep		15B25
553	Copenhagen H. ... ... arr		21 28
	INWARDS		June 13 to Sept. 14 Thurs. and Suns.
	Copenhagen H. ... ... dep		11C40
	Esbjerg ... ... { arr		16 50
	{ dep		17 15
	Newcastle ... ... (next day) arr. abt.		18A00

A—Convenient British Railways services are available between Newcastle and principal stations in the North of England and Scotland. Passengers are conveyed free between Newcastle Central station and the steamer berth at Newcastle Corporation Quay, No. 11 Wharf
B—Special boat train
C—" Englaenderen " 1st and 2nd Class. Seats may be reserved in advance

The address of

BRITISH RAILWAYS
GENERAL AGENCY
in
SCANDINAVIA
is
Norrmalmstorg I, STOCKHOLM 7

Telegrams: Britrailway Stockholm   Telephone: Stockholm 21/86/90

This page and next page: As elsewhere, the 1960s were a decade of critical change, and the sad fact is that, while at the decade's end the story of the passenger ships serving the Tyne was as interesting as ever (and would remain so), the railway connection was almost destroyed. One last spurt of railway effort was this development from the *British Railways Continental Handbook* in the country booklets well examined in the Harwich chapter. The one containing Tyne shipping services (as well as Harwich and Humber material) was *Scandinavia and Finland* which would be published through to 1973. This is it in 1963 with its John Cort cover. The two pages used show Olsen's Norway route, an AHL sailing from the Humber, and the DFDS service which, in the early 1960s, appears almost as a token presence compared with how DFDS were to expand their Tyne sailings. The vessel was the revolutionary, though by then antique, 1925 motor ship *Parkeston*. Her DFDS career ended in 1964. Note that DFDS were then sailing from downstream of the Tyne Bridge at 'Newcastle Corporation Quay No.11 Wharf'.

This series of brochures would later have to cope with the closure of Tyne Commission Quay and bustitution. One paragraph towards the bottom of p.22 reflects the new breeze, in yet another reference to the car-carrying train from London.

Scandinavia & Finland

by train and ship

John Coit

SERVICES AND FARES

BRITISH RAILWAYS

26 May to 28 September 1963 inclusive

The Newcastle DFDS sailings were, in the main, DFDS brochures already seen at Harwich. There were brochures issued solely for the Newcastle–Esbjerg sailings, and a run from about 1958 until 1963 with this artwork were focused by name (inside) on the pioneering *Parkeston*. *Parkeston* was replaced by *Kronsprins Frederik* for the summer 1964 timetable.

TO SCANDINAVIA
AND
THE CONTINENT
VIA NEWCASTLE-ESBJERG

1963

DFDS
THE UNITED STEAMSHIP COMPANY LIMITED
COPENHAGEN

TO SCANDINAVIA
AND
THE CONTINENT
VIA NEWCASTLE-ESBJERG

DFDS
THE UNITED STEAMSHIP COMPANY LIMITED
COPENHAGEN

1968

The next sight of the route in 1968 shows more change. On the cover of the Newcastle brochure that year was a nice image of the *Kronsprins Frederik*, but the brochure specified the sister – *Kronsprincesse Ingrid*. In effect the Tyne was receiving cast-offs from Harwich where the car ferry revolution was making its impact. The leaflet made it clear that DFDS expected and wished to carry cars to Denmark but did not make it explicit that they would still need to be craned on.

Winston Churchill had sent the *Kronsprincesse Ingrid* to the Tyne in 1967. Later the Churchill would become closely associated with the river. The Ingrid was replaced by the *Princessan*, and then the *England* (in 1974). The Esbjerg service was moved to Tyne Commission Quay (*Princessan* was working from there by 1970). *Winston Churchill* first became a Tyne regular in 1978. This was not on the Esbjerg run but on a new route to Gothenburg which was a collaboration with Tor Line. She certainly graced the cover of the Gothenburg brochures.

On 5 July 1992, she was entering the Tyne from Esbjerg, and still this 1967 ship had another four years before her withdrawal. Charting the DFDS changes would be complex but in 1992 she was in Scandinavian Seaways colours although with the DFDS funnel logo this was really a re-branding exercise. One Scandinavian Seaways item I only know of by repute, although dating only from 1993 (the year in which a route from Newcastle to Hamburg was opened on 2 April), has the *Winston Churchill* proudly featured on an opening day brochure. A file can fill with the already obsolete Scandinavian Seaways material but, as on the Humber, the rail connection had become marginal.

The last three decades of Tyne passenger shipping have been very complicated and it is not the brief of this volume to examine this.

Just one hint of the complexity comes in this Norway Line brochure. 'Complexity' is chosen very deliberately. Several reports in *Ships Monthly* have to be interpreted and, reading them, it is not difficult to see just how much intriguing literature the 1980s must have produced. The 1985 season was a key season. The Bergen–Stavanger services had been in decline in the hands of Bergen Line/Olsen (as a joint operation since 1976) and then even with DFDS for a while after 1982. A new company was formed called Norway Line, and one of the regular favourites was chartered: the 1966 *Jupiter*/*Black Watch* and *Venus*/*Black Prince*, adding to their name-changing abilities a whole saga of working the Tyne–Norway service for a range of operators.

Here then is the 1966 *Jupiter* on the cover of the 1989 Norway Line brochure. By then she had been sold from Bergen Line to Norway Line.

250

Other modern names whose Tyne-based literature can be found include Color Line which was a consortium of Norway Line/Fred. Olsen/Jahre Line (1991–98) and, from 1999, Fjord Line (DFDS bought Fjord in 2006). It is no surprise that classic names appeared on yet another generation of ship.

On 17 July 1993, the Tyne was playing host to the Tall Ships and, through them, first the *Winston Churchill* and then the *Venus* threaded their way out to sea. There are no Tall Ships in the image but all the spectators visible had not come just to see the Norway ferry off the Shields. This 1974 vessel spent four years, 1990–94, in this *Venus* incarnation before a move to DFDS. While this *Venus* was in service, the 1966 *Venus* had become once and for all Olsen's cruise ship *Black Prince*. The older *Venus* had last worked to the Tyne in 1986, and in 1987 became the full-time cruise ship which in 2005 she remained. Her sister the 1966 *Jupiter* had finished working to the Tyne in 1990 after which the *Venus* of this image succeeded her.

Opposite: The variety which it would be so intriguing to archive must not blind one to the fact that these are vehicle ferries. There is a vestigial market in public transport connections and so, since 1970, quite a tale could be unfolded around the bus connections to Tyne Commission Quay, which continue to be operated. For a number of years Tyne & Wear PTE were directly responsible for these and this public body with huge transport interests in the Metropolitan County bought, in 1976, a small batch of second-hand Bristol VR 1972 double-deck coaches to operate the connection from Newcastle Central station. These were quite exceptional vehicles and many might remember their yellow bulk sitting outside the station. Did they gain their own illustrated publicity? I do not know – the service is not very obvious in the TWPTE timetables I have examined. Usually the connection is a feature somewhere in the shipping operators' own literature.

Which paucity of information makes these two Go-Ahead Northern-issued brochures all the more interesting. Round about deregulation (I suspect) in 1986 they took over the operation and some brochures have been issued to directly promote it. Note that the vessel tied up behind is Norway Line (the *Jupiter*'s name is in one view) although the buses are decorated for DFDS Seaways or Scandinavian Seaways (DFDS all-over livery vehicles are present in 2005).

Inside, the brochures are multilingual and it is evident their target was not just the long-distance traveller using the train but also the incoming Scandinavian intent on a shopping spree in Newcastle. They are not actually dated but come from 1990 plus or minus three years. Obscure from one angle, truly fascinating from another. There will be bus enthusiasts in a transport of delight over the dual-door Eastern Coach Works-bodied Leyland Atlantean (always a rare combination) in special DFDS Seaways livery. This is what makes the subject tick.

THE NORDIC LINE

SERVICE
327

NEWCASTLE
CENTRAL STATION
TO

NORTH SHIELDS
TYNE COMMISSION QUAY
FOR

SCANDINAVIAN FERRIES

GO-AHEAD NORTHERN
TYNE DISTRICT

Above: Railway-related shipping has maintained a relationship with the Tyne through to the twenty-first century. One of Newcastle's established nightclub venues in 2005 is the former landmark Stranraer–Larne ferry, the Denny built *Caledonian Princess*, re-christened *Tuxedo Princess*.

The famous Shields ferries gained an official railway connection when taken over by the Tyneside PTE who, in the late 1970s, became railway operators with their Metro system. Nowadays the organisation is called Nexus and its two direct operations are the Metro and the Shields Ferries.

The volume can end most appropriately by revealing that an Eastern Region railway ferry built for the Tilbury–Gravesend route continues to carry passengers on the Tyne and was in action off the Shields that July 1993 day when the Tall Ships left. Here is the 1961 *Catherine* ready to sail from the Newcastle quayside.

Right: Over a decade later and she was still a feature of the river and had appeared in several pieces of Tyne Leisure Line literature, like this brochure. Look carefully and Newcastle's famous bridges are staring down on two former British Railways ships.

RIVER·TYNE·CRUISES

"A Venue With A Difference"

Select Bibliography

ABC Shipping Services (monthly), various publishers, various issues consulted.

Alsop, John, *The Official Railway Postcard Book* (John Alsop, Bedford, 1987).

Anon, *General Information about Sealink* (Sealink, 1976).

Bradbury, G.T. & Quayle, H.I., *The Felixstowe Railway* (Oakwood Press, Blandford Forum, 1978).

Carpenter, Reginald, *Container Ships* (Model and Allied Publications, Hemel Hempstead, 1971).

Christie's South Kensington, *British and Irish Travel Posters* (Christie's South Kensington, London, 1999 & 2000).

Clegg, W. Paul & Styring, John S., *British Nationalised Shipping* (David and Charles, Newton Abbot, 1969).

Collins, Michael J., *Life & Times Series: Freightliner* (OPC, Sparkford, 1991).

Cone, Phillip J., *100 Years of Parkeston Quay and its Ships* (Phillip J. Cone, Harwich, 1984).

Cooke, Andrew, 'The Fred. Olsen Cruiseships' in *Ships In Focus Record 18*, 2001.

Cooke, Andrew, 'A Safe Haven' (Harwich) in *Ships Monthly*, May 2004.

Coote, Jack H., *East Coast Rivers from the Humber to the Swale* (Yachting Monthly, London, 1981).

Coote Jack H., *East Coast Rivers from the Air* (Yachting Monthly, London, 1986).

Cowshill, Miles & Hendy, John, *DFDS: The Fleet* (Ferry Publications, Kilgetty, 1998).

Cowshill, Miles & Hendy, John, *Winston Churchill* (Ferry Publications, Kilgetty, 1991).

Cox, Bernard, *Pleasure Steamers* (David and Charles, Newton Abbot, 1983).

Credland, Arthur G., *The Wilson Line* (Tempus Publishing, Stroud, 2000).

D'Orley, Alun A., *The Humber Ferries* (Nidd Valley Narrow Gauge Railways Ltd, Knaresborough, 1968).

Dix, Frank, *Royal River Highway* (David and Charles, Newton Abbot, 1985).

Firth, J., 'The Humber Ferry Service' in the *Journal of the Transport Ticket Society*, May 1980, Chester.

Foster, Colin, *North Eastern Record Volume 1* (Historical Model Railway Society, London, 1988).

Greenway, Ambrose, *A Century of North Sea Passenger Steamers* (Ian Allan, Shepperton, 1986).

Greeves, Ivan S., *London Docks 1800–1980* (Thomas Telford Limited, London, 1980).

Groundwater, Ken, *Maritime Heritage Newcastle and the River Tyne* (Silver Link, St Michael's, 1990).

Haresnape, Brian, *This is Sealink* (Ian Allan, Shepperton, 1982).

Haws, Duncan, *Merchant Fleets: Britains's Railway Steamers* (TCL Publications, Hereford, 1994).

Ian Allan ABC series: various titles and editions.

Keys, Dick & Smith, Ken, *Ferry Tales Tyne–Norway Voyages 1864–2001* (Newcastle Libraries, Newcastle-upon-Tyne, 2002).

Longbone, Bryan, 'New Holland: A Backwater of Distinction' in *British Railways Illustrated*, October 1982 (Irwell Press, Oldham).

Ludlam, A.J., *Railways to New Holland and the Humber Ferries* (Oakwood Press, Oxford, 1996).

Martin, Kirk, 'BR Firemen – 1975 Ferries of the Humber Estuary' in *Railway World*, December 1975 (Ian Allan, Shepperton).

McCall, Bernard, *Coasters Around Britain* (McCall, Barry, 1989).

Middleton, Alan, *It's Quicker by Rail! The History of LNER Advertising* (Tempus Publishing, Stroud, 2002).

Murphy, Michael and Laura, *The Ocean Ferryliners of Europe Vol. 1: The Northern Seas* (David and Charles, Newton Abbot, 1987).

Norden, Greg, *Landscapes under the Luggage Rack* (GNRP, Bugbrooke, 1997).

Peacock, Thomas B., 'Transformation at Felixstowe' in *Modern Railways*, June 1987 (Ian Allan, Weybridge).

Riedé, Leo, *Holland from the Air* (Reader's Digest, 1987).

Ripley, Don & Rogan, Tony, *Designing Ships for Sealink* (Ferry Publications, Kilgetty, 1995).

Ships Monthly, Burton-on-Trent, many issues (especially Ships Datafile on DFDS in February 2002).

Simper, Robert, *The River Orwell and the River Stour* (Creekside Press, Woodbridge, 1993).

Simplon Postcards: The Ship Postcard Website, http://www.simplonpc.co.uk/

Strugnell, Kenneth Wenham, *Seagates to the Saxon Shore* (Terence Dalton, Lavenham, 1973).

Thompson, Michael, *Hull Docklands* (Hutton Press, Beverley, 1990).

Vallance, H.A., 'Across Denmark by Lyntog' in *Railway Magazine*, October 1951 (Tothill Press, London).

Westcott Jones, K., 'Parkeston Quay and the Antwerp Service' in *Railway Magazine*, November 1951 (Tothill Press, London).

Widdows, Nick, *Car Ferries of the British Isles 1992/93* (Ferry Publications, Narberth, 1992).

Widdows, Nick, *Ferries of the British Isles & Northern Europe* (Ferry Publications, Narberth, 1998).

Williams, David L., *Glory Days: British Ferries* (Ian Allan, Hersham, 2003).

Wren, Wilfrid J., *Ports of the Eastern Counties* (Terence Dalton, Lavenham, 1976).